# Patents, Copyrights & Trademarks

## FOR

# DUMMIES®

## 2ND EDITION

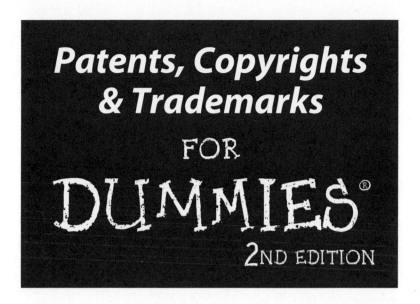

# Patents, Copyrights & Trademarks

## FOR DUMMIES®

### 2ND EDITION

by Henri Charmasson and John Buchaca

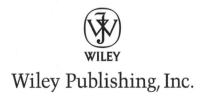

Wiley Publishing, Inc.

**Patents, Copyrights & Trademarks For Dummies,® 2nd Edition**
Published by
**Wiley Publishing, Inc.**
111 River St.
Hoboken, NJ 07030-5774
www.wiley.com

WILEY

# About the Authors

**Henri Charmasson** is an attorney with a 35-year career in the field of intellectual property (IP) law. He has been a naming adviser to major corporations. Henri is also an inventor with his name on 15 U.S. patents and an entrepreneur who sits on the board of several small business corporations. In his early engineering career, Henri designed computer hardware. Henri has authored several articles and delivered lectures on patent, copyright, trademark and trade secret topics, and written an authoritative treatise about the art of naming companies and branding new products. Born, raised, and educated in sunny Provence, France, he's found in California the ideal place to exert his enterprising spirit.

**John Buchaca,** also an Intellectual Property law attorney, is a former software engineer and occasional inventor, and has worked with Henri for more than 15 years. Indeed, when Henri wrote the first edition of this book, John regarded himself as the "first dummy." Before becoming a lawyer, he worked in ocean acoustics analysis and modeling and computer programming. His undergraduate degree is in applied mathematics. But his highest claim to fame (according to Henri) is to be married to Henri's daughter and to be the father of two of Henri's grandchildren. He lives in San Diego, California where he is a partner at Charmasson, Buchaca & Leach, LLP, an IP law firm.

# Dedication

To Marcia and Mari

# Authors' Acknowledgments

Thanks to our editorial team and particularly to our project editor, Corbin Collins, who tactfully coached us into expressing many arcane legal principles in limpid prose.

## Publisher's Acknowledgments

We're proud of this book; please send us your comments through our Dummies online registration form located at www.dummies.com/register/.

Some of the people who helped bring this book to market include the following:

**Acquisitions, Editorial, and Media Development**

**Project Editor:** Corbin Collins

   (Previous Edition: Mike Baker)

**Acquisitions Editor:** Tracy Boggier

**Copy Editor:** Corbin Collins

   (Previous Edition: Laura Peterson)

**Editorial Program Coordinator:**
   Erin Calligan Mooney

**Technical Editor:** Michelle Falkoff

**Media Development Producer:** Jenny Swisher

**Editorial Managers:** Jennifer Ehrlich

**Editorial Supervisor and Reprint Editor:**
   Carmen Krikorian

**Editorial Assistants:** Joe Niesen, David Lutton,
   Jennete ELNaggar

**Cover Photos:** © Comstock

**Cartoons:** Rich Tennant
   (www.the5thwave.com)

**Composition Services**

**Project Coordinator:** Kristie Rees

**Layout and Graphics:** Carl Byers,
   Christin Swinford, Abby Westcott

**Proofreaders:** Melissa Bronnenberg,
   Bonnie Mikkelson

**Indexer:** Potomac Indexing, LLC

**Publishing and Editorial for Consumer Dummies**

   **Diane Graves Steele,** Vice President and Publisher, Consumer Dummies

   **Joyce Pepple,** Acquisitions Director, Consumer Dummies

   **Kristin A. Cocks,** Product Development Director, Consumer Dummies

   **Kathleen Nebenhaus,** Vice President and Executive Publisher, Consumer Dummies, Lifestyles,
      Pets, Education

**Publishing for Technology Dummies**

   **Andy Cummings,** Vice President and Publisher, Dummies Technology/General User

**Composition Services**

   **Gerry Fahey,** Vice President of Production Services

   **Debbie Stailey,** Director of Composition Services

# Contents at a Glance

# Table of Contents

# Introduction

. . . . . . . . . . . . . . . . . . . . . . . . . . . . . . . . . . . . . . . . . . . . . . . . . .

*W*elcome to *Patents, Copyrights & Trademarks For Dummies, 2nd Edition!* We'll try to make your visit as pleasant and enlightening as we can.

In our technology-driven world, intellectual property (IP) represents the major asset of most business enterprises. If the phrase *intellectual property* leaves you puzzled, this book will help you navigate its reefs and shoals and show you how to acquire and protect your share of this form of wealth.

Have you always thought you might be the next Thomas Edison or Danielle Steele? Has your company recently developed a bold new corporate logo or motivating trademark? Perhaps you're thinking of a new concept in software, one that can revolutionize the entire world of cybernetics. Or maybe you've just dreamed up the latest in "latest things" — something to rival the iPod or camera phone.

If so, you've come to the right place because having the great idea, creating a magnificent work of art, or starting the next fad is only the first step to cashing in on your creativity and hard work. Next up is protecting your intellectual property. But, obviously, you know that. You've been enticed to pick up this book (and buy it, we hope) by those three not-so-little words: patents, copyrights, and trademarks. We're guessing you want to find out more about these matters. Well, you're about to find out all you need to know (but were afraid to even think about). You're entering the exciting world of IP rights. Well, maybe the term *exciting* is pushing things a bit, but give us a break, we're IP attorneys after all.

## About This Book

In this book we explain, in layman's terms, the basic nature, function, and applications of intellectual property (IP) rights, including how you can acquire and wield them effectively against your competitors, or exploit them lucratively through licensing agreements and other rewarding schemes. Each of the main types of IP protection — patents, copyrights, and trademarks — is covered in its own complete part. We also dedicate a chapter to the too-often overlooked subject of trade secrets.

After reading this book, you'll have a solid grasp of the processes involved in acquiring, registering, maintaining, and protecting the intellectual property rights due you and/or your company. You'll be able to make informed decisions and speak confidently with the IP professionals you meet along the way. And you'll have the tools and knowledge to take care of much of the work involved in the various research and registration processes.

However, this book is no substitute for legal advice from a specialized professional. When you deal with intellectual property and IP rights, you face many complex legal issues. There's only one definite answer to any legal question: *It depends.* So make sure that you have a competent professional advisor to guide you through the legal muck.

*Note:* Although the authors recommend that companies always prominently display their commercial identifiers (names and brands), preferably in bold, uppercase letters, to make them stand out and emphasize their legal status, for practical and aesthetic reasons, the publisher has opted to follow the industry standard of spelling brand and trade names with their accepted, conventional spellings throughout this book. This usage should not detract readers from appreciating the importance of highlighting your marks and other commercial identifiers whenever they are used on signs or advertisements.

# Conventions Used in This Book

We use the following conventions throughout the text to make things consistent and easy to understand.

- ✔ New terms appear in *italic* and are closely followed by an easy-to-understand definition.

- ✔ **Bold** highlights the action parts of numbered steps.

- ✔ Sidebars — text enclosed in a shaded gray boxes — contain information that's interesting to know but not necessarily critical to your understanding of the chapter or section topic.

- ✔ We regularly use the abbreviation *IP* to refer to intellectual property. It's one of those IP lawyer things we just can't shake.

- ✔ Throughout the book, we provide *estimates* of fees you may run into in your quest to sew up your intellectual property. Many U.S. Patent and Trademark Office fees are changed at least once a year (usually in October), sometimes substantially. Fee estimates here are based on the most recent published fee schedule at the time of this writing. Failure to pay the full applicable fee can result in a missed deadline and lapse of your application, patent, or trademark registration. Always check the current fee schedule on www.uspto.gov before sending a payment.

> ✔ When we use the term *you,* we are, of course, referring to you the reader. But for those tasks, jobs, and other assorted legal hoops where we advise you to consult an IP professional — and there are many of them — *you* often refers to both you and the professional.

# Foolish Assumptions

In order to channel the sea of IP information into a single book that's helpful to you, we make a few assumptions about you, the reader. See whether one or more of these shoes fit:

- ✔ You have a penchant for entrepreneurial adventure.

- ✔ You're running a business. Even the smallest commercial enterprise, such as an outdoor coffee cart, can benefit by making intelligent use of IP — creating an inspiring business name, for example.

- ✔ You're a budding or accomplished sculptor, painter, playwright, choreographer, musician, or songwriter, or you're involved in some other type of artistic activity.

- ✔ You're a writer, publisher, or computer programmer, or are in another profession that takes advantage of the products of your creative mind.

- ✔ You're a scientist, engineer, or inventor.

- ✔ You're a college student considering a career in the field of IP law.

- ✔ You're a business lawyer, executive, or middle manager and want to understand some aspects of IP rights.

If we've hit the mark with any of the previous descriptions, this book is for you.

# How This Book Is Organized

*Patents, Copyrights & Trademarks For Dummies,* 2nd Edition, is organized so that you can easily access the information that you need. We've put the material in six parts, each with chapters related to a common theme. We now give you a preview of coming attractions. Projector, please.

# Part I: Corralling Your IP Assets: Intellectual Property Basics

Part I talks about intellectual property and briefly describes how patents, copyrights, trademarks, trade secrets, and other IP rights safeguard your IP assets. We also include the basics of dealing with IP professionals, such as agents, attorneys, and examiners.

# Part II: Going for the Gold: Patenting Your Product

Part II deals with perhaps the most complex type of IP protection: the patent. Here, we explore which types of inventions qualify for a patent and whether you should patent your invention based on costs and other considerations.

We show you how to better your odds of getting your patent by doing a search to see whether your invention is really original and useful. We then explain, in detail, how to go about getting that patent — getting professional help, preparing your patent application, following up on your paperwork, and dealing with the patent office examiner.

Throughout Part II, we also show you how to protect your invention during that perilous period when your application is active (and somewhat public) but not yet protected by a patent. All that for the price of admission!

# Part III: Asserting Your Copyrights

Part III talks about the wide variety of creative works, from symphonies to software, that can be protected with a copyright. And we give you some good news and bad news. The good news is that you may already have exclusive rights to some of your works; you just need to make sure to keep them. The bad news is that if you created something original while employed by someone else, you may not have any right to it. But we help you maneuver that maze here in Part III.

# Part IV: Protecting Your Commercial Identity

Part IV gives you the lowdown on commercial identifiers — basically, the process of putting an exclusive brand on your goods and services. We define the various types of identifiers (such as trademarks, servicemarks and membership marks), show what makes a good mark and what should be avoided, and talk about how a good commercial name can give you a leg up on the competition. We also show you how to search to make sure your mark is unique and how to register and effectively use it in commerce.

## Part V: Making Your IP Rights Work for You

Part V gets into what you can do after you acquire your U.S. patent, copyright, or trademark. We tell you how to protect your IP overseas, how to employ your IP to the greatest possible advantage to make some money, and how (and when) to go after those who infringe on your rights — the bad guys.

## Part VI: The Part of Tens

The icing on your IP cake, this section contains some valuable information that you absolutely need in convenient top-ten packaging. What kind of valuable info, you ask? Good question. Here's a good answer: Common misconceptions about IP rights, things not to do in a patent application, frequently asked copyright questions, and blunders to avoid when selecting a business name.

## The CD-ROM

A big part of our job is to blast through the mountain of available information regarding intellectual property and present our nuggets of wisdom. Inevitably, details are left out. That's where the enclosed CD-ROM comes in. In this miracle of plastic and aluminum, you'll find additional materials, ranging from forms to examples of back-and-forth communications with patent and trademark examiners. In a pinch, the entire body of U.S. IP laws is included as a surefire cure for insomnia.

## Icons Used in This Book

Marks tips and tricks that you can put to use to make your life easier while you're protecting and profiting by your IP.

Highlights something to keep in mind while working on your patent, copyright, or trademark.

Alerts you to common mistakes that can trip you up and to other factors that may prove hazardous to your market image or your financial or legal health.

Indicates projects or examples from real-life IP cases. At times, the names have been changed to protect the innocent — and infamous.

Examples of actual text — paragraphs and passages — that you can use in legal documents, and other legal observations.

A hint that the information is a bit more complex than most of the fine and fascinating points we raise throughout the book. Although still interesting, you can skip it if you want and not miss out on any need-to-know advice.

Points out resources you'll find on the CD.

# Where to Go from Here

One good thing (of the many good things) about a *For Dummies* book is that you don't need to read it from beginning to end to access the information you need. The book is designed to let you get in and get out, only focusing on the information you need. Simply turn to the part, chapter, or section that contains the info you want to know. Only interested in creating a catchy new product name? Turn to Chapter 16. Want the scoop on copyrights? Turn to Part III. It's easy — you won't need a compass to get around. Of course, you can read the entire book, and truthfully, we'd be thrilled if you did.

We do suggest that you read Chapter 1, which provides an overview of the main IP components, if you have questions about which IP tool can best meet your needs. After that, let the index at the back and table of contents at the front of the book be your guides. And then just follow the signs, which in this case are headings and those handy little icons.

# Part I

# Corralling Your IP Assets: Intellectual Property Basics

The 5th Wave    By Rich Tennant

# In this part . . .

If you're reading this page, you probably have an invention, a creative work, a trademark, or some other piece of intellectual property that you want to guard against all the copycats out there. Well, you've come to the right place. In this part, we give you an overview of intellectual property (IP) in all its glory and tell you why protecting these assets is important. We map out each IP instrument — patents, copyrights, and commercial identifiers — showing how they each protect a different type of IP asset. We also talk about ways to treat your IP as a trade secret, by restricting access to information, using confidentiality agreements, and taking advantage of other tools at your disposal. And we discuss hiring an IP professional (when, why, and how), working effectively with an attorney or agent, and estimating how much the whole process can set you back.

# Chapter 1

# Marshalling Your IP Tools

*W*elcome to the world of intellectual property — which is abbreviated IP. If you've created, invented, or named something that you're selling, you already have intellectual property. And that property could be quite valuable. What if you'd invented the Segway scooter or written the first *For Dummies* book? Wouldn't you like to be able to cash in on it? Exploiting your IP assets for your own financial gain and, at the same time, pursuing those who may infringe on your precious but fragile rights to those assets (called IP rights) is what this chapter and, in general, this book are all about.

## Defining Intellectual Property

What is intellectual property? Although we've encountered many true and effective definitions — including *information that has commercial value, a proprietary product of the mind*, and *things protected by patents, copyrights, and trademarks* — none of them is quite complete. Here's the one we like best:

*Intellectual property* is intangible creations of the mind that can be legally protected.

Because IP has no physical form, we can give you a better idea of what it is by providing examples of what it isn't. Intellectual property is not

- The new and wondrous machine that you developed in your garage, but the invention embodied in that machine.

- The marvelously efficient cholesterol-reducing pill you see advertised on TV, but the formula and the process used in manufacturing that pill.

- The physical portrait that an artist made of you, but the aesthetic expression of the artist's talent reflected by the painting.

- The riding mower you reluctantly start up every Saturday, but the brand name that embodies the reputation of the product and its manufacturer.

Now, if you'd be so kind as to refer back to our earlier, scintillating IP definition, we'd like to expand on it. Intellectual property is made up of two components: assets and rights.

## Assets

IP *assets* are intangible creations, such as the invention, the formula and process, the expression of artist's talents as reflected in a painting, and the brand name.

## Rights

IP *rights* are the legal protections that secure each IP asset against its unauthorized use by others. One or more of the following legal protections can be used to secure IP rights:

- **Patents:** Obtaining a patent protects the invention from outright thievery.

- **Trade secrets:** Keeping a formula or manufacturing process confidential safeguards it against imitators.

- **Copyrights:** Holding a copyright shields artistic expression against copying by others.

- **Trademarks**: Adopting a trademark as a brand name keeps it and its market reputation yours and yours alone.

- **Contractual rights**: Licensing the right to use someone else's invention, for example, gives rights to the licensee while allowing the patent holder to profit from her invention through royalties.

## A very short history of intellectual property

Although the origin of patents dates back to medieval Europe, the U.S. patent was invented by a bunch of short-breeched fellows in powdered wigs, mostly lawyers, who met in Philadelphia in the 1780s. However, incorporating IP into the laws of the United States was not a slam-dunk. Thomas Jefferson was viscerally opposed to all shades of monopolies, including patents. Ironically, our Jeffersonian Democracy was put in place in Philadelphia in the absence of the Sage of Monticello. At the time of the Constitutional Convention, Jefferson was minister plenipotentiary to France, busily courting the Parisian ladies (relax, by then he was a widower). It is rather Alexander Hamilton who deserves credit for including a patent and copyright clause in Article II of the U.S. Constitution.

Some IP rights — copyrights, trademark rights, and trade secrets in particular — attach themselves automatically upon the creation or use of the IP assets without your ever having to lift a finger or spend a cent. Obtaining other IP rights — patents, specifically — requires you to put up a pretty good fight and spend plenty of money.

What happens when you don't protect your IP assets? Sorry, Charlie, but an unprotected IP asset is up for grabs — anyone can copy it, steal it, or change it for the worse (possibly damaging your good reputation). The bottom line is that your unprotected IP will fatten the bad guy's bottom line.

But there's more to IP assets and rights than mere talk of patents, copyrights, and trademarks, and that's what this chapter is all about. First of all, you must verify that you in fact own that IP asset you want to protect, you have to make sure it's original, and you must know how to secure all the IP rights that can apply to it. And last but not least, you have to know how to get the professional advice you need. Curtain, please.

# *Exploring the Patent Process*

We may as well start with the most well-known (though not the most practical) form of IP protection: patents. A *patent* is a temporary legal right granted by the government as a reward for a unique invention, giving the inventor, for a few years, a way to keep others from stealing the fruits of his or her labor — the invention.

While we're on a roll, how about another definition? Patent law defines an *invention* as a technological advancement that is useful, new, and isn't obvious to a person with ordinary skill in the field of technology. Inventions can take many forms, from a machine or device to a method or process; from a new composition to a new use of an old product; from a man-made organism to a new plant created with or without sexual fertilization (yes, most plants have sex, too). See the sample patents on the CD (documents B1–B19).

If you're wondering whether your latest and greatest gadget idea actually fits the bill of a bona fide invention, check out Chapter 5, which details the types of patents and the inventions covered by each.

## Obtaining a patent

To get a patent from the United States Patent and Trademark Office (USPTO), you must file an elaborate application that completely describes your invention. Don't worry — we cover the nuts and bolts of this application in Chapter 8. The USPTO rigorously examines your application — see Chapters 9 and 10 for all the gory details. If you pass the test, you're granted permission to pay a hefty fee so those nice people at the USPTO can afford to print your patent and take a long, well-deserved summer vacation. After all, they think they earned it by making you sweat blood for the last two years. Chapter 11 covers that info, minus the vacation itinerary. Yes, two years is typically the *minimum* amount of time it takes to get your application approved — if, of course, the moon is right and the gods are with you.

Make no bones about it, the patent process is costly in terms of both time and money, not to mention blood, sweat, and tears. So if you're thinking you may want to head down this road, you need to be sure that a patent is indeed the best path for protecting your IP. Chapter 6 provides you with other options and an exercise to help you decide whether a patent's the right choice. The first stop in your journey will likely be to conduct a patent search before pouring a bunch of money into a possibly doubtful application — Chapter 7 provides a road map for that side trip.

## Putting a patent to good use

Emblazoned with fancy lettering and a big, shining seal with blue ribbons, a framed patent makes an impressive conversation piece on your living room or office wall.

Oh yeah, you can also use it to threaten imitators with lawsuits if they're using and abusing your invention. Basically, a patent is a license to sue someone. If the copycat answers with an obscene gesture, you can mortgage everything you own down to your grandfather's dentures and file an infringement lawsuit. If the Force is with you, the litigation goes well for your side, and your adversary is flush with greenbacks, you'll make a bundle. You can also exploit your patent by selling it, or licensing (renting) it in exchange for royalties. Find out what else you can do with your patent in the section "Putting Your IP to Work at Home and Abroad" at the end of this chapter.

 Yes, a patent has teeth, but those teeth come at great expense. So looking beyond patents at your other IP rights is a good idea, too. You can also buy insurance policies that cover some of your litigation costs. We discuss that issue in detail in Chapter 21.

# Copyrighting Your Creations

Although derived from the same constitutional mandate as patents, copyrights resemble them only superficially. A *copyright* is a temporary right giving a creative person exclusive control over the use of an original work of authorship. And what is that? An *original work of authorship* (OWA) is a textual, graphic, plastic, musical, dramatic, audio, or visual creation.

Interestingly, even if pretty much the same thing has already been done before, you can still obtain a copyright if your work wasn't copied from or influenced by the pre-existing work. For example, just think of how many books have recounted the life stories of the Kennedys. Don't forget: Unlike a patent, a copyright protects the *form* in which an idea or concept is expressed, not the idea or the concept itself.

Copyright basically doesn't extend to abstractions or to anything technical or functional. For example, an idea for a new TV program isn't protected by copyright. But the way the idea for the show is developed and played out is protected. The copyright on a cookbook prevents you from copying the way the various recipes are expressed, selected, and arranged in words or images. But it doesn't prevent you from freely using the very same recipes and even incorporating them step by step into your own cookbook (because the steps are actually a technical process) as long as you don't express them in the same style, compile them in the same order, or arrange them in the same format. We go over this idea/expression distinction in great detail in Chapter 12.

## Lassoing a copyright

Check this out: After you've created an original work of authorship — such as the doodling you decorated your geometry book with while Miss Squareroot explained the quadrature of the circle — all you need to do to get it copyrighted is relax and have a glass of chardonnay to our health.

---

## Computing copyrights

The copyright law is always 10 or 20 years behind technology. In their attempt to catch up, Congress has characterized computer programs as copyright-protectable writings. This legislation gives programmers and the entire software industry an effective security tool. In a computer program, the choice of words or lines of computer code and their respective positions in an instruction represent the creative portion of the program and are critical to its operation.

The fact that others cannot copy this specific language greatly expands the scope of copyright protection for software. We explain in Chapter 12 how the courts separate the unprotectable, functional aspect of the program from the protected way its various components are expressed. Although patents also are available to protect innovative processes within a given computer program, the industry relies heavily on copyrights to protect its software.

---

Seriously, that's it! Copyright attaches automatically as soon as the work is shown in a perceptible and reproducible form without the need for any formality. That means that as soon as you print out your great American novel, it's already copyrighted. That's a big advantage over patents. If, however, you want to sue someone for infringement — or worse yet, someone sues you — you need to prove that it's actually your original work. That's why you should make it official and apply for a registration of your copyright with the Copyright Office, submitting a copy of your creation as proof of your authorship. You'll find an example of copyright registration in Chapter 14.

### Nailing the bad guys

You can use your copyright in much the same way you use a patent — to pressure and sue an infringer. Copyright litigation tends to be much less expensive than patent disputes.

## Proclaiming Your Identity: Trademarks and Other Commercial Handles

Trademarks are only one species within a class of IP assets called *commercial identifiers* that you use to distinguish your company, product, or services from others. The three basic types of commercial identifiers (which we cover in more detail in Chapter 15) are as follows:

✔ **Company identifiers:** A company is identified by its legal name (for example, General Motors Corporation) and often by the logotype that adorns its buildings and letterhead (General Motors or the familiar blue-and-white GM emblem).

✔ **Service identifiers:** The services that a company offers to the public — such as automotive maintenance or fast-food restaurant services — usually are identified by a servicemark. It can be a word or phrase (Mr. Goodwrench, McDonald's), logotype (the golden-arched *M* you see on a ubiquitous fast-food chain), or the shape and decoration of a building (the KFC brand of restaurant service outlets).

✔ **Product identifiers:** Trademarks (brand names) are the most familiar product identifiers and can even take the form of a single letter, or a mere design or symbol, such as the swoosh mark on a popular brand of athletic gear. Any fanciful and nonfunctional characteristic of a product or package can act as a product identifier — for example, the ribbed bottle of a large soft-drink company or the pink color of a glass-wool insulation material. These nonfunctional characteristics often are referred to as *configuration, design marks,* or *trade dress,* which, like trademarks, can be registered at the state and federal levels.

Commercial identifiers constitute the IP rights that we consider to be most neglected, misunderstood, and underestimated by entrepreneurs in their new industrial, commercial, educational, or scientific ventures. Watching new businesses spend *lots* on money on iffy patent applications always puzzles us because they're obviously neglecting the wondrous marketing tools provided by good commercial identifiers.

Company image, product fame, or a reputation for providing quality service are critical aspects of a business that can benefit from and be greatly enhanced by the right choice and use of pleasant and motivating monikers, logos, and distinctive and attractive packaging. However, coming up with an identifier that's a hit with customers isn't easy, so we devote the whole of Chapter 16 to providing some insight in making such a selection.

Likewise, in Chapter 15 we detail all you need to know about the ins and outs of developing marks and names that the courts will protect. We also explain how the degree of protection awarded to company identifiers and other commercial names depends mainly on the distinctiveness of the name.

A great name can be the most valuable asset of a company. A name deserves a lot of attention and appropriate protective measures, such as federal registration and proper usage. But a great commercial identifier won't do you any good if it duplicates an existing identifier — so before you begin the registration process, discussed in Chapter 18, you'll want to do a search to make sure no one else is already using your brainchild (or something close). We explain trademark searches in Chapter 17.

# Keeping It Under Your War Bonnet: Trade Secrets

**REMEMBER**

In certain circumstances, keeping your invention secret can be as effective as obtaining a patent.

Kiss and tell only on a need-to-know basis. The best way to keep a commercially advantageous piece of information, such as a manufacturing method or customer list, away from your competitors is to take advantage of laws that protect trade secrets. A *trade secret* is a very important and inexpensive IP right. Don't let anyone in on a trade secret other than the people who necessarily need to know about it.

Not every type of commercially advantageous material can be safely and practically kept under lock and key. Whenever that happens to be the case, and you can't keep some information as a trade secret, then you need to rely on other types of IP rights — patents, copyrights, or trademarks — for protection.

In Chapter 4, we explain how you can implement a trade secret strategy and how the law provides for enforcement of trade secrets in case of negligent or intentional disclosures. We also discuss the trade-offs between patents and a trade-secret policy.

# Let's Make a Deal: Looking at Contractual IP Rights

A specific category of legal contracts (explained in Chapter 20) are intended to deal with IP rights. They provide contractual IP rights to all parties. For example, a company may acquire the contractual right to manufacture a patented product while the inventor obtains rights to a percentage of the sales proceeds, called *royalties*. Even if you are not an inventor or computer programmer, you may acquire contractual rights to inventions or software that you can exploit in place of or in addition to their creators.

Similarly, after you acquire your patent, trademark, copyright, or commercial identifier, you can profitably sell or lease it to others. You can transfer your IP rights through an *assignment* (the outright purchase or sale of the IP right) or a *license* (an agreement allowing another individual or business to use your IP rights). For example, if you want to publish a book, you must either buy the copyright from the author using an assignment or obtain the author's permission to publish the work under a license.

When you hire employees or commission independent contractors to do a job for you, you can enter into written and signed agreements stating that any technological advancement or original work of authorship that results from their employment or commission belongs to you. This is often called a Proprietary Rights Agreement. See Chapter 13 for information on assigning and licensing copyrights and Chapter 15 for information about commercial identifiers.

The contract should always be in writing and be signed by all parties to the agreement.

You can also acquire contractual rights to intellectual property by buying a *franchise* for a specific type of business — fast-food and dry-cleaning franchises are among the more common ones. In Chapter 20, we explain how a franchise constitutes a classic and convenient way of exploiting a bundle of IP assets and related IP rights.

# Putting Your IP to Work at Home and Abroad

You can use IP assets and rights in many ways. Developing and protecting your intellectual property assets and rights can give you an edge over the competition by discouraging unscrupulous competitors, developing new revenue sources, and increasing the value of your company. (We talk about each of these aspects in detail in Chapter 2.)

Because IP rights are rare exceptions to antimonopoly and antitrust laws and regulations, their use is strictly limited. When you misuse your teddy bear to beat your little sister, your mom confiscates the bear. The rules haven't changed with regard to IP rights. The usual penalty for an abusive misuse of an IP right, such as threatening someone who is not in fact infringing, is forfeiture.

When you take advantage of your IP assets within the confines of your own company, basically exploiting your own invention, you face little risk of running afoul of the law. However, when you're forced to use your IP rights against others outside of your company who infringe upon them, you need to be more careful. Trust your IP litigation attorney to know how to stay within the bounds of the law. Check out Chapter 3 to find out how to select and work with an IP professional. IP specialists, like any other attorneys, are bound by strict confidentiality obligations and are subject to discipline and loss of their license to practice if they breach these obligations. Therefore, you can reveal your most sensitive knowledge or information to your attorney. There's no need to make her sign a confidentiality or non-disclosure agreement because she's already bound by law to absolute discretion.

You'll be happy to know that almost all industrialized countries have IP laws that are roughly similar to the ones in the United States. Because acquiring a copyright doesn't require any application or other formality, you can readily defend and exploit your copyright all across the planet, at little cost.

By contrast, patents and trademarks require local applications and examinations in almost every foreign land, which we detail in Chapter 19. Application and attorney fees tend to be even higher abroad than they are in the United States, and proceedings can drag on for years. A foreign patent program is not for the fainthearted and requires substantial financial resources.

# Chapter 2

# Fencing In the Herd

• • • • • • • • • • • • • • • • • • • • • • • • • • • • • • • • • • • • • • • • • • • • • • • • •

## *In This Chapter*

▶ Taking an inventory of your IP assets

▶ Developing new IP

▶ Planning an appropriate IP protection strategy

• • • • • • • • • • • • • • • • • • • • • • • • • • • • • • • • • • • • • • • • • • • • • • • • •

*I*n any serious endeavor, logic and pragmatism pay off. You can be logical by following a well-defined plan. You need to be pragmatic by using your resources efficiently and remaining within budget. Although you may not yet be involved in any kind of business activity, the minute you start dealing with intellectual property (IP), you're talking about assets that can be financially valuable. Therefore, developing an IP acquisition and protection strategy is a must for a business venture of any size. Briefly, your IP strategy should include evaluating your IP assets, deciding what type of IP rights would best protect them, searching to make sure that they can be protected, and going for every form of IP protection available to you.

## *Questioning Your Motives*

When you implement an IP program, getting carried away and spending beyond your needs and means are easy mistakes to make. One of the biggest errors is going after a patent when a copyright, good commercial identifier, or trade-secret policy would better serve your needs at a cheaper cost. If you're motivated by pride, and your goal is displaying a patent on the wall behind your desk, you need to find an easier ticket for your ego trip.

We know of three good reasons for developing and protecting an IP asset:

✔ Gaining an edge over your competitors

✔ Creating a revenue source

✔ Enhancing the value of your business

IP rights can be aptly compared with an interest in real property. They can be sold, leased (see Chapter 20), or used by you or your company.

Some businesses may require greater protection than others. In situations where competition is weak, absent, or unlikely, investing in patents makes little sense. For example, due to the likelihood of being sued for personal injury as a result of product failure and huge liability insurance cost, there is little competition in the crash helmet manufacturing business, and hence less incentive to patent helmet designs. By contrast, in the highly competitive field of pharmaceuticals, a company wouldn't dare release a drug after heavy development costs without a solid IP protection package. Back in the late 1800s, it would have been foolish to move your ranch from the safety of Pennsylvania, surrounded by peace-loving and law-abiding Quakers, to the middle of *banditos*-infested Texas without bringing along a few extra rifles.

## Keeping your competitors at bay

Almost every IP right gives you a way of excluding others from doing something that interferes with or competes against a vital part of your business. When you can tolerate competition and still maintain a reasonable income, you may forget about IP protection and spend your resources on marketing or some other more productive and lucrative activity.

However, we can't conceive of a business that wouldn't benefit from acquiring at least *some* IP rights. At a minimum, your business can capitalize on the protection afforded by a trade secret program, which could prevent, or at least deter, former associates or employees from using your manufacturing or marketing methods or stealing a customer list. At the other end of the spectrum, acquiring a patent, copyright, and/or trademark can give you a huge competitive advantage in the market and legal clout to stifle copycats.

Oftentimes it's helpful to look at what your competitors can do if you decide *not* to protect some IP right. Without a barbed-wire fence, your neighbors' cattle would come and drink from your well. After those strays deplete your meager water resources, your ranch isn't worth its tumbleweeds.

## Developing a new revenue source

After you acquire IP rights, you can generate income with them by licensing someone to manufacture your product or by leasing your commercial identifier to another organization to market products under your brand name. You can also franchise other folks to manufacture or sell your goods and services under your guidelines. Under any of these arrangements, you earn money any time someone makes, sells, or uses your goods or services.

Some business ventures may limit themselves to securing solid protection for a product or technology and then licensing the IP rights to others, sometimes to former competitors. Licensing IP rights is like renting out real estate. You maintain title to the property (the IP assets and rights) while collecting "rent" in the form of *royalties* (see Chapter 20). Say a young entrepreneur launches a new line of sporting or casual garments, enhances his product line with an attractive brand name and logo, and then licenses the brand to other manufacturers after it is established. He then gets out of the business — except, of course, for opening envelopes containing the quarterly royalty checks and laughing all the way to the bank. When they're planned and marketed well, IP rights can be an essential part of your product line.

If you don't want to get out of the business completely, you can maintain the right to continue manufacturing your product by granting only *nonexclusive* licenses to one or more manufacturers. However, the royalty rate is lower than for an exclusive license (again, see Chapter 20 for more).

## Adding value to your business

When the time comes to sell your business, you can get more for it If your

- ✔ Products are protected by patents.
- ✔ Proprietary computer programs are covered by copyrights.
- ✔ Brand names are unique, motivating, and not copyable by competitors.
- ✔ Goodwill —the reputation of the business — is transferable under the business name that is fictitious and not your family name.
- ✔ Customer list has remained secret.

But you don't have to sell your business merely to capitalize on its IP-enhanced value. If you need to raise more capital or borrow money, your IP can provide a boost to your net worth, making your stock more attractive to investors and offering collateral security for the lender to consider.

# Implementing an IP Program

Developing an IP acquisition and protection strategy is a must for business ventures of all sizes. Although such a strategy probably is more elaborate for a major corporation than for a small business, the recommendations that we make in the sections that follow apply to all commercial and professional enterprises, regardless of size. These components — taking stock of your IP assets and mapping out a strategy for protecting those assets — are the essential part of an effective IP acquisition and protection program. (By *acquisition,* we mean developing and safeguarding your own IP assets and IP rights and only occasionally buying some of these rights from someone else.)

Businesspeople often are unaware that they may actually be using IP assets already developed or created by themselves, their employees, associates, or contractors, including inventions and other technological advances, computer programs, and other original works of authorship. Because these assets go unrecognized (and unprotected), they often remain in the hands of their developers and creators or fall into the public domain. Nothing is more frustrating than discovering that an asset you thought you owned belongs to a former employee or contributor who becomes your toughest competitor.

## Taking stock of your IP assets

Begin implementing an IP protection program by taking an inventory of the intellectual property you already have. Begin with the following steps:

1. **Identify innovations in products or manufacturing methods that you and your associates or employees developed in the last few years, including older technology that may have fallen into public domain.**

   These are assets that may benefit by patent or trade-secret protection.

2. **Gather all software, instructional manuals, or promotional literature developed or published under your authority for the last five or six years — which is the grace period you have to go after copycats.**

   These items are good candidates for copyrights.

3. **Look at all your commercial names and logos, including business identities, product brands, and packaging.**

   This itemizes the assets that should be protected by a registered mark. Try to think of any other information that could benefit a competitor, like customer lists or suppliers.

These are definite trade secrets. After you gather this information, you have an inventory of the IP assets that you can protect with a variety of IP rights.

Before investing in protecting what you already have or acquiring more IP assets, your assets should be the best they can be. You can always improve inventions and processes, and you can boost the marketing and legal strengths of commercial names with some adjustments and selective use. Likewise, before investing in acquiring IP asset protection, make sure your widgets, assembly lines, and logos are terrific. Copyrightable material — such as manuals, books, graphics, and computer programs — are the exception here. Copyrights attach as soon as the work is put on paper (or saved to disk). Nevertheless, make sure that you revise and update these documents to include any improvements you've made to the assets they represent.

## Pinning down your trade secrets

In general, whenever you know that your inventions can't be readily reverse-engineered — that is, your competitors can't figure out what's going on by breaking down or analyzing them — you can keep the inventions confidential and thus protected by a tight trade-secret policy. Chemical compositions are prime candidates: Someone may be able to detect every chemical element in a new plastic material or eyedrop medicine, but a competitor is unlikely to determine the amount of each element or the mixing process with any level of practical precision. In many cases, keeping the formulae, dosage, and mixing parameters as a trade secret ensures protection against imitators. We tell you more in Chapter 4 about the pros and cons of secreting rather than patenting.

## Managing outsiders contributions

A common business mistake is thinking that you automatically have the rights to property you've obtained through the labors of others, including your employees. Acquiring an asset and obtaining the IP right that attaches to it are two different things. You must take some precautions and legal steps to get all the rights to what you acquire from others.

The law distinguishes between objects that are the embodiment of their underlying IP asset and the IP rights protecting that asset.

For example, if you hire a painter or a photographer to produce a portrait of you and you pay for those professional services and for copies of the art-work, you may expect to acquire all rights to the use of those materials. After all, you bought the thing, right? You may feel free to make copies, distribute those copies to your fans, or draw a mustache and devil horns on some of them. You'd be dead wrong. Those kinds of acts are restricted by the copyright that automatically attached to the artwork the minute it was put in a perceptible or reproducible form — in this case, on a canvas or photographic film — by the artist. Because you didn't specifically buy the copyright, in most cases, the artist or photographer retains control over how that material can be used, including, in some cases, making alterations (more about copyright in Part III). For now, just know that what you think you're paying for isn't always what you get. A written contract should be signed at the time a contractor or employee is hired that clearly specifies who owns what.

If you're the employee, contractor, or other contributing party, you need to insist upon retaining some rights to use the material that you contributed; otherwise, you may paint yourself into a corner. One day, you may need to incorporate part of that material into another project, only to find that you no longer have the rights to what you created because all aspects of your art have been assigned to your former customers. Under those circumstances, you have to adopt a new style and develop a new stock of frequently needed material.

## Covering copyrighted creations

Even though all original works of authorship are automatically copyrighted, registering them is important if you want to profit from them or take infringers to court. Periodically gather and evaluate all textual, graphical, and audiovisual material, including technical and promotional works, photographs, computer programs, and microchip masks. You then need to register your copyright claims in the U.S. Copyright Office (USCO — see Chapter 14 for all your registration needs). You also need to establish a procedure for periodically updating your applications for registration.

## Encouraging technological advances

To promote inventiveness and technological breakthroughs, a company needs to ensure that all valuable contributions are protected and encouraged by

- Implementing a record-keeping system to document new developments.
- Devising a reward program for its creative employees.

Preparing complete written disclosure of potential inventions and submitting them to a patent attorney or agent is important. The attorney or agent helps you decide on a case-by-case basis whether you need to file a patent application or treat the breakthrough as a trade secret. This decision is extremely critical in further helping you achieve your desired scope of protection within the constraints of your company's budget (see Chapter 4).

## Calling in the © police

Here's an eloquent demonstration of the effectiveness of a well-planned IP protection policy: An advertising agency's art department produces sketches that are used in a promotional campaign aimed at potential customers. Every few weeks, they collect and bind copies of the artwork and deposit and register them as unpublished works. A competitor got hold of one proposal, underbid the agency, won the account, and put the artwork on a billboard. A few days later, the agency's attorney, armed with the copyright registration and without having to go to court, convinced the customer to take that billboard down and reclaimed the advertising contract for his client.

## *Preserving identity and brand names*

Commercial names — specifically a company's business name and logo and more significantly its brand names — determine how a company is perceived in the marketplace. In fact, these commercial names are vehicles upon which all of a company's marketing programs ride. Few brand names that you see every day are outstanding. In fact, many are downright inadequate. Some brand names are counterproductive because they impede rather than bolster the promotion of the goods and services they identify. How are *you* faring? Do you have gems in your jewel box or merely lumps of coal in your stocking? You'd better find out and act accordingly.

If budgetary constraints limit your ability to both protect your product *and* polish your commercial image, we recommend favoring the latter. Establishing a good brand-name program is cheaper than patent protection, and you get much more bang for your buck. (Chapters 15 and 16 have the scoop on creating effective commercial identifiers and avoiding bad ones.)

Be methodical in assessing your commercial names by

- ✔ Taking a hard look at all your current commercial names and logotypes.
- ✔ Rating their promotional value via the criteria defined in Chapter 16.
- ✔ Phasing out the ones that don't make the grade and replacing them with more judiciously selected monikers.

Registering your commercial names on the federal register and, for extra protection, on some state registers (described in Chapter 18) greatly enhances your legal clout when you have to weed out copycats. Consider registering

✔ All your brand names as trademarks and your business identities as servicemarks with the U.S. Patent & Trademark Office.

✔ Copyrights of logotype graphic components in the USCO as visual art.

Don't overlook the fact that an attractive and non-functional product shape or ornamentation, such as the unique shape of a bar of soap or a whimsical design on the side of an athletic shoe, can be recognized as source identifiers and registered as trademarks, just like brand names. For example, the fanciful shape of a perfume vial and the bright stripes across a pesticide package are distinctive packaging that can be registered as trademarks. Even the recognizable sound of a motorcycle exhaust pipe, the unique smell of a detergent, the sound of a lion's roar at the start of a movie, and the springy feel of a textile product can be deemed registrable nonvisual marks.

If you don't have these kinds of unique identifiers for your product line, your designers should create them! The more unique and distinctive your product, the easier it becomes for you to prevent your competitors from copying it.

## Developing contractual procedures

Contractual engagements, which are essential for implementing your IP protection strategy, always need to be secured in writing. You need to consider contractual agreements with the following:

✔ Potential inventors and others who contribute to technological assets. Agreements with them ensure your ownership of their work products.

✔ Computer programmers, writers, artists, photographers, music writers, producers of audio-visual works and sound recordings, microcircuit mask designers, choreographers, architects, and others who contribute copyrightable works to your business. These kinds of agreements make you or your company the legal author and copyright owner when contributors' creations come to life. They also obligate these contributors to transfer any copyright they acquire to you or your company.

✔ All associates, employees, representatives, and some contractors, suppliers, visitors, and customers who guarantee confidentiality.

For these agreements to be effective, a competent IP attorney must draft them. Don't rely on a personal-injury or criminal-law practitioner or even a business attorney, because they may not know the latest developments in IP law. These well-meaning but often unqualified lawyers routinely rely on forms plucked from outdated manuals or may even use the wrong form for the job altogether. An IP specialist (see Chapter 20) can save you money and keep you out of trouble when drafting agreements to implement IP programs by

✔ Combining necessary contractual agreements into a single document.

✔ Ensuring that the contractual agreements extend to employees, employers, and agents of the parties signing them.

✔ Forbidding personal use of confidential material by the parties.

✔ Making sure that the agreement conforms to local rules and regulations.

✔ Charging a fair fee for legal work and not merely for clerical tasks.

# Chapter 3

# Calling in the Cavalry and Picking Up the Tab

*In This Chapter*

▶ Knowing when you need an accredited intellectual property professional

▶ Finding and selecting a professional at home and abroad

▶ Keeping an eye on the bottom line

*I*f you're like most people, the idea of hiring a professional, especially one who has "Attorney at Law" tagged after her or his name, can send cold shivers down your spine, put goose bumps on your arms, and set your heart palpitating like a loose muffler.

Yes, attorneys are expensive, probably even more so than you think, especially if they specialize in intellectual property (IP) cases. To get an idea of the total costs, just take a peek at the section "Assessing the costs," later in this chapter. But hang on — we show you ways to mitigate the high cost of professional services. First, you have to accept that you'll need a professional's services sooner or later and make the best of an unsavory but highly beneficial reality. What counts is that you know what kind of help you need and how to get it.

## Getting the Help You Need

Let's face it, you need professional help — and no, we're not questioning your mental fitness. You need professional help when diving into IP waters because acquiring and using IP rights to protect and exploit IP assets are essentially legal procedures. And as you know, laws are inherently characterized by nuances, exceptions, and loopholes. IP laws are no exception. Over the last 20 years, the need to harmonize U.S. IP procedures with those of other industrialized countries and the huge volume of IP applications and filings have brought many changes in IP law. These changes require **increasingly** complex and expensive procedures. The days when a garage **inventor** could successfully navigate a patent or trademark application through **the** U.S. Patent and Trademark Office (USPTO) with the help of a how-to manual are, sadly, over.

Take a gander at documents E1 and E2 on the CD to get a whiff of these proceedings' complexity.

Law students spend years studying this stuff, bringing a level of **expertise to** the table that others can't easily duplicate. By steering you clear of **legal pit**falls, the IP professional saves you the time, grief, aggravation, and **expense** of having to refile a defective application or other paperwork. More **impor**tant, a professional makes sure that you don't miss any critical **deadlines and** lose the opportunity to acquire the IP protection you need.

This book, helpful as it is, is no substitute for engaging the services of a competent IP specialist should the need arise in your situation.

## Identifying the right person for the job

Because IP is such a vast and complex field, many professionals limit **their** practice to narrow specialties, such as patent applications, trademark causes, IP litigation, or entertainment copyright cases. It's up to you to **retain** the professional most qualified to handle your case.

### Registered patent attorney and agents

Registered patent attorneys and agents are accredited by the USPTO to **rep**resent individuals and companies in matters related to patent applications. They also handle trademark applications in the same agency.

To be registered, attorneys and agents have to meet the following **criteria:**

- ✔ They must have a technical or scientific education or experience (typically an engineering or scientific college degree).

- ✔ They must pass a rigorous examination on patent application **procedures.**

A list of registered attorneys and agents can be searched online on the **USPTO** Web site at www.uspto.gov.

### Using a patent attorney

Any attorney admitted to the bar in a state can interpret the law, apply it **to** your case, give you legal advice, file and prosecute trademark applications, and represent you before judicial or administrative authorities, including **the** USPTO and the U.S. Copyright Office. However, only an attorney or an agent registered to practice in the USPTO can represent you in a patent application. In almost all foreign countries, IP matters are handled by agents and rarely by an attorney, solicitor, or barrister.

### Using a patent agent

Because a patent agent's fees are generally lower than an attorney's, you may want to hire an agent. However, you must clearly understand the limitations of his or her authority.

A *patent agent* can conduct an anticipation search on your invention and give you an opinion of whether your invention is patentable. He or she can prepare and file your patent application and represent you throughout the examination of the application.

However, a patent agent can't interpret any law beyond the issue of patentability, tell you whether your invention infringes upon an existing patent, or advise you about what your patent will cover and how it'll be construed by a judge in any future infringement lawsuit.

A patent agent is at a real disadvantage when it comes to drafting the claims in a patent application. (In Chapter 5, we show you why the claims are the most important part of a patent application.) Because agents have no training in litigation, they may not understand how your claims might be interpreted by the court if you need to stop an infringer at some point.

If you can live with these limitations, consult a patent agent, but you may want to also look for a "back-up" attorney in case you run into an issue that falls outside the agent's authority or expertise.

### Non-registered IP attorneys

Certain well-intentioned business and corporate lawyers won't hesitate to tackle IP matters (other than patent applications) — which they are indeed authorized to do but are not necessarily competent to handle. Many are very knowledgeable and do their best but are clearly out of their league when it comes to the latest developments in IP law.

Be particularly careful if you approach an attorney who's not an IP specialist. Question the legal eagle about her competence and experience — something you should do whenever consulting an attorney. You may, for instance, ask her whether she has read this book! (Our publisher will love that line.)

A young entrepreneur consulted an IP lawyer when he was threatened with an infringement lawsuit for the use of his company and brand name, which he thought his business attorney had *cleared* (searched). When the IP lawyer phoned the business attorney, he discovered that the business attorney had checked for the availability of the name in the records of the local secretary of state, which only showed that no corporation existed by that name in the state. The search didn't discover that the name was already used as a trade name elsewhere in the United States. The entrepreneur had to change the corporate name, letterhead, signs, stickers, labels, and packaging, at significant cost and loss of *goodwill* (business reputation) already accumulated under that name.

## Qualifying an IP professional

To ensure that the person you hire is the right one for the job, interview several candidates and ask some hard questions before you make your final decision. Lawyers and agents will gladly supply you with references and samples of their work and answer these questions:

- ✔ What is your technical background?
- ✔ How long have you been practicing in this field of law?
- ✔ Are you familiar with my area of technology?
- ✔ Have you assisted clients in obtaining patents related to my invention?
- ✔ How many patent applications have you handled?
- ✔ How many patents have you obtained?
- ✔ Do you draft licenses and other IP contracts?
- ✔ Do you issue infringement or non-infringement opinions?
- ✔ Who else, besides you, will be working on my case?

## Unaccredited individuals and companies

Some individuals and companies offer various IP services, such as patent, copyright, and trademark searches (see Chapters 7, 13, and 17). Many advertise extensively in the yellow pages and professional publications. Although they can do some legwork for you, their services are limited and don't extend to any kind of legal matter. For example, a company may conduct a trademark availability search and come up with a list of similar marks and trade names already in use. However, it can't give you a legal opinion as to whether the use of that mark would infringe on the rights, if any, of the users of the uncovered marks and trade names. In Table 3-1, we provide a breakdown of the services offered by various IP professionals.

| Table 3-1 | Authority and Competence of IP Professionals and Service Companies | | | |
|---|---|---|---|---|
| *Action* | *Registered Patent Attorney* | *Registered Patent Agent* | *Attorney Not Registered to Practice with USPTO* | *Unaccredited Individual or Company* |
| Conduct a preliminary search on your invention | Yes | Yes | Yes | Yes |
| Give you an opinion of whether your invention is patentable | Yes | Yes | Yes | No |
| Prepare and file a patent application on your behalf | Yes | Yes | No | No |
| Represent you throughout the examination of the application by the USPTO | Yes | Yes | No | No |
| Give you advice on issues of patentability | Yes | Yes | Yes | No |
| Give you advice on issues of patent coverage | Yes | No | Yes | No |
| Conduct a mark availability search | Yes | Yes | Yes | Yes |
| Interpret mark availability search results | Yes | No | Yes | No |
| Help you register a mark | Yes | No | Yes | No |
| Help you register a copyright | Yes | No | Yes | No |
| Represent you in court in any IP matter | Yes | No | Yes | No |
| Give you legal advice on an IP matter | Yes | No | Yes | No |

# Finding and Retaining an IP Professional

The best and safest way to find a competent IP professional is by referral from someone who has used that professional's services in the past and been satisfied. You do have some other options, though (listed here in order of our preference):

- ✔ Ask for a referral from an attorney you know and trust.
- ✔ Consult an attorney referral service, such as your local Bar Association, or check the yellow pages.
- ✔ Check the U.S. Patent Office Register of Attorneys and Agents available online at www.uspto.gov.
- ✔ Sift through listings of IP professionals in the yellow pages under *Intellectual Property Law, Patent Attorneys* or *Patent Lawyers, Patents* or *Patent Searches,* and *Trademarks and Copyrights.*

## Giving up a piece of the action

Fledgling entrepreneurs are always short of cash and often eager to offer their IP professional a part of their business, technology, or invention as payment for services. If you're tempted to do so, here are a few things to think about first:

- ✔ A part owner of your company or its assets may have some say about how the business is run. Have a clear, written understanding about these matters to prevent a costly dispute.

- ✔ You don't yet know what your business or IP is worth, so you may be giving up too much for the services you're trying to secure. Later, you may find yourself without enough remaining assets or ownership of the business to obtain the capital and resources you need. Don't sell yourself short. Wait and see where you're going before making that kind of trade.

- ✔ A part-of-the-action fee arrangement is fraught with many dangers for an attorney

or patent agent because the likelihood that a conflict of interest will eventually develop is high. This places the IP professional at a disadvantage because of the strict duty of loyalty imposed by professional codes of ethics. Although it's not your problem if the professional runs into trouble with his state bar association or the USPTO, we would seriously question the prudence, integrity, and professionalism of an attorney who takes such a risk. Get the entire financial arrangement in writing and get a second opinion from another attorney.

- ✔ Giving a piece of your invention or company to someone must be done in a legal business framework. Accepting anything of value, including legal services, in exchange for a percentage of future earnings from the invention is always a serious violation of state and federal security laws. You can go to jail for that.

When you're ready to retain or hire an IP professional, insist on an engagement contract or retainer agreement that clearly spells out all the services, terms, and conditions of your professional relationship.

Here is a partial checklist of the most important things to include:

- ✔ What the IP professional will do for you.
- ✔ Which professional in the firm will handle your case.
- ✔ How much and when you have to pay for the services.
- ✔ What additional costs and fees you may encounter.
- ✔ How you can terminate the agreement and hire another professional.
- ✔ Whom the IP professional will represent: you, your associate or partner, your company, or the man on the moon.

This last point is particularly important. You may ask your IP professional to do something that isn't beneficial to your associate or your company. An eventual conflict of interest that wasn't properly anticipated can lead to at best additional time and expense and at worst a nasty legal fight.

# Staying within Your Meager Means

Legal services are expensive and eat up the lion's share of the money you spend to protect your intellectual property. We're going to give it to you straight here (you may want to be sitting down), but don't panic — we also give you some advice on keeping your IP protection expenses within your budget.

## Assessing the costs

Here's the skinny on some hefty prices. Don't be surprised if your IP specialist quotes you hourly rates between $200 and $500. Registered patent attorneys often charge $250–$450 an hour, while registered patent agents often charge $200–$300. Keep in mind that fees and costs, including government charges, often change and may not be the same in all places. The following sections contain some sample budgets for common basic services, using average attorneys' rates.

### Patents

Before applying for a patent, and after reading Chapter 7, you may decide to conduct a preliminary search to explore what has already been done in your field and to get a professional opinion about whether a patent is right for you. Here's roughly what a search may cost:

| | |
|---|---|
| Invention preliminary search (no attorney opinion) | $500–$750 |
| Review of search results and attorney opinion | $700–$1,000 |
| Total | $1,200–$1,750 |

Assuming you don't encounter any complications, a formal patent for a simple mechanical invention may cost you about $5,000. A more complex invention could run $10,000 to $20,000. Here's a detailed breakdown for a U.S. utility patent covering an electro-mechanical device of medium complexity:

| | |
|---|---|
| Preliminary interview and draft of application | $5,000 |
| Drawings and filing fee | $1,500 |
| Review of examiner report with attorney | $500 |
| Answer/amendment | $1,000 |
| Publication | $300 |
| Issue fee and cost of copies | $760 |
| Total | $9,060 |

Any complication, such as interference or opposition, potentially doubles or triples these figures. Appealing an adverse ruling may call for $5,000 up to . . . who knows? It depends on how high you want to climb the judicial ladder.

Costs associated with a design patent covering only the ornamental aspect of a device (as seen on documents B6 and B7 on the CD) run to about one fifth of those for a utility (functional) patent application given above.

### Copyrights

Here's the good news — relatively speaking. The registration and deposit of copyrighted material costs less than $1,000, unless you face complex issues of ownership or copyrightability.

Registration of a copyright for a computer program:

| | |
|---|---|
| Preliminary interview and preparation of application | $500–$1,000 |
| Filing fee and miscellaneous charges | $60 |
| Total | $560–$ 1,060 |

## Exercising caution with TV invention-development services

Gee, by now those commercials touting invention development and marketing companies probably sound pretty enticing, don't they? What a savings they represent compared to the fees we just quoted you! Our advice? *Beware!* This industry is riddled with abuses. Many of these companies prey upon the ignorant, the naïve, and the elderly, taking inventors' money and never returning a cent to their trusting victims.

Several states and the federal government have had to intervene, shutting down some of these long-established firms. A few states, namely California and Michigan, even adopted laws that severely restrict the ability of these companies to siphon money from their clients.

If you do choose this route, be as prudent as you are when selecting an attorney. Insist upon proof of prior performances by asking how much money the company has doled out in the past and how many customers have received those disbursements. Ask for references and check them out thoroughly. Interview and compare. And keep in mind that only a licensed IP attorney can give you valid legal advice. Remember that if it sounds too good to be true, it probably is!

### Trademarks and other commercial identifiers

When you select a mark or trade name, you want to make sure that it won't infringe upon a commercial identifier already in use (see Chapter 17). Here is what each availability search may cost you:

| | |
|---|---|
| Word mark availability search (no attorney opinion) | $350 |
| Legal review of search results and attorney opinion | $600 |
| | |
| Total | $950 |

A trademark or servicemark registration can set you back $1,000 to $3,000.

Here are the details for registering a design trademark in two classes:

| | |
|---|---|
| Preliminary interview and draft of application | $850 |
| Filing fees and drawing | $850 |
| Review of examination report with attorney | $450 |
| Answer/amendment | $900 |
| | |
| Total | $3,050 |

### Protection abroad

You should budget between $50,000 and $150,000 for overseas patent protection and between $10,000 and $30,000 for trademark registration. All this to cover only 10 to 20 foreign countries. See Chapter 19 for more on international patents and trademarks. There is no filing required to obtain copyright coverage overseas.

## Managing the expenses

Your IP attorney can help you properly allocate your resources and minimize IP-related expenses. Here is a short list of what she can do for you:

✔ Give you short-term and long-term estimates of all fees and costs.

✔ Show you how to strategically spread the protective measures over a number of years so you don't have to blow the entire budget all at once, and give you time to figure out whether your product is really as good as the famous Tea Kettle whiskey of yesteryear.

✔ Devise the least expensive approach for protecting your intellectual property — such as applying for a copyright, configuration mark, or design patent application instead of the more expensive utility patent, or by implementing a trade-secret protection program using confidentiality agreements and other procedures.

✔ Tailor your IP protection program to your basic needs. However, if you need to go into the witness protection program, this book won't help.

✔ Give you some peace of mind and a bill for her services — not necessarily in that order.

Patent agents can only give you cost estimates. They can't plan an IP protection strategy involving more than patent applications because of their limited area of practice.

## Doing it yourself

Throughout this book, we point out some things you may do yourself. However, the savings may be minimal and may not be worth the risk you're taking. Our experience tells us not to rely on what the client has done on his or her own. An IP pro would rather start from scratch than try to unravel the mangled mess of an inadequate patent application. The best thing you can do is carefully prepare the background material, as we suggest in Chapter 8.

## Paying the piper

You can pay for IP professional services in one of three common ways:

- ✔ An hourly fee
- ✔ A fixed amount for the whole job
- ✔ A combination of the two

If you agree to an hourly fee, request a complete estimate of all the costs over the life of the project, such as filing fees, copying and mailing costs, foreign agent charges, and maintenance fees. *Maintenance fees,* also called *annuities,* are paid to patenting authorities during the life of a patent. In some countries, the annuities are due from the date of filing the application. Be prepared for an estimate having a wide range of costs because it is very difficult at the outset to predict what will happen over the life of the project.

If you're going to pay a fixed fee, ask about other expenses, such as government charges, drawing costs, and copying charges that may not be included. In all cases, clarify how and when you must make the payments.

# Working with Foreign IP Professionals

You must have a representative in every foreign jurisdiction in which you file a patent application and often for every application to register a mark. Most U.S. patent attorneys and agents maintain working relationships with IP professionals in industrialized foreign countries. There is more on this in Chapter 19.

In all cases, you need to pay the foreign IP professionals' fees and government charges. Usually, neither you nor your attorney has any control over these costs, but you should always ask for a rough estimate when you file overseas. Because foreign costs tend to be substantially higher than in the United States, don't forget to take those expenses into account when preparing your IP budget and laying out your IP protection strategy.

# Coordinating with Other Professionals

Don't forget to keep your other advisors informed about your IP program.

- ✔ **Keep your business or corporate attorney aware of all your IP activities.** It's a good idea to give him copies of all your major correspondence with IP professionals. Your patents and marks may be put to good use in some distributorship and representative agency agreements.

- ✔ **Inform your CPA, comptroller, and other bean counters about your IP expenses.** Acquiring a patent or developing a trade secret can have important tax implications, and you don't want to miss lucrative amortization or depreciation deductions. Proceeds from the sale of licensing of an invention may benefit from special taxation rules, and your technological acquisitions and research program may qualify for tax credits.

- ✔ **Make your PR and advertising agency fully aware of the marks you acquire and register.** Those marks can be effectively put to work in your promotional campaigns. As we explain in Chapter 16, your advertising and marketing people can play an important role in selecting your commercial identifiers.

# Chapter 4

# Trade Secrets: Often-Overlooked IP Tools

*In This Chapter*

▶ Defining trade secrets

▶ Combing your business operation in search of trade secrets

▶ Safeguarding your trade secrets

Trade secrets are the most overlooked and misunderstood IP tools. Yet, in many cases, they offer an attractive substitute for patents: You don't have to file applications with a government agency and don't have to pay multiple fees. Best of all, you seldom have to hire an IP professional. Here we explain what qualifies as trade secrets that the law can protect. And we show you how to implement a set of company procedures to safeguard these valuable assets.

During the Palaeolithic Age, the first Cro-Magnon individual who devised a clever method to shape a shard of flint into a sharp, two-edged spearhead didn't go around demonstrating the new technique to everybody around, including those brutish Neanderthals still roaming the banks of the Dordogne River. We can safely speculate that this advantageous chipping method was for a long time practiced in the deepest recesses of a cavern, its secret carefully hidden from competing clans. Twenty thousand years later, trade secrets are again gaining a lot of attention, and for good reasons.

# Taking a Gander at Your Operation

Even if you think you don't have trade secrets because you and your staff are open, candid, trusting, and trustworthy, you may have information not readily available to the public that gives your company a competitive edge. We're not talking about any cloak-and-dagger scenario or about those skeletons in your file cabinets — but take, for example, your customer list. How would you feel if one of your former associates, or perhaps the employee who maintained that list, jumped ship, joined your closest competitor, and started using that list to solicit your best customers? Other examples might include someone revealing the identity of your supplier of a hard-to-find component, the parameters of a tricky manufacturing process, the way your financial resources are allocated, or the details of your next marketing campaign.

The first thing that comes to mind upon hearing the phrase *trade secret* is usually some kind of chemical formula or a wild concocting process. And yes, this type of information is best qualified for trade secret protection. You may be surprised to discover that most trade secret litigations don't revolve around the theft of secret formulae, but around the stealing of commercial information that is often not patentable or even that novel.

Examples of business-related scoop suitable for trade secret protection:

- ✔ Customers' identities
- ✔ Names and phone numbers of key contact purchasing person
- ✔ Marketing strategy
- ✔ Price lists
- ✔ Identities of suppliers
- ✔ Salespersons' commissions bonuses and other perks
- ✔ Customer soliciting approaches
- ✔ Identities of consultants
- ✔ Sources of ancillary services (branding, package design, jingles and other advertisement creators)
- ✔ Research and development projects
- ✔ Budgets and resource allocations
- ✔ Contractual arrangements
- ✔ Cash reserves
- ✔ Salaries

Imagine you're in the very competitive field of outdoors advertising and want to silk-screen a new type of plastic panel with your customer's logo. But the paints and inks commonly used in silk screening won't stand up to harsh weather. Then you discover a small ink manufacturer in Minnesota whose products adhere permanently to the plastic. The identity of that manufacturer constitutes a valuable trade secret that you'd be wise to carefully protect.

Turning to technical information, we have

- ✔ Chemical formulae.
- ✔ Synthesizing processes.
- ✔ Recipes that involve more than mixing of common ingredients.

✔ Manufacturing sequences.

✔ Using a commercially available substance for a new purpose.

✔ Metallurgical treatments.

✔ Computer programs including source programs and flowcharts.

The list is far from all-inclusive. If we had to put a broad label on what may constitute a trade secret, we would have to say it is anything competitively advantageous that can be subject to a modicum of confidentiality.

The law (with minor variations from state to state) defines a trade secret as information, including a formula, pattern, compilation, program, device, method, technique, or process, that:

> (1) Derives independent *economic value,* actual or potential, from not being generally known to the public or to other persons who can obtain *economic value* from its disclosure or use; and

> (2) Is the subject of efforts that are reasonable under the circumstances to maintain its secrecy. (The Uniform Trade Secret Act is document D15 on the CD.)

As laws go, this one appears straightforward and very concise. Alas, it was found to be too concise by lawyers and judges, who have qualified it with jillions of appellate court decisions that put the devil in the details. The key phrase in the definition is *economic value.* That's a business advantage so long as your competitors cannot readily get access to your secret. That advantage need not be current, but can be merely potential.

A trade secret cannot exist without a commercial setting. The closely guarded chili recipe the family got from your eccentric Aunt Maude is no trade secret — at least not until you decide to enter the chili business).

Having navigated the commercial hurdle, the definition of a trade secret is broad enough to cover every conceivable type of commercially useful information. So, pardner, where's the devil gone hiding? Hold on to your galluses (that's suspenders for you city slickers). Here are a few exceptions that confirm the rule. Something is *not* a trade secret if

✔ It can be readily ascertained without extensive research by your competitors, such as by reverse engineering. A milk route customer list is no trade secret if all your competitor has to do is follow your truck.

✔ It's not used in connection with a commercial activity.

✔ It is already known by someone not bound to secrecy, like software on your hard drive that has been accessed by your computer technician.

✔ It is inevitable that the alleged secret information, due to its nature, would be disclosed by one of your former associates or employees. Few jurisdictions will prevent your former marketing director from taking the same position with your competitor. Protecting employee mobility appears to be the courts' major concern.

✔ Its commercial advantage doesn't result as much from its secrecy as from its very nature. For example, a generous discount or low-margin bidding policy is an obvious competing strategy that need not be learned from a competitor. What we may call the "duh!" exception.

In the case of your customer list, its trade secret status won't prevent your competing former employee or representative from using it in merely announcing her new employment or association as long as she doesn't at the same time solicit those customers. Courts have articulated many other exceptions to trade secret status based on the peculiar circumstances of each case. The most common reason for denying protection of an alleged trade secret is the court's finding of a loophole in the plaintiff's security policy.

# Patenting or Secreting?

Chemical formulae, manufacturing and business processes, and other technical information are things you can either protect with patents or keep secret — for example, a process devised by a bank or other financial institution for managing investment accounts. It uses several algorithms to allocate monies between various investment portfolios. Market-related factors as well as customer profile criteria are processed to achieve maximum return. It would be relatively easy to keep the key elements of the operation under wraps and beyond the reach of competitors. The account-managing process could also be the subject of a utility patent application. Which is best?

The main advantages of treating a new development as a trade secret are

✔ It needs not be disclosed to the public in a patent application.

✔ The life of a trade secret is not limited to the 20 years normally associated with a patent. A trade secret will last as long as you can keep it under your hat. The Coca-Cola soda recipe is a good example.

✔ The costs for preserving a trade secret are relatively insignificant compared to the amounts involved in obtaining and maintaining a patent.

✔ Trade secrets can give value to things that aren't even patentable. Let's say Dr. Winkeye decided to sell his lucrative snake oil business and chose the highest bidder (who had signed a confidentiality agreement). It wouldn't matter that the snake oil is really just cherry-flavored tonic water. As long as the true recipe remains hidden, the company has value. Had Dr. Winkeye decided to seek a patent and failed, his company and his "Eau de Pigeon" tonic would have been worthless.

With trade secrets, you unfortunately run a substantial risk that another party may independently discover the same thing and even secure a patent for it. If that happens within one or two years of your original discovery, the patent owner may be able to exclude you from the market.

Albert, a chemist, developed a new antibacterial agent for use in pharmaceutical as well as industrial applications. The molecular base of his concoction was very different from what had been used in the past and required a complex synthesizing process, so he opted for keeping his discovery as a trade secret rather than applying for a patent. Soon he had water-purification agencies and pharmaceutical laboratories requesting his product all over the world. Unbeknownst to him, X Co., a large foreign pharmaceutical company had been working for some years on a similar germicidal preparation. X Co. was successful in obtaining patent protection in most industrial countries. After four years of lucrative operation, and just when he was about to merge his whole operation with another pharmaceutical manufacturer for a lot of money, Albert faced patent infringement suits in one country after another. The merger fell through. Lacking a defensive position, Albert was shut off from his lucrative contracts and nearly lost the ranch.

A patent, in contrast, provides you with

- ✔ A way to prevent your competitors from using your creation for a guaranteed 20-year period.

- ✔ The most powerful legal deterrent against copycats. However, the cost of pursuing a patent infringement lawsuit is astronomical.

- ✔ Considerable value to your business and help in attracting investors.

You must balance these advantages against the following drawbacks:

- ✔ Obtaining a patent is a lengthy (two to five years if no appeal), costly, and tortuous process that can seriously tax your financial resources.

- ✔ You must spill out all the details of your invention in the application that will become public, typically after 18 months.

- ✔ After 20 years from the application filing date, the patent expires and anybody can then practice your invention.

Inventions that are practiced by way of a computer program can get a certain degree of protection under the copyright covering the program itself (see Chapter 11), either by itself or in combination with a trade secret. Chapter 13 explains how to safeguard a trade secret when you register your copyright.

# Safeguarding Your Trade Secrets

For something to qualify as a trade secret, the law requires that you make efforts that are reasonable under the circumstances to maintain its secrecy.

## Creating a trade secret policy

You can maintain secrecy and enforce the confidentiality of your trade secrets by establishing a company trade secret policy and putting someone in charge of enforcing that policy. Such a policy may involve any of the following:

- ✔ Have all members of your staff, contractors, outside consultants and advisors, critical suppliers, or anyone else who may be exposed to any sensitive information sign a confidentiality agreement. Make it a part of your employment contracts. You may be wise to add some customers and casual visitors to the list of folks signing a confidentiality agreement.

- ✔ Restrict access to certain areas of your place of business.

- ✔ Stamp some documents SECRET or use some other confidential legend.

- ✔ Limit the circulation of confidential documents.

- ✔ Lock away sensitive material.

- ✔ Include appropriate warnings and directives in your employee manual.

- ✔ Schedule periodic meetings with your staff to go over trade secret policy.

- ✔ Obligate by contract those persons and companies to whom you license your trade secret to implement the same precautions and procedures.

## Trying for limited disclosure

When dealing with governmental agencies such as the Food and Drug Administration (FDA), the Environment Protection Agency (EPA) or other regulatory institutions, you may be asked to divulge your product formula. You should first attempt to negotiate a *limited disclosure*. For example, the FDA may be satisfied with a description of your cosmetic preparation as containing only "natural, aromatic plant extracts." The EPA is more interested in a list of ingredients than their dosage. If that approach fails, you may ask for *confidential treatment* of your formula. Your application will be sealed, and your secret conditionally protected — *conditionally* because a government's secret classification remains open to challenge by private party.

You don't necessarily need to adopt *all* the measures just mentioned, but you do need to exercise reasonable precautions. You need to ensure that any leak that may occur can only be the result of gross negligence or breach of duty for which you can get some legal remedy. No breach of duty can occur if your rules aren't clearly set, understood, and diligently practiced. Courts will enforce reasonably drafted and implemented trade secret protection policies by issuing restraining orders or injunctions against anyone breaching your trade secret policy and against the beneficiaries of the indiscretion. Compensatory damages can also be awarded.

A word of caution about confidentiality agreements: Like any contract, confidentiality agreements are only worth the money you are able and willing to spend enforcing them through the courts. It's best to avoid having to rely on them. Instead, beef up your security procedures and only look at the agreement as a last line of defense. Agreements with foreign individuals or companies are particularly problematic. Enforcement overseas turns out to be practically impossible. The wording of the agreement must bind not only the company recipient of the trade secret, but also the agent signing the document and all the other principals and employees of the company. This is an area where the assistance of a competent IP attorney is a must.

## Understanding how loose lips sink secrecy

It is important to note that just because an employee signs a confidentiality agreement, that doesn't mean you are home free. If that employee starts blabbing your secret to others, and the secret gets out, your only recourse may be against that employee. And if that employee only owns a change of clothes and the horse he rode in on, those items may be all you can get in compensation for the loss of your million-dollar secret. With a little savvy, you can fire from both barrels and combine patents and trade secrets, as demonstrated by the following example from a real case.

Tim, a garage tinkerer, came out with a way to treat chunks of Styrofoam or polyurethane with a metallo-plastic composition and give them the appearance and consistency of hardwood or solid metal. He also devised many applications in the field of cabinetmaking, architectural moldings, and decorative artifacts. He filed for and was granted a patent covering the composition application process that would be difficult to keep under secrecy.

After obtaining his patent, Tim spent many hours of trial and error refining his composition for easy application, immunity to weather conditions, and long life. This time, Tim opted for trade secret protection, and put in practice a very stringent security protocol to prevent any leakage of his formula to his competition. He moved the production of his composition to a separate and secret location away from his Styrofoam and polyurethane processing factory. That location was manned by a few trustworthy employees, all sworn to secrecy. The composition formula and mixing method were disguised by adding several unnecessary but harmless substances and processing steps. Moreover the disclosure provided to the EPA in order to obtain a nontoxic classification was limited to a list of basic ingredients, omitting dosage and the preparation process. The basic formula was locked away, and its access was subject to multiple restricting procedures.

After several years, and despite many attempts by competitors, no one has been able to duplicate Tim's unique composition. The patent is about to expire, but our former tinkerer, by now a millionaire, will enjoy many more years of monopoly in his field of endeavor. What distinguishes Tim from the unfortunate Albert, the chemist in a previous example? Luck — but also a wisely balanced use of both a patent and trade secret protection.

Be aware that you cannot withhold any critical aspect of your invention when you file your patent application. You must spill the whole can of beans. You can reserve for trade secret protection only techniques that don't directly relate to the invention and don't constitute its best embodiment or that you have developed after your application filing date.

There is no application, registration, or other type of governmental involvement in devising a trade secret policy. You face no long wait for approval and no expensive filing fee — just some advance planning, discipline, and a bit of legal work by your IP attorney to draft a few confidentiality agreements.

After reading the preceding chapters, you may be starting to realize that applying for a patent can be lengthy, expensive, difficult, and unpredictable. Given the current anti-patent mood of Congress and the latest Supreme Court decisions raising the bar for patentability, the case against patenting is getting stronger. Smart entrepreneurs, small businesses, and even some large corporations are showing considerable interest in trade secret protection — one of the oldest and by far the most affordable IP protection tool.

# Part II
# Going for the Gold: Patenting Your Product

The 5th Wave          By Rich Tennant

"In order to file for a plant patent, you need to describe what sets your beanstalk apart from other beanstalks. Besides the giant."

# In this part . . .

Getting a patent can be tough, no question about it. But we're here to guide you through the entire process of preparing and filing the patent application. In this part, we introduce the basics of the patenting process, including the legal and practical definitions you need to get a handle on before you enter the world of patents, and the criteria you and your invention must meet to qualify for a patent. At every step of the way, we illustrate how your hired gun — your IP professional — can clear obstacles from your path.

Acquiring a patent is probably the most complex, expensive, and time-consuming type of IP protection process. Because getting a patent can be so difficult, we help you evaluate whether you should really apply for a patent or use another way to protect your IP.

For similar reasons, making sure that no one else has already come up with your device is the way to go before you start the application process. So we show you how to do an anticipation search to see whether your invention is new, non-obvious, and useful — because these factors determine whether your invention is really patentable.

We then give you tips on preparing your patent application, help you push it through the patent office and deal with the patent examiner, and finally, show you how to get that coveted piece of paper.

# Chapter 5

# Understanding Patents and How They Work

$A$ patent is the most common, effective, and valuable IP right, but it also happens to be the most misunderstood. In this chapter, we untangle for you, one step at a time, the knotty complexity of patents so that you have no doubts about what a patent is and whether you can get one. (Chapter 6 gets more into whether you really want a patent as part of your IP strategy.)

## Defining the Nature of the Beast

A *patent* is a temporary, limited legal right granted to an inventor by the government to prevent others from manufacturing, selling, or using his invention. It's a loaded definition. Read it again. The most important words:

✔ **Temporary:** Patents last for a specified number of years, not forever.

✔ **Limited:** The right associated with a patent is not absolute but very specifically limited and subject to the right of any other person who happens to own a dominant patent related to the same subject matter.

✔ **Right . . . to prevent:** A patent allows its owner to go to court and *ask* a judge to stop someone from doing something. But remember, what's good for the goose is good for the gander. An inventor isn't immune from a superior *right to prevent* held by another patent owner as illustrated in the "Understanding the limits of your rights as a patent owner" section in this chapter.

A patent doesn't give its owner the *right* to do anything with the invention. Instead, think of it as veto power over someone else trying to do something with it. A patent allows the owner to stop others from using, manufacturing, selling, licensing, or otherwise exploiting the specifically covered invention. And that may require a trip to a federal courthouse and paying huge lawyer fees if the infringer isn't deterred by your threat of litigation.

## What your patent can do for your country

The U.S. Patent & Trademark Office (USPTO) is in charge of the United States patent system. The patent system is a limited exception to the general free competition and antimonopolistic principles that underline our body of laws because it gives one person sole control of a possibly important technological field. Yet, in a roundabout way, patents still ensure fair competition among all citizens. A patent gives the inventor incentive to disclose and use his precious invention and, to quote the U.S. Constitution, "promote the progress of science and useful arts."

A patent also publishes the nuts and bolts of the invention, giving the public knowledge of the invention very early on, even though the inventor gets about a 20-year head start in exploiting it. When the patent expires, the inventor can no longer prevent anyone from using the invention or manufacturing and selling anything that falls within that previously taboo area of technology — free competition reigns again, and the country is richer for the technology.

## What your patent can do for you

A patent can be a powerful legal tool that affords you, as an inventor, businessperson, or entrepreneur, the sole right to your technology and a competitive edge in the market. The patent reserves, exclusively for your benefit, an area of technology corresponding roughly to your invention. (We explain in Chapter 8 how the scope of a patent is defined.) For the life of the patent, you can exclude others from making, selling, or using any machine, device, composition of matter, method, process, plant, or design that falls within the technological area defined by the claims in your patent.

After your patent is granted, you can go into business yourself to practice the invention, free of competition. You can also license your patent rights to someone else (a *license* is a lease that allows another party to exploit your invention. In most cases, it is just a promise by the patent owner not to sue the holder of the license). If you've invented something really valuable, potential licensees will be lining up for the opportunity to pay you handsome royalties for the right to profit by your invention.

Or you can *assign* (sell) the patent outright for a bundle, giving the new owner the patent's exclusive benefits for the remaining term of the patent.

# Dissecting the Beast: Three Patent Types

The USPTO issues three kinds of patents:

- **Utility patent:** This patent is the type most people think of when they talk about patents — protection for technological advances and innovation. A utility patent applies to the way something is made, how a device operates, or a process for accomplishing some utilitarian purpose. The subject of a utility patent must result from human activity (and not be a product of nature). It can be any one of the following or an improvement on any of them:

    - A manufactured article, such as barbed wire or a plastic horseshoe.

    - A machine, such as a corn picker or a six-shooter.

    - A composition of matter, such as a fertilizer or a saddle wax.

    - A process for making or doing something, such as a method for braiding barbed wire or a schedule to maximize land use by alternating crops and cattle grazing periods.

    The invention can also be a combination of these things. A new use of an old machine can be patented as a process — for example, using a pesticide to control weeds.

- **Design patent:** This type covers a new and original ornamental shape or the surface treatment of a manufactured article. For example, the cut of a dress or the shape of a table lamp or an automobile body may be protected by a design patent.

- **Plant patent:** Applies to characteristics of a new plant that has been asexually reproduced (by grafting or selective cuttings — without seed manipulation). A new variety of plant, no matter how reproduced, can also be the subject of a utility patent. See document B13 on the CD.

You can't patent a law of nature, such as a mathematical theorem, or a physical phenomenon or property, even if you are the first to discover or articulate it. Einstein couldn't have gotten a patent on his famous equation $E=mc^2$. However, he could have patented the nuclear reactor that implemented that equation.

## *Understanding the limits of your rights as a patent owner*

Under your patent, you can sue anyone who manufactures, sells, markets, or even uses your invention without your permission. It doesn't matter that you, as the patent owner, might be excluded from all those activities yourself under someone else's patent — you still can sue, which can lead to the following conundrum. Say that Jane has a utility patent covering a widget. You've developed a modification to the widget that makes it more efficient and cheaper to produce and have been granted a patent covering the improvement. Jane wants to modify her widget according to your invention, but can't do so without your permission. You, on the other hand, can't make or sell the improved widget without her permission. The solution is to get together and strike a deal. Here are your options:

- ✔ You give her the exclusive right to use your improvement for a fee.
- ✔ She gives you permission, for a fee, to make and sell the improved widgets.
- ✔ Each of you agrees not to sue the other and goes into business using the other's invention without exchange of money.

We see this all the time, so it bears repeating. Receiving your patent does *not* give you the right to make or sell your product. Your product can still infringe someone else's patent.

If you own a design patent, your rights are more restricted. You can't prevent others from using your patented ornamental design on an article that is unrelated to your original one. However, you can prevent others from making the same or a similar article adorned with a similar styling or decoration. It doesn't matter if the article itself is very common and in the public domain.

Say you've patented a new style of silverware that has cylindrical handles with garlands of oak leaves spiraling over their entire lengths. You can prevent others from using the same design on forks, spoons, knives, and serving pieces. If the judge likes you, she may let you convince her that the same style applied to other household items, such as letter openers, hair brushes, and combs, would be an infringement of your patent rights. However, you can't prevent someone else from using your design on columns, fountains, and other things that aren't commonly purchased together with or from the same retail outlets as silverware. But if you flip to Chapter 12, we show you how a copyright on the oak-leaf garland gives you that kind of protection.

A plant patent gives you the right to exclude others from asexually reproducing, selling, or using the plant. It doesn't prevent creation of the plant by fertilization and seeding (sexual reproduction).

## Tracing a patent's life span

Each type of patent has a different life span. Here are the details:

- **Utility patent:** The life span of a utility patent is determined by the application filing date:

  - A utility patent filed before June 8, 1995, will remain in effect until the 17th anniversary of its issue date.

  - A utility patent filed on or after June 8, 1995, is good until the 20th anniversary of the earliest priority date claimed by the applicant. The *priority date* can be the filing date of the application or the filing date of a prior domestic or foreign application that disclosed at least part of the same subject matter. A priority date based on a provisional patent application (see Chapter 8) doesn't count.

- **Design patent:** Granted for a term of 14 years from its issue date.

- **Plant patent:** Determined in the same way as a utility patent.

A patent can expire before its term if it's declared invalid by a court, recalled by the USPTO, surrendered or dedicated to the public by its owner, or cancelled for failure to pay one of the periodical maintenance fees (discussed in Chapter 11).

The term of a patent may be extended beyond the time frames just listed under specific circumstances, usually to compensate the owner if the government significantly delayed the application process while, for instance, reviewing a decision of the patent examiner or getting the invention approved for sale by the Food and Drug Administration (FDA). When your patent is about to issue, the USPTO calculates and notifies you of any term extension attributable to the delay.

# Checking Out the Mechanics: Specifications and Claims

A patent doesn't define any particular device, machine, composition, or process, but sets aside an area of technology just for you. You may compare it to the deed to your house. The deed doesn't spell out the layout of your house and how many bedrooms and bathrooms it has; it describes only the limits of your property by reference to certain landmarks, geographic orientations, and topographic coordinates.

But enough theory — it's time to take a look at how a patent works. Two primary parts of a patent get most of the job done:

✔ **Specification:** This is a description of what the inventor considers to be the best way to practice the invention, accompanied by drawings if necessary. It must be detailed enough to allow a skilled person to practice the invention itself without undue experimentation.

✔ **Claims:** These constitute the legal component that defines the area of technology, based on the specification, that is reserved to the patent owner. Each claim defines a different scope of coverage.

In the following sections, we introduce you to some actual patents, pointing out these two important components in each one. In Chapter 8, we take an in-depth look at how the specifications and claims are drafted, and in Chapter 21, how they are interpreted.

## Lining up a utility patent

Check out the first patent on the CD (document B1). This is a very basic U.S. utility patent for a very simple invention — namely, an imitation wax seal. Each section of the patent has a specific purpose:

✔ The *Abstract* gives a general idea of what the invention is all about.

✔ The *Field of the Invention* tells you the areas of technology involved.

✔ The *Background of the Invention* gives you the reasons and purpose of the invention.

✔ The *Description of the Preferred Embodiment of the Invention* provides an example of the best way to practice the invention.

✔ The *Claims* define the legal boundaries of the patent coverage.

In Chapter 8, we explain how the patent application drafter uses each section to make a case for patentability.

Everything from the Field of the Invention through the Description of the Preferred Embodiment of the Invention and the drawing figures is called the *specification*. But the specification doesn't tell you exactly what this patent covers or, more precisely, what the owner of the patent can prevent others from doing. For that you have to look at the claims, which are on the third page of the application in column 2.

This patent has eight claims, but 1 and 8 are the most important. Claims 2 through 7 just add more details to Claim 1. Notice that Claim 1 is more concise and recites fewer components (no mention of a document) than Claim 8, and it gives it a broader scope than Claim 8. You might say that with claims, less is more.

The shorter the claim, the broader the coverage. A claim defines what the other guys can't do. If your claim lists many elements, you can only sue someone who makes, promotes, sells, or uses a gizmo containing every one of those elements. If you reduce the number of elements recited in the claims, then there are more gizmos out there that include those fewer parts, and more bad guys to sue! Don't go any farther until you have fully grasped this claim concept. It is the foundation of most of what follows. Please, repeat after us:

> Short claim — more coverage — broad patent.
> Long claim — less coverage — narrow patent.

You got it.

In many patents, the actual coverage is broader than the structure described in the specification, but this isn't always the case. In some patents, the coverage is extremely narrow, as you can gather from the long list of items recited in the claims. Determining what a patent covers requires a complex, expert analysis, as you discover in Chapter 21. Let's warn you for now that a patent seldom is what, at first glance, it appears to be.

## Sketching out a design patent

The first design patent on the CD (document B11) is addressed to a paintball gun barrel muzzle.

Note the simplicity of a design patent. It doesn't have an elaborate specification, only the front page and a drawing (a patent drawing usually comprises several figures). In a design patent, the disclosure consists of a line drawing and a brief description of each view. Only one claim is allowed in a design patent, written with a mandatory formal wording.

In a design patent infringement action, the judge or jury compares the accused device to what is shown in the drawing. The infringement test doesn't require an exact sameness, but only a similarity that could confuse an unsuspecting buyer. More on this in Chapter 21.

## Grafting a plant patent

Document B13 is a plant patent for a lily plant. This is a hybrid patent with elements from both a utility and design patent. The specification, including the drawing, discloses the main characteristic of the new plant in substantially the same manner as in a utility patent, except that a photograph may be substituted for the line drawing. You must word the claim formally, as in a design patent. This patent would be infringed by the asexual production and sale of a plant having the same general characteristics illustrated in the document.

# Playing by the Rules: The Three-Part Patentability Test

To qualify as patentable, the invention must fall under one of the three patent types we outline in the section "Dissecting the Beast: Three Patent Types," earlier in this chapter. U.S. law then requires the invention to pass through a series of elaborate tests to meet the three-pronged *patentability test:*

- ✔ **Utility** (practical usefulness, even design and plant patents need to be of some use)
- ✔ **Novelty** (innovativeness, it's gotta be new)
- ✔ **Non-obviousness** (something that isn't immediately apparent to a skilled person)

We discuss these requirements in detail in Chapter 10.

The reason for these laws is to guarantee consistency when granting patents. However, the tests are rather complex, with many accommodations for special cases. In the following sections, we explore each of the hurdles the invention must clear and then provide you with a checklist that you can use to make sure that your invention meets the requirements necessary to receive a patent.

## Making yourself useful

The *utility test* determines whether your invention has any use in the real world. This is an easy one. As long as you can dream up some kind of application for your invention, you won't have any problem passing the utility test. You don't even have to prove that the invention actually works, *except* in the case of some medical inventions. (If you claim a therapeutic treatment or drug that smoothes saddle sores, you must prove its effectiveness by producing laboratory or clinical test results.)

## Developing a novel approach

The *novelty test* requires that you've developed an original way to solve a problem. Your invention will be compared to everything that has been created in the past, which is called the *prior art.* Contrary to what you may think, the newness test is rarely insurmountable. Your patent can't be denied unless a prior art device, machine, or process includes *all* the basic components of your invention as recited in the claims. For example, if you invent a watercraft with a hull made of plastic sheets heat-welded together, it would be considered new even though you found a similar craft in a prior patent that had glued components. But you may have some problem with the next test.

# Avoiding the obvious

The *non-obviousness test* is the crux of the matter and is also the toughest one. To pass, the difference between your invention and the prior art must not be obvious to a person with ordinary skill in the relevant field. The problem with the obviousness test is defining that mythical person with ordinary skill in the field. For example, he wouldn't be your typical weekend do-it-yourselfer or a design engineer, but a good technician who knows or has access to all prior art information in the field of the invention.

Another way to look at it is to say that your invention is not obvious if it provides a solution to a long-standing problem in an offbeat way or, as the courts like to put it, by *teaching away* from the prior art. The two tests are illustrated in the following examples.

### Stating the obvious

Say you are an artist who molds statues and other artifacts out of polyester or other types of *thermosetting resin* (in which the resin hardens with increased temperature, instead of melting). You also sprinkle flakes of aluminum and other metals into your resin in decorative patterns. This type of resin is commonly used to cast countertops and bathroom vanities, so to an ordinary bathroom fixture builder, there's nothing new or non-obvious in your process.

However, while experimenting with different types and sizes of metal flakes, you realize that by reducing the size and increasing the number of metal particles, you can color the entire material in various hues, for example, red with copper dust, silvery gray with aluminum, and so on. If you conduct an anticipation search (see Chapter 7), you won't find your invention in the prior art, but you'd be dead wrong to think that you can get a patent. Even though you've come up with a new product and fabrication process, a patent examiner will probably reject your application for being obvious because a "person with ordinary skill" would expect a change of color when large quantities of small metal particles are scattered in the resin.

### Making the best of a non-obvious situation

Let's take our example a little farther. Being a curious inventor, you notice that the resin reacts with the metal particles, coating each one with a thin layer of oxidation. You now mix the resin with a metal powder made of extremely fine particles. When the metal particles are almost completely oxidized by reaction with the resin, you discover that you've created a new composite material whose physical properties are substantially different from those of past composites. You also observe that your compound conducts heat more like a metal than a plastic substance, but doesn't conduct electricity.

Can you get a patent on that baby? You bet you can! Your results wouldn't be obvious to anyone with ordinary skill in the fields of plastics and electrical insulators. For years, electrical engineers have been looking for a material that insulates electronic components from one another and effectively dissipates the heat the components generate. Congratulations! You found an unexpected solution to a long-standing problem in electrical assemblies. (Actually, someone else did. For those interested in this technology, check out the sixth patent (document B6) on the CD.)

## *Making a list and checking it twice*

We've got to warn you that the following rules are mysterious, obscure, and foggy. But they are important, and you'll have to refer to them on several occasions. So, douse the fire, put away your harmonica, and concentrate.

If you're still a little fuzzy after reviewing the following list, don't worry. If you *fully* grasp these concepts, you'd be able to pass the patent bar exam — and no one is asking you to do that. If you decide to go after a patent, your attorney will investigate these matters with you. So for now, just be aware of these rules and make an initial analysis of how your invention would score.

- ✔ **The invention must be useful.** The utility test can be satisfied if you can show that the invention is practical.

  A method for growing parsley in your nose may appear totally crazy and useless. Who would want to grow an herb in his nasal cavities? But who is to forbid such an innocent activity? Certainly not the USPTO. After all, you might relish the fragrance of fresh parsley. What better way to satisfy your olfactory fetish than to keep a sprig of it in your nose at all times? It could also measurably reduce your carbon footprint (by removing $CO_2$ and producing oxygen). This argument, as silly it may sound, is enough to establish utility.

- ✔ **The invention must have some credibility.** If you apply for a patent on a product or process that runs contrary to the laws of physics, you'll be asked to provide persuasive evidence that it actually works. Typically you don't need a working prototype to apply for a patent. But, applications for perpetual motion machines are routinely rejected because of the inventors' failure to convincingly demonstrate that their contraptions work.

The USPTO demands laboratory or clinical proof that pharmaceuticals are effective. If you claim a new formula to treat hair loss, don't waste time and money filing a patent application unless you have solid test results or the means to conduct appropriate and successful clinical trials.

✓ **The invention must be practicable.** You must be able to practice the invention with existing components and materials. For example, if your invention requires milling a component down to a micron range, and no equipment is available to do so, your invention is indeed useless.

✓ **The invention can't have been previously known or used by others in the United States before your date of invention.** If someone else had possession or knowledge of the invention before you did and didn't willfully conceal it from the public or abandon it, you're out of luck. It doesn't matter that you came up with the invention on your own and didn't know about the other dude.

✓ **The invention can't be patented or described in a printed publication before your date of invention anywhere in the world.** The fact that your invention was known or used for a long time in a foreign country doesn't prevent you from obtaining a patent under the previous entry. But if a printed description of it is readily available to the public before your date of invention, anywhere or in any language, you're out.

✓ **The invention can't be patented or described anywhere in a printed publication more than one year before you file your application.** If someone prints or tries to patent an invention that you had first, you'd better hurry up and file. If you wait more than a year, it won't matter that your date of invention came first. The critical date is not the date of invention but one year prior to the filing date of the application.

✓ **The invention can't be in public use or on sale in the United States more than one year before you file the application.** This clause relates to your own prior activities as well as those of others. However, an experimental use isn't considered to be a public use, so your secret research and development activities are exempt — another good reason to use confidentiality agreements (see Chapter 4).

✓ **The inventor can't abandon it.** *Abandonment* means not intending to pursue an invention by use or patents. It may be proved by an unjustified long inactive period before filing a patent application or putting the invention on the market. Your prior knowledge of the abandoned invention won't prevent a later inventor from getting the patent.

✓ **The inventor can't get a foreign patent before filing an application in the United States, unless the foreign application was filed less than one year before the U.S. application.** Almost all countries impose this one-year deadline from the filing in a foreign jurisdiction. (See Chapter 19 and the Paris Convention — document D12 on the CD.)

✔ **The invention must not be described in someone else's patent or published patent application filed in the United States prior to the date of invention by the applicant.** This rule doesn't require that somebody knew about or used the thing prior to your date of invention, only that the other guy's patent or published application discloses it. However, knowledge and use of the invention abroad (without description in a publication) doesn't, by itself, prevent a later U.S. inventor from obtaining a patent. Most patent applications are published (open to the public) about 18 months after the filing date.

✔ **The applicant must be the inventor.** The applicant must have come up with the invention on his own and not learned about it on vacation.

✔ **The applicant must be the first to file an application for patent in the United States.** This new requirement has been introduced in a patent revision bill now being discussed in Congress and expected to become effective in early 2009. Under current law, priority between competing patent applications is given to the applicant who was first to invent. It'll be a lot easier to verify which inventor was the first to file than it has been to determine who was the first to come up with the invention. Lawyers like us make quite a few bucks fighting that battle on behalf of our clients. We're sure you'll share our despair. Be aware that the new rule will establish a race to the USPTO that you'd better not lose. You've got to be first. Don't procrastinate — file as soon as possible!

✔ **The invention must not be obvious to a person with ordinary skill in the field at the time of the invention.** This is the last and toughest of the rules. Countless court decisions have struggled with this requirement of non-obviousness. Review the "Avoiding the obvious" section.

# Chapter 6

# Testing the Patent Water Before You Dive In

*In This Chapter*

▶ Nailing down your invention

▶ Determining whether a patent is right for you

▶ Making the most of your time and money

*P*rotecting a technological breakthrough with one or more patents isn't a trivial undertaking. The complexity, costs, and long delays that accompany such a project necessitate a clear understanding of the process and a thorough exploration of alternative, more practical, and less expensive approaches.

But don't let us scare you — we've no intention of discouraging you from applying for a patent. Far from it. A patent can be an effective protection tool that provides you with a lucrative source of income. However, we've seen many inventors jump into the patent-application fray with no reasonable prospect of seeing it through to a successful completion. If you think you have a patentable invention after reading Chapter 5, take a deep breath and follow us through the prepatent exercises we describe in this chapter. But don't waste too much time weighing the pros and cons. If someone else files for the same invention before you do, you may be out of the game.

## Assessing What You Have

The first step in attempting to protect an invention or other technological breakthrough is formulating a clear vision of your idea and determining what rights you have to it. Be prepared for some surprises.

## Defining the invention in writing

At first glance, preparing a written description of your invention may seem like a childish exercise, but that's what patent attorneys do to sharpen the invention before actually drafting an application. So, follow their lead. Go over your notes, drawings, and models and write down an accurate description of your new device, process, or composition. You need to be as concise as possible — 15 lines at the most — without missing any key features that make your invention new and unique. Help yourself by drawing a little sketch of your invention with cross-reference numbers that refer back to the written description.

Focus on the nuts and bolts of the invention in your description — how it's made and how it operates, rather than its advantages and commercial applications. Keep in mind that you're not drafting an advertising pamphlet, but a technical paper. Such a description will become the cornerstone of the patent application, so make sure that it's technically accurate and complete. This description is also exactly what a professional needs to conduct a patent anticipation search.

## Qualifying the invention

Now, you must determine whether your invention qualifies for a patent. You don't need to do the detailed analysis of a patent examiner, but we want you to be sure that your invention exceeds the basic patentability threshold. Don't waste your time pursuing a patent process that's already doomed to failure because of an inherent flaw in your invention or idea.

Rising above the *basic patentability threshold* first means finding out whether your invention fits into one of the three categories of patents — utility, design, or plant patents. Then pit your invention against the critical patentability factors — novelty, utility, and non-obvious nature — that make up the three-part patentability test we describe in Chapter 5. If your invention still looks good, you can double-check your findings against the patentability checklist, that bunch of hoops you must jump through to get a patent, as we discuss in the last part of Chapter 5.

When you get to the last part of the patentability test — the one about whether your invention is something that would be obvious to someone of ordinary related skills, don't waste too much time wracking your brain: That happens to be the million-dollar question to which a patent examiner or a judge named Regis will provide the final answer.

## Coming up with an inventor

Be brutally honest in assessing whether you alone conceived the invention or whether someone else made suggestions or contributed to the concept. You also need to know whether anyone else refined or improved the device when you built the prototype or model. Maybe a co-worker or your 10-year-old whiz kid helped you out. Regardless of the circumstance, make sure that you acknowledge any helpful outside contribution now. Any contributor may have rights that are equal to yours and therefore must (by law) be listed as a co-inventor on the patent application.

Determining exactly who came up with your invention is an extremely tricky but critical legal issue that requires the advice of a competent intellectual property (IP) professional.

## Figuring out ownership

Ownership of an invention and patent is related to but still a separate issue from inventorship. We look at it from two perspectives: securing ownership of contributions to the invention by others and ensuring ownership of your own creations.

### Acquiring contributions

Taking care of your invention's ownership issues early in the game lessens the likelihood that you'll run into problems later. It's not unusual for a former associate, employee, neighbor, or relative to claim a role in a commercially successful invention, so watch out for that cousin Ernie who's always giving you advice you don't need! Troublesome people always seem to crawl out of the woodwork to claim their shares of the loot at the most difficult times in an entrepreneurial venture.

If anyone contributed to your invention, secure your exclusive ownership through agreements with that contributor, regardless of who's named as inventor on the patent application. You can use the same type of agreement discussed in Chapter 13 in connection with copyrights. Ask your IP attorney to draft an invention and patent transfer agreement that fits your circumstances and complies with your state laws and local restrictions on invention assignments (transfers), which we mention in the next section.

### Claiming your own creation

If you invent something in your role as an employee, chances are you have no right to that invention, even if you invented it entirely on your own. You need to establish that you own your invention, so check through these sticky points before proceeding with a patent:

- ✔ Employment intake forms often include invention-assignment clauses that folks sign without much thought. Unless state law forbids or restricts such an agreement, even an invention made entirely at home and using your own resources in any technological field may actually belong to your boss.

- ✔ A business may have a *shop right* (a right to freely use your invention) if any part of its facilities was used in developing that invention.

- ✔ Even an unwritten agreement to work together on a project or an advance of funds can trigger the establishment of a legal partnership where everything belongs to all the joint venturers in common.

- ✔ Federal law provides that if the invention was developed as part of a governmental project or under a government grant, Uncle Sam gets a piece of the action.

Don't waste time and money on something that may not be yours. If you have any concerns in this area, consult an IP professional.

## Selecting the filing entity

In the United States, an inventor must sign and file the patent application (except for a provisional application, discussed in Chapter 8), even if the inventor doesn't own the invention. However, in most foreign countries, the application can be signed and filed by the inventor or the owner of the invention. If the inventor is dead or incapacitated, a legal representative, such as an executor, heir, administrator, guardian, or conservator can sign and file the application with documentary evidence of his or her authority.

Identifying the filing entity gets a little trickier when inventors can't be found or refuse to cooperate and sign the application. We've seen it happen. An employee-inventor becomes frustrated after realizing she doesn't own her inventions and quits her job or refuses to help the employer get a patent. When that's the case, anyone who can show a documented right to the invention, including a co-inventor or employer, can file on behalf of an absent or unwilling inventor. The procedure requires an earnest attempt to notify and offer the missing party the opportunity to join in the application.

# *Making Sure that 10-Gallon Hat Is Right for You*

So you think you have a patentable invention. It's all yours, and you have the right to file a patent application. Now you get to play homesteader and decide whether this patent is the fertile valley of your dreams where after years of hard work you'll harvest the fruits of success . . . or starve.

## *Comparing the pros with the cons of the patent game*

Applying for a patent is a lengthy, expensive, and uncertain endeavor. Therefore, you should understand all the alternative, less-taxing approaches for protecting your invention. You may want to use one or more of those approaches rather than or in addition to the patent application.

First, though, look at the advantages and disadvantages of applying for a patent. The advantages:

- **Broad scope of protection:** Can extend to a broad field of technology beyond your own imagination.

- **Powerful anti-competition tool:** Business people are wary of infringing patents because of high litigation costs and damages awards.

- **Increase in the value of your business:** A patent portfolio is a must if you want to raise capital.

Not to be ignored, the disadvantages:

- **High costs:** The costs are extremely high and unpredictable. Patenting is a continuous process often requiring multiple applications to cover all aspects of the invention and subsequent improvements. And that's without even thinking about enforcing your patent against some infringer. (Make sure you're sitting down when you get to Chapter 21.)

- **Your secret is out:** You must bare it all in your application, making it easy for others to use your invention as soon as the patent expires or to design around the manner you have claimed it in your application.

- **Long wait for (relatively) short-lived protection:** The protection lasts 20 years at the most from your earliest application filing date.

The bottom line: Don't sell the range to raise money for the seed.

# Exploring alternative routes

If you decide that the advantages aren't worth the disadvantages of applying for a patent, you might still secure a substantial degree of protection for your invention. These following approaches are easier, less expensive, and can usually be completed in less time.

### Looking at trade secrets

If you're dealing with a chemical or process invention or other improvement that you don't have to expose to your customers or to the general public and can keep under your sombrero, a patent application may not be the best approach.

Check out what Chapters 1 and 4 have to say about using a trade-secret strategy. The most serious risk is that someone else will independently discover the invention you're keeping secret, file a patent application, get a patent, and cause you considerable grief.

In general, keeping an invention a trade secret is a great idea when the useful life of the invention is relatively short — less than seven years. The odds against someone else discovering the same invention and obtaining a patent during that period are in your favor.

### Backing up your trade secret with a covert patent application

If you think your invention will give you a strong competitive edge for seven or more years, it may be prudent to keep the invention a secret, and also back up your trade secret by filing a patent application within the first year of putting it into general use. If somebody spills the beans, you can let your application turn into a patent whose priority right goes back to your original filing date. Taking advantage of the fact that patent applications are initially held in secrecy, you begin by filing a provisional application (see Chapter 8). This provisional application is relatively inexpensive and is good for 12 months. This gives you 24 months of back-up protection. If at that time, your trade secret looks like it's holding up and not likely to be broken in the future, you can abandon the patenting process. But if you're still concerned, you can file a scaled-down formal patent application with only one or two claims at a relatively low cost.

If you're not interested in foreign patents, you can file a request that your application not be published at the 18-month anniversary from priority (see Chapter 9). Your technology won't be made public until you allow the formal application to turn into a patent, no earlier than two or three years down the line. You can even extend the covert application process time to several more years by stringing up a line of continuation patent applications and making sure none of them is published (see Chapter 9). This clever strategy is now under attack in Congress and in the USPTO. Laws and regulations have been drafted, but not yet implemented, to limit the number of patent applications that an applicant can present covering the same subject matter.

### Getting protection under a copyright

As we explain in Chapter 2, copyrights are typically so simple and inexpensive to secure that they always need to be part of your IP protection strategy.

Copyright doesn't cover facts, concepts, or processes the way a patent does. It does, however, cover the way that a concept or process is expressed. We apologize for this legal nicety, but it's nothing trivial (see Chapter 1). Making the copyright-for-patent substitution may be particularly applicable for protecting:

- ✔ **An invention that uses a computer program:** Relying on copyright protection is particularly effective if you've invented a type of process or method that's implemented with a computer program. But remember, the copyright covers only the written part of the program and not the actual process.

  Say you've developed a complex process for shredding recyclable rubber, melting it, and turning it into a paste that can be molded at room temperature for 24 hours before it cures into a resilient body. The method consists of multiple steps involving precise temperature and timing controls which must be automatically managed by computer.

  A copyright on the computer program prevents others from copying your specific application but doesn't prevent anyone who's familiar with your process from independently devising essentially the same process and writing an original computer program to achieve the same results. But you can charge anyone with copyright infringement who copies any part of *your* software while trying to devise such a process. Along with copyright protection, you need to keep *your process* confidential as a trade secret. (See Chapter 12 for info about registering a software copyright without revealing your trade secret.)

- ✔ **Style and ornamentation:** Instead of seeking a design patent to protect the style or ornamentation of your product, a simple copyright may do the trick. The styling or ornamentation must stand separately from the product, meaning it must be detachable from the product (it can be reproduced independently) for copyright to protect it. Using a table lamp made from a statue as an example; the statue itself, independent of the base, stem, and shade, is protected by copyright.

Although clothing style and fashion can only be protected with a design patent, you can copyright surface embroidery and other decoration that can stand separately from the garment.

✔ **Peripheral material:** Manuals, promotional material, packaging, presentations, lectures, and handouts qualify for copyright protection. Making sure that peripheral materials are properly copyrighted goes a long way toward substantially stifling your competitors.

Because of its inability to cover concepts and processes, a copyright won't extend to some parts of a manual, mode of operation, or game rules because of their essentially functional aspects (see Chapter 12).

### Going design rather than utility

A design patent is intended to cover purely decorative and nonfunctional aspects of a product. However, we've seen cases where a design patent turned out to be a more effective tool than a utility patent in quashing an infringer. Remember that's the crux of the matter — being able to stop a copycat in his tracks. On the CD (documents B6 and B7) we show both design and a utility patent on the same product.

In one case, the product was a wallet designed for law enforcement officers. A section of the wallet featured a fabric pad onto which a badge could be pinned and a flap that covered the badge so that the wallet could be used without revealing the owner's profession. The wallet was protected by both utility and design patents, but a competitor, as most copycats do, simply duplicated the whole thing down to the shape of the flap. While presenting the case to a judge, the patent holder's attorney relied exclusively on the design patent when asking for a restraining order pending a trial. The similarity of the accused's article to the patented wallet was enough to persuade the judge to grant the order. Had the attorney relied on the utility patent, the judge would've required expert testimony about prior art and other complex, costly procedures. The defendant gave up and settled the case the next day.

The protected appearance of your device may be so striking that a copycat would find marketing a competitive product difficult without using the same look. For instance, look at the distinctive shape and ornamentation of the canister packaging for Morton brand of cooking salt. Can you imagine yourself picking up salt presented in a totally different container? You automatically rely on the look of the product and don't have to read the brand name to know what you're buying.

You can add to your design patent sufficient material to support a utility application. Later on, and before your design application issues, you can file a divisional utility application. Be careful. This maneuver can be dangerous if there isn't enough descriptive material to support your later utility claims.

### Appreciating trade dress

*Trade dress* isn't about what the saloon girls wear. In general, it covers the way a product or service is presented to the public, and can be protected by a configuration mark. In effect, a *configuration mark* acts pretty much like a design patent by protecting the look of a product or service establishment. Furthermore, a configuration mark, contrary to a design patent, can be established quickly and inexpensively and lasts as long as the configuration is used in commerce. Notice that a configuration mark does not need to meet the novelty requirement the way a patent does.

Product packaging trade dress is treated differently from product design trade dress. You can only obtain a configuration mark on a product design after the public associates that design with your company through a period of exclusive use. This is also known a *secondary meaning* and applies to acquired distinctiveness in all trademarks, not just configuration marks (more in Chapter 15). Some packaging, or trade dress like the taco shop discussed below, can be inherently distinctive and thus does not require secondary meaning.

Trade dress, independent of the product or package, must be both distinctive and non-functional. To be distinctive, it must be different than anything else on the market. To be non-functional, the styling or ornamentation must not present any advantages other than aesthetic ones.

However, the non-functionality rule does have a hair-splitting exception: An *arbitrary* combination of functional characteristics can qualify for protection as a configuration mark. Say, for example, you want to open a taco shop with a little character, a nonlegal term for trade dress. At the entrance, you mount a tilting garage door. You serve drinks from coiled hoses hanging from the ceiling like grease guns. The seats are steel benches covered with wire mesh and the table feet are made of chrome car wheels. The door, drink dispensers, benches, and wheels are all functional elements, yet the entire combination is arbitrary. This combination is protected as trade dress.

You may ask: Why, with all the advantages of a configuration mark, would anyone ever bother filing a design patent application? That's easy . . . design patents have their own merits. First and foremost, a design patent carries all the prestige of a patent. Second, it can be acquired and enforced independently of any commercial activity. A configuration mark, by contrast, exists only when associated with a business. (In Chapter 15, we show you how to select and protect a configuration mark.)

### Recognizing the role of commercial identifiers

All this protection stuff we've been talking about serves only one purpose. It gives you an edge over the competition. The same can be said of good *commercial identifiers,* so don't overlook the marketing power of a good trademark, servicemark, or a company name.

Look at all the products around you. Almost every one of them has a trademark prominently displayed on it. Now see how many patent numbers you can find. Two, one, or none at all? In most cases, the market position of a product or service is enhanced more by its brand and packaging than it is by a patent.

Would you consider buying fabric fastener strips under any other brand than Velcro? Do you see much advertising for this product on TV or in magazines? Nope. The name does the marketing. You want another motivating brand name? How about Cover Girl brand of cosmetics? After all, what do many young ladies aspire to be or look like? A glamorous cover girl. Check out Chapter 16 to discover how to create powerful names.

# Starting Things Off on the Right Foot

The wild blue yonder of patents and patent applications is no place for a rookie pilot's first solo flight. Even though explosive legal issues lurk behind every cloud, you can do some of the work without waiting for professional advice or assistance. You can also use the guidelines that we provide in Chapter 7 and conduct a preliminary search to find out exactly what has previously been done in the area of your invention. A little preliminary digging can't hurt if you don't waste too much time on it.

## Making a record of your invention

As you develop your product or process, take copious notes that include plenty of illustrative sketches, preferably in a bound notebook with numbered pages. Use a pen, not a pencil, and don't erase but cross out your mistakes. Once in a while, ask a trusted relative or friend to review your notes, date, and sign the last written page, stating that on the specified date, she or he read the notes and understood the invention.

If you keep your notes on a computer, print them out periodically, have your witness sign and date every page, and keep them in a file. These precautions are necessary because you need to know how to create a legally admissible document. Don't waste your time sending a description of your invention through the mail to someone else or to yourself. The time stamp on the postmark won't hold up in court as proof that you owned the invention at that particular point in time.

Your well-kept notebook, however, has many uses. It can

✔ Provide your IP professional with a complete history and disclosure of the invention. He or she, in turn, may see something in some of your earlier and now discarded designs that deserves a patent.

✔ Provide convincing evidence of the date that you first conceived the invention and reduced it to practice, which is especially important when you're trying to prove to the patent examiner that you came up with the invention before it was known or used by others in this country, or before it was patented or described in a printed publication here or abroad. (See the last section of Chapter 5.).

✔ Help you organize your thoughts, providing an easy review of your progress and helping you avoid reinventing the wheel.

## Using the disclosure document program

Under the *disclosure document program,* the USPTO allows you to file an informal description of your invention that isn't examined but is kept secret for two years. If you file a patent application within two years and mention the earlier filing, the informal description becomes part of your application file although you don't get the same statutory priority as a provisional application. If you go past the deadline, your description is destroyed.

This program is obsolete and is mainly used by unscrupulous invention development companies to make you believe they've "filed" your invention in the USPTO. You're better off filing a provisional application, as we discuss in Chapter 9.

## Be first in line

A congressional bill titled The Patent Reform Act of 2007, whenever it is adopted, will bring radical changes in the way patents are applied for and granted. Most significantly, an eventual conflict between two contemporaneous inventors will no longer be resolved in favor of the party who was the *first to invent.* Instead, the patent will be granted to the *first to file* her application. This radical change puts a big premium on early filing. You must apply for a patent as soon as you have defined your invention, or even sooner; that is before you've worked out all the minute details. You can always file a more complete *continuation* application later, as a substitute or supplement to your initial application. Alternately, you may opt to start with a *provisional* application (see Chapter 9 for definitions of provisional and continuation applications).

An early or even premature filing is particularly indicated if you have reasons to believe that others are working in the very same field of technology. But you have to be careful with whatever you file. Every piece of paper, including discarded provisional applications, may be used against you later to show some minute restriction to how the language of your eventual patent is interpreted.

Considering the hassle and added costs of preparing and filing a provisional application or a subsequent continuation application, the decision about what to file and when can throw you in a hobble. Before you get your spurs all tangled up, consult your IP practitioner.

# Chapter 7

# Hoping It Ain't There:
# The Patent Search

In This Chapter

▶ Deciding to conduct a preliminary online patent search

▶ Developing a search strategy

▶ Understanding search results

▶ Doing other types of patent searches

*P*reparing and filing a patent application takes a lot of time and a good chunk of change. After pushing that application through the U.S. Patent and Trademark Office (USPTO) and shelling out all that cash, how would you feel, some 15 months down the line, if the patent examiner says that a complete description of your invention can be found in patent number so and so? (See Chapters 8 through 11 for a more detailed trip down the long and winding road to a patent.)

You can find out whether your invention is old hat or is innovative enough to deserve its own patent by conducting an *anticipation search,* also called a *patentability search* — a careful study of published patents and other documents relevant to your invention that make up the so-called *prior art*. An anticipation search is also the most common type of search, so we begin this chapter with it. (Other types of searches are described in "Looking at Other Patent Searches," at the end of this chapter.)

No law says you *have* to do an anticipation search before filing your patent application. But by first looking at prior patents, as well as technical books and other publications in the area of your invention, you can save yourself a lot of money and avoid a great deal of embarrassment. Further, the results of the search can help you or your IP professional prepare a better — not just cheaper — application.

Most inventors don't understand what they can gain or lose by conducting a preliminary patent search, or whether one is even indicated. In this chapter, we talk about the pros and cons of doing a search, how to conduct one, and how to interpret what you find. We also provide some tips to the "do-it-yourself" searcher.

# The Preliminary Online Search: What Did We Do without the Internet?

Before the Internet, we spent lots of time scanning trays and trays of index cards in musty libraries under the judgmental, enforcing eye of the assistant librarian, often getting nowhere. But now, anyone with a mouse, an itchy index finger, and an afternoon to kill can do a pretty decent preliminary anticipation search.

The *preliminary* online search should *not* be confused with a full-blown anticipation search, which is best conducted by a professional searcher and where the results are analyzed by an IP professional.

The best place to start a preliminary online search is at the USPTO Web site (www.uspto.gov) which is structured to service both the knowledgeable old hand as well as the greenhorn. Afterwards, you can try a broad-based Internet search by using Google, Yahoo!, or other search engine.

Google has recently launched its own U.S. patent search service at www.google.com/patents, now under beta testing. The site currently does not appear to state whether your searches remain confidential or what Google may be doing with the records they keep of your search. Therefore, we focus our discussion on using the USPTO Web site.

As always, you should be careful when typing information into a field on a Web page, even if it's one as presumably trustworthy as that of the USPTO. Currently, the search section at the USPTO is *not* necessarily secure. Although it may be unlikely, there are dozens of ways for your information to get diverted into the wrong hands.

The search at the USPTO Web site is keyword based, which sounds good at first but more often than not yields spotty results. You see, unfortunately, most patents are not written by normal people. They're written by a loony bunch of IP professionals who seem to have an odd-word fetish. Instead of describing a spring as . . . well . . . a *spring*, these wacky characters are more likely to call it a *resilient biasing member*. So, a good keyword search includes lots of synonyms. Keep a thesaurus handy. Keep in mind that you're not looking for a prior patent that shows every detail of your invention, but something that comes close to it or might suggest its main features.

From the USPTO's Patents main page, begin your search by clicking the "How to Search" link and then (after reading the helpful info) click the "Search patents now" link. You can restrict your search to a specific field, such as *Title* or *Abstract*. Play around. If you get too many hits, narrow the full text search to just the title, or add another key word. For more details on this type of searching, see "Examining patent documents," later in this chapter.

Search published applications as well as issued patents. The USPTO divides these two types of references into two separate databases. Also, if you've already hired a patent attorney or agent, you may want her to conduct a quick preliminary keyword search for you. Most IP professionals have had some experience doing these types of searches and may find just what you're looking for quickly and inexpensively.

# Upping the Ante: The Professional Anticipation Search

So you've pulled an all-nighter, drunk a whole pot of coffee, but you found nothing resembling your invention at the USPTO Web site or on the rest of the Internet. You're starting to feel a little confident. And, although you don't admit it to yourself, you're starting to think about whether you're going to retire to Hawaii or Florida.

But now is the time to splash some cold water on your face. In our experience most inventions that are brought to us turn out to be unpatentable — even after a favorable result to a preliminary patent search. This means that you should treat the favorable result as just another rung on the ladder to getting a patent, nothing more.

So far your journey to a patent has used up a lot of brain cells, but there hasn't been much out-of-pocket expense. The next step requires you to decide whether or not to turn on the spigot attached to your wallet and hire a professional searcher.

Hiring a professional searcher is a tough decision, but it may be the most important one. A professional search can tell, with much greater confidence than you can, whether your creation is patentable. However, because a professional search delays the filing of your patent application, isn't cheap, and is no guarantee that you'll get a patent, you shouldn't jump into it without weighing the pros and cons. So let's do that.

## Compelling reasons to do a professional search

If your search uncovers something very close to your invention, you save yourself the cost and aggravation of filing a patent application only to have it rejected after two or three years of futile pursuit. But don't despair; you can possibly use this information to improve and refine your invention or to help you draft a more focused and convincing patent application — one that forestalls the examiner's rejection of the invention in view of the closest prior art. Avoiding even one sweaty round in the ring duking it out with the examiner can save you more than the money it costs to do the search.

Perhaps the best reason to do a professional search: It gives you some peace of mind and confirms that you and your invention are starting down the right road.

## Some valid reasons for skipping the professional search

One potential hazard of doing a thorough patent search is that while you're waiting for the results before filing your application, someone else may file for a similar invention. And he'll end up with the patent — not you.

As we explain a little later in this chapter, no one can ever safely rely on a search to positively conclude that your gadget is new and deserves a patent, or that there's absolutely nothing patentable in its design.

The high cost of a professional search and interpretation, which could set you back $1,000 to $1,500, is another reason some people avoid doing one. And extending a search to technical publications may end up costing more than the preparation and filing of the application itself.

You could file a quick-strike provisional patent application of the type described in Chapter 8 right off the bat to nail down an early filing date. Later, after you receive your search results, you can file a more thorough provisional or a formal patent application.

## Deciding whether a professional search is right for you

Why would anyone bother with such a time-consuming and costly procedure instead of just filing the patent application? It's all a matter of balance — weighing the peace of mind that a successful search can give you against the high cost in time and money.

We can only help you by suggesting a simple, reliable, cost-effective approach: Do a professional anticipation search only if you suspect that your invention may not be new.

A search may be a good idea if your invention meets two or more of these criteria:

- ✔ The invention is relatively simple.
- ✔ The invention belongs to a low-tech field.
- ✔ The invention isn't fully developed.
- ✔ The invention is marginally useful or practical.
- ✔ The invention uses very old or obsolete technology.
- ✔ The invention is just another version of a very common device.
- ✔ The invention closely resembles something that already exists.
- ✔ The invention is outside your area of expertise.

## Getting a second opinion

Like every inventor, you may tend to overestimate the importance and novelty of your creation. Before you get carried away, get a second opinion from an expert in the field. Let your technical expert (or a patent attorney) review the criteria listed in the preceding section and give you an educated guess as to whether your invention is unique before you do a long and expensive search. (Check out Chapter 3 for more on dealing with patent agents and attorneys.)

Finding someone who's willing to stick his neck out and give an opinion without the benefit of a search may be hard to do. You may have to agree, in writing, not to hold it against him if he guesses wrong.

# Conducting Your Own "Professional" Anticipation Search

In the classic film *All About Eve,* Bette Davis's character says, "Fasten your seat belts — it's going to be a bumpy night." We can say the same of conducting and analyzing your own thorough patent searches. So buckle up and bear with us on a trip through some arcane, Byzantine, convoluted, disorienting, eccentric, foggy, and goofy legal concepts.

When you perform an anticipation patent search, you're trying to anticipate how the patent examiner will deal with your application. Therefore, your search shouldn't be limited to looking through documents for something resembling your invention. You also need to analyze what you find under the rules of patentability to decide whether your invention qualifies for a patent. To do this, you must step into the shoes of a patent examiner and

✔ Look for information about the area of your invention, commonly called the *relevant prior art* as defined in the next section.

✔ Apply the patentability test described in Chapter 5 (the whole utility, novelty, and non-obviousness thing, that is) to your invention in view of the relevant prior art to determine whether your invention is patentable.

## Looking for relevant prior art

When rejecting patent applications, examiners have been known to rely on prior publications as diverse as the writings of Homer, the ninth-century BC Greek poet, scholarly papers of all types and languages, and, of course, domestic and foreign patents.

We've seen a patent application for a wet suit rejected because of a drawing of a medieval suit of armor published in an encyclopedia circa 1900!

Accordingly, prior patents are not the only source of prior art. Any other published document can be used against your application. However, not all prior technology related to your invention is legally admissible against your patent application. Drawn from patentability tests in Chapter 5, the following prior patents and publications *don't* qualify as relevant prior art:

✔ Anything done in a foreign country that wasn't described in a printed publication and is not generally known in the United States.

✔ Anything that wasn't disclosed, published, patented, or generally available in the United States more than one year ago.

✔ Anything that falls outside the *analogous field* of your invention. That field includes anything that you as an inventor would look into while developing your invention and that is directly pertinent to your invention. In a landmark decision, a court ruled that paper stapler technology is outside the analogous field of surgical staplers used to repair digestive organs.

The Internet makes it much easier for anyone to publish potential prior art. Your wife's nephew's best friend's older brother Scooter could have posted on his blog the idea of a Bluetooth fountain pen that automatically inputs chicken scratch handwriting into a computer text file (see document B7 on the CD). Without any discussion of accelerometers, wireless data communication protocols, and character-recognition software, Scooter's blog entry may be enough to qualify as prior art and torpedo your broadest claims to the concept.

## Moving beyond keywords

Believe it or not, by Valentine's Day, 2006, the United States had issued 7,000,000 patents. A patent examiner could use any of these millions of documents (including expired, cancelled and abandoned patents, or even published applications) as proof that your doodad is neither new nor non-obvious.

It's almost impossible to contemplate sifting through such a mountain of documents without using keywords. However, keyword searches have their limitations. It is often very difficult for the search engine and the searcher to come up with all useful synonyms. Plus, the full text of many earlier patent documents have yet not made it into many searchable databases. The USPTO database only provides the full text of U.S. patents issued after 1975.

To move beyond the limitations of keyword searching when doing your antic-ipation search, you need to take advantage of *patent classifications*.

Patents are grouped into a number of technological classes, allowing you to limit your search to the fields of technology most related to your invention. You can find the appropriate classifications in the *Manual of Classifications* published by the USPTO (`www.uspto.gov/patft/`). This manual covers all fields of technology, organized according to international standards. After you find the class or classes that relate to your invention, you can use them to retrieve both U.S. and foreign prior patents. If your invention is simple and well defined, you can limit the search to just one relevant class.

## Examining patent documents

Searching patent documents can be as difficult and frustrating as looking for a wayward golf ball in a thorny thicket along the fairway. You have to sort through odd language while looking in lots of out-of-the-way places for your idea. Just as you may miss a ball caught in the bushes if you look only at the ground, you have to look at all sections of the patent document.

But don't fret — here's a short course in navigating utility patent documents on the USPTO Web site. An issued patent, or a published patent application, can be divided into five sections:

✔ The *reference section,* shown on the front pages of the patents, gives information that identifies the patent. Besides the patent number, title of the invention, name of the inventor, name of the assignee (owner), if any, filing date, and identification of related applications by the same inventor, the section also includes international and U.S. class numbers and a list of related documents under the legend *References Cited.*

The class numbers refer to the standard technological classes where the subject invention falls. The related documents are prior publications that were cited during the patent application examination because they contain material related to the invention.

When viewed online, each cited reference is typically a hyperlink. Further, there is a link to subsequently issued references which the patent you're looking at was cited against under the heading *Referenced By.*

✔ The *abstract* gives you a very concise, but often very narrow, description of the invention, which is usually illustrated by a representative figure of the drawing.

Don't conclude that the patent isn't relevant to your invention just because you don't recognize your baby in the abstract or the illustration This info can be very misleading as to the true contents of the document. Look at the whole enchilada.

✔ The next pages carry the drawing figures with reference numbers that identify the components of the depicted devices. Some chemical patents that can be described with molecular diagrams alone don't have a drawing.

✔ The subsequent pages of typed text, arranged in two columns, under appropriate section headers, give you

  • The field and background of the invention.

  • A summary that's meatier than the abstract.

  • A brief description of each drawing figure.

  • A detailed description of the inventor's preferred embodiment of the invention. This description is the meat of the document — go over this section with a fine-toothed comb.

✔ After an opening phrase, such as "What is claimed," you find a numbered list of one-sentence definitions (technically called the *claims*) of what the inventor considers to be his contribution to the art — in other words, his invention. Don't let the formal and circuitous wording of these documents confuse you. Refer to Chapter 5 to get an idea how claims must be read. If necessary, grab a pencil and a sheet of paper and draw a diagram of the described structure.

# Organizing and conducting the search

You must map out a search strategy by deciding where and how to search. The following are your options.

### Searching manually or electronically

You can conduct "professional" anticipation searches in two basic ways: manually and electronically.

✔ You can search manually in the library of the USPTO in Arlington, Virginia, or in one of the USPTO depository public libraries in major U.S. cities. Begin by thumbing through reference manuals, such as the *Manual of Classifications,* for a list of patents to look at. Then get paper copies of those patents, kept by class in so-called "shoe boxes." In a depository library, you must look through microfilm copies of the patents.

To find a USPTO depository library near you (commonly called a Patent and Trademark Depository Library or PTDL), go to www.uspto.gov/go/ptdl/ptdlib_1.html.

✔ You can run electronic searches on the USPTO Web site. You can do keyword searches on the full text of U.S. patents issued after December 1975 and U.S. patent applications published after 2000. You can only view *images* of pre-1975 patents. Also, most PTDLs provide computer access to the USPTO databases.

Electronic searches are often inadequate very practical if the field of technology is more than 25 years old.

Considering that your patent application can be rejected because of a prior description in any domestic or foreign published document, you also need to review available foreign patent applications. You can access European patents and published applications at the European Patent Office Web site (www.epo.org), the Japan Patent Office Web site (www.jpo.go.jp/), and published international Patent Cooperation Treaty (PCT) applications at the World Intellectual Property Organization Web site (www.wipo.int/portal/). The full text of patents in many other countries and patent abstracts translated into English are available by paying for a subscription to databases maintained by Delphion (www.delphion.com), or Thomson (www.thomson.com).

### Searching strategies

Many professional searchers have their own approaches and connections for conducting an anticipation search, which they keep very close to their vests, much like trade secrets. But here are two effective searching strategies, one based on our own experience and the other straight from a Patent Office publication. If these approaches look too complicated, hire a professional.

### Do-it-yourself (and it's not home improvement)

If you're willing and able (and have plenty of strength and fortitude), you can try to do the search yourself. There are two ways to do this.

Because the best searching strategy is one that's thorough and also saves time and money, here's our own shortcut approach that you should try first:

1. **Locate the latest patent that's most closely related to your invention by conducting an electronic keyword search in the most pertinent class.**

   For example, if you invented a new formula for an epoxy glue, you may want to try searching *resin adhesives*.

2. **If that patent doesn't completely describe the invention, find the *References Cited* listing on the first page of the patent, and if online the *Referenced By* listing.**

3. **Check out two or three of the most recent U.S. patents on those lists.**

4. **Repeat Steps 2 and 3, going back in time through the cited references and the *Referenced By* list on each newly found patent until you have reviewed at least 15 patents.**

Promptly abandon links that deviate from the invention and concentrate on the ones that look most promising.

Remember, it's not over till it's over. An anticipation search isn't complete until you find what you don't want to find — an exact description of the gizmo you invented. By definition, you could search forever, so it's up to you to decide when to stop searching.

When searching online, the connection to the USPTO Web site is not necessarily secure. If you are afraid that someone is snooping in on your plans to create the next solar-powered outhouse, try entering keywords that are addressed to the closest prior art you are aware of, instead of keywords that summarize your invention. For example use *toilet* and *powered,* not *solar-powered.* Then follow the prior steps without entering any additional information.

A more elaborate approach is the multi-step search strategy recommended by the USPTO that you can find at `www.uspto.gov/go/ptdl/step7.htm`. Here are the steps in a nutshell:

1. **Look at the classification definitions in the *Manual of Classifications* to identify all the classes your invention fits into.**

2. **Browse through the titles of patents listed to help narrow down the class list.**

   Note the classes related to your invention.

3. **Retrieve the list of all patents in those corresponding classes.**

4. **Check the weekly *Patent Official Gazette* and add to that list all patents issued during the current week.**

5. **Repeat these steps for all the patents remaining on your list.**

   Review the abstract of each patent and eliminate those that don't relate to your invention. Note that the *Gazette* is also posted on www. uspto.gov.

Be sure to have plenty of coffee handy: This job takes a few hours!

Don't forget to look at published patent applications as well as issued patents. Some of these applications may have been filed before your invention or been published more than a year ago, thus making them relevant prior art.

An anticipation search must look at everything the patent document discloses, teaches, and even suggests. For example, don't overlook a design patent document just because it deals only with the ornamental aspect of an object. Check out any design patents in the same class as your contraption because a drawing in a design patent may depict something that anticipates your invention.

### Getting professional help

At some point in your search, you may feel like you're in way over your head. But you don't need to drown — just call in the lifeguards (in this case, a professional searcher).

The most valuable professional assistance you can get for an anticipation search is from a reputable searcher, preferably one based in the Washington, D.C. area, who can conduct searches in the USPTO Library. A professional searcher routinely consults an examiner assigned to the department where your application will be processed. Because each patent examiner reviews applications in a limited field of technology, he can readily point out the closest prior art. The professional searcher doesn't have to be registered to practice before the USPTO. Someone with a technical background may be all you need. Don't forget to safeguard your disclosure by having the non-attorney searcher sign a confidentiality agreement.

You can find professional searchers online or in the yellow pages under *Patents*, *Patent Attorneys*, *Patent Lawyers*, or *Patent Searches*.

## Giving yourself an opinion: Analyzing your search results

You have found a stack of patents and documents related to your invention. Now what? It's time to act like a patent examiner and apply the novelty and non-obviousness tests, outlined in Chapter 5, to your invention in view of the relevant prior art found during the search.

Would a patent examiner reject your application based on this material? As with all legal concepts, many nuances and exceptions blur the rules about novelty and non-obviousness. The prosecution of a patent application is like a court battle. Patent attorneys and patent examiners often fight like cats and dogs and seldom find common ground.

Only in a clear and blatant case of exact duplication can a layman safely conclude that the invention is not patentable. Usually, only a competent patent attorney, after a careful analysis of the search results, can provide a reliable opinion of non-patentability.

To locate a patent attorney or agent, try www.uspto.gov/web/offices/dcom/olia/oed/roster/.

Don't forget to keep all the prior art you found during the search and send it to the USPTO with your patent application or shortly thereafter. As the inventor and applicant, you must be completely candid with the USPTO and disclose anything that may be pertinent to your application. Failure to do so could be considered a fraudulent act and cause your patent to be voided.

---

## Beware: Search results are always full of holes

Patentability standards are very subjective. After you find out what's been done in the past, you must make an educated guess about how a patent examiner will apply those findings to your invention. The more you know about patent law, the more accurate that guess will be. Unfortunately, there's no black-and-white answer. You may want to refer to Chapter 1 to find out what types of things are more patentable.

Most anticipation searches only look at U.S. patents and published patent applications and overlook a vast volume of prior material such as technical books, foreign patents, and scientific articles. Ignoring this material can make for some unpleasant surprises if potential competitors come to light later in the process. Whoops — your educated guess just became a wild-goose chase!

Compounding the problem is the fact that patent applications are held in secrecy until published, some 18 months after their filing date. While it is secret, the file of a patent application, commonly referred to as the *file wrapper* or *file history,* is open only to the inventor or owner. Therefore, the hundreds of thousands of patent applications filed over the last year and a half won't show up during a search. By the time your application reaches an examiner's desk, many of those pending applications may be published or turned into patents. If one of those pending applications, lurking like a shark underwater, discloses your invention, the patent examiner will cite that document in rejecting your application. You can see now that your wild guess looks more like a shot in the dark. The moral of the story: No matter how thorough your search, the results are always full of holes.

# Looking at Other Patent Searches

An anticipation search is the most common type of patent search, but some-day you may need one of these three other types of patent searches: *infringement*, *state-of-the-art*, and *title*.

## Infringement search: Stepping on someone's toes

An *infringement search* is a totally different kettle of crabs from an anticipa-tion search. If you're about to or have already manufactured and sold your thingamajigs, you may worry that someone will get you for infringing a patent you've just found. Before you panic, find out from an attorney whether you're really infringing on an existing patent. What you see in a patent isn't always what's legally covered. That patent may be very easy to get around.

An infringement search is extremely complex and requires a thorough study and analysis of currently active patents and published patent applications in your field. Our best advice? Consult an experienced patent attorney who has studied zillions of patent infringement cases. Check Chapter 21 to find out more about patent infringement.

An infringement search, also called a *freedom to operate* search is essentially a combination of an anticipation search of unexpired patents for every impor-tant element of a product or process coupled with a thorough analysis and legal opinion of the scope and validity of all the patents that turn up. This type of search is so expensive and fraught with caveats and CYAs that it is only useful to large corporations.

## State-of-the-art search: What's the latest

A *state-of-the-art search* is often conducted as part of a program of research and development or to gain expertise in a technical field. It requires looking at the latest patents in a particular field, but has very little to do with getting a patent. In most state-of-the-art searches, inventors review the most recent advances in that field, not just patents. It's a very detailed and technical search of electronic databases and Internet sites. You probably wouldn't do a state-of-the-art search by yourself — it's usually a job for engineers, scien-tists, and other research and development types.

## Patent title search: Finding the owner

A *patent title search* finds out the current owner of a patent. To be fully effective, the sale of an ownership interest in a patent (legally called an *assignment*) must be recorded in the USPTO, which keeps a chronological record of all assignments and other recorded transactions related to a patent. This record is keyword searchable at the USPTO Web site, where you can find the current owner of any patent.

# Chapter 8

# Preparing Your Patent Application

*I*f you take our advice, you'll let your patent attorney or agent prepare your utility patent application for you. But he or she can't do a good job without your supportive participation. You're the one who came up with the invention after all. In this chapter, we give you a basic understanding of the purpose, structure, and function of the patent application, so that you can efficiently and effectively assist your IP professional.

If you're after a design or plant patent, you might be able to prepare and file the application yourself, following the guidelines in Chapter 9 and using the information you download from the USPTO Web site (www.uspto.gov). These design and plant patent applications don't require the highly legalistic claim language (discussed later in this chapter) of a utility patent application. With a little common sense, basic writing skills, and a willingness to follow directions, you can write a complete disclosure of your new plant characteristics or a sound and convincing description of each figure in your design application drawing. This chapter, therefore, deals almost exclusively with preparing a utility patent application.

## Understanding the Patent Application

A patent application is a formal request addressed to the United States Government for the exclusive legal right to a certain area of technology. Your primary goal when preparing your patent application is to make that area of technology as broad as possible within the scope of your invention. Your patent may eventually cover inventions that are inconceivable today but that fall within your exclusive area of technology.

The strength of your patent depends as much on the skills of your attorney or agent to persuade the patent examiner to grant legal rights to the broadest area of technology as it does on the merits of your invention. However, the patent examiner's duty is to make certain that your patent doesn't carry more rights than your invention deserves.

Patents aren't granted for the asking. The complex application process often takes unexpected turns into long appellate detours, procedural sidetracks, and disappointing dead ends. The process breaks down into three major phases:

1. **Preparing the application:** For patents, preparation is definitely the key to success, and that's what this chapter is all about.

2. **Filing the application:** It's more than just tossing forms in the mail. We cover the nuts and bolts of filing in Chapter 9 — which you definitely want to check out if you're flying solo with a design or plant patent application.

3. **Pushing the application through the USPTO:** Technically, this phase is called the *prosecution*. At this point, your attorney may have to answer communications from the patent examiner or state your case before one or more appeal tribunals.

# Choosing Between Formal and Provisional Applications

One of the first choices you and your legal eagle have to make is whether to file a formal application or a provisional application.

✔ A *formal application* (a *non-provisional* application in USPTO-speak) is the most common type of utility patent application upon which a patent can be granted. It's subject to examination as soon as it's filed. But, given the enormous backlogs, few applications are examined during the first six months after their filing dates.

✔ A *provisional application* isn't really an application because no patent can issue from it. It's never examined and must be followed by a formal application within one year of its filing date. A provisional application essentially contains a complete disclosure of the invention and therefore establishes a *priority date* over any subsequent disclosure of the invention and a *priority right* against the subsequent application for the same invention by another person anywhere in the world. A provisional application is kept secret. If no formal application follows within a year, the provisional application is destroyed and never made public.

A provisional application is a gimmick instituted to level the playing field for foreign applications among nations (see Chapter 19 for more).

## Making things formal

A formal application is the most direct, and thus the quickest, route to a patent. We recommend starting with a formal patent application if

✔ You want to get a U.S. patent as soon as possible. Your invention is already on or about to hit the market, and it's likely to be copied by your competitors. You're gonna need that patent to stop them in their tracks.

✔ You expect your invention to have a relatively short life, like four to seven years. Electronic and software inventions often fall into that category. Although the law allows you to sue an infringer up to six years after the infringing act, you want to stop those copycats ASAP. Business method patent applications in particular tend to invite added scrutiny (some say deliberate foot dragging) by the USPTO and may be pending for several years.

The formal application is the quickest, most prestigious route — but it's also the most expensive at the outset and can't be added to after filing. Instead, it must be complemented or replaced by another application, having a later priority date to cover any new improvement.

## Starting with a provisional application

A provisional application offers a convenient way to file a complete disclosure of your invention and establish an early priority date without the high cost of drafting a formal application. The filing fee for a provisional application ($105 for a small business) is about one fourth of the fee for filing a formal application ($435 for a small business).

You can also file additional provisional applications to add improvements to the invention for up to a year, at which point you *must* file a formal application. Mark your calendar —don't miss your application's filing date.

In general, filing a provisional application can be a good idea, especially if any of these circumstances apply to you:

✔ Your invention isn't fully developed, and you expect to make significant improvements within the next few months.

✔ You're in no hurry to get your patent, but want to establish early priority rights. Because your invention won't hit the market for three or four years, you can postpone the expenses associated with a formal application for a year (including those incurred in dealing with the patent examiner). In the meantime, your provisional application establishes a record of the invention that trumps applications by subsequent inventors.

✔ If you want to keep your invention confidential as long as possible, you start by filing a provisional application, and file a formal one right on the one-year anniversary with a request for non-publication. Your invention will become known only when the patent is granted, some three to four years after you file the provisional application (one year of provisional status and two or three years of formal prosecution). For more on deciding whether to publish your application, see Chapter 9.

✔ You want to add an extra year to the life of your patent. A provisional application isn't taken into account when calculating the earliest filing date — so you get 21 years instead of the usual 20 (see Chapter 5 for more information on the life span of a patent).

The disclosure in a provisional application must be sufficient for a person skilled in the field to implement all aspects of the invention you want to cover later in the formal application. Because patent professionals usually are more adept at appreciating all the patentable features of an invention than the inventors are, having a qualified professional review or prepare your provisional application may be wise. (Inventors tend to focus more on technical features that they think are valuable and overlook vast areas of technology they could have controlled.) The improved quality and breadth of the provisional application can end up being worth the added expense of professional preparation or review.

Note that you can petition to change the provisional or formal status of an application from either one to the other within one year of its filing date, subject to the payment of all applicable fees. It's unlikely that you'd change the status of a provisional application into a formal application because it wouldn't contain a disclosure of any interim improvement and good legal patentability arguments. But, changing a formal application into a provisional one is common in order to avoid examination and delay publication.

Even though claims are not required in a provisional application, its usually a good idea to include some claims as part of your disclosure. Make sure that you keep them very broad.

## Going international

Optionally, you may start by filing an international formal patent application covering a number of countries, including the United States. We explain the procedure in Chapter 19.

# Deconstructing the Patent Application

A well-drafted utility patent application should contain the following:

- ✔ **Abstract of the invention:** A concise description of the invention in one paragraph of 150 words or less. The abstract gives a general overview of the invention. As shown in the utility patent examples (documents B1–B10 on the CD), it ends up on the front page of the patent.

  If you can, try to use lots of different key words and synonyms in the abstract. Many people search abstracts rather than the entire text of patents. With lots of key words, potential licensees searching for patents may have an easier time finding you.

- ✔ **Drawing:** An illustration, in as many sheets and figures as needed to support the disclosure. You don't need to be an artist. But you do need to be able to show the important functional parts of your invention. When in doubt, keep it simple.

- ✔ **Reference to any prior application:** A short statement that ties the application to any provisional or other previously filed application by the same inventor that discloses the whole or part of the invention. (This part isn't allowed in a provisional application.)

  In order to claim priority to the earlier non-provisional application you need to state the relationship (for example, "divisional" or "continuation-in-part"). For a lengthy example, see the Related U.S. Application Data on the front page of document B5 on the CD.

- ✔ **General field of the invention:** A one- or two-sentence summary of the area of technology affected by the invention.

- ✔ **Background and circumstances of the invention:** Give a good argument for the need for the invention and the problems it resolves.

- ✔ **Summary of the invention:** A condensed explanation of the nuts and bolts of the invention, its utility, and, if necessary, its honest, broadly stated advantages.

- ✔ **Description of each figure of the drawing:** A short sentence explaining each figure.

- ✔ **Description of the preferred embodiment of the invention:** A description of what the inventor considers the best implementation of the invention. It's not necessarily what was built and sold, but what would be built and sold under the best practical circumstances. This part refers to the figures in the drawing.

- ✔ **Formal definition of the invention in the form of at least one claim that defines the area of technology over which you want exclusivity.**

It takes a well-rounded IP practitioner to draft a good patent application. The strength of the eventual patent depends on the completeness of the specification and claims. If you're a tech-savvy good writer, you can write an acceptable description of your invention. But the specification isn't the most important part of a patent application. What legally defines the rights of the patent owner and the area of technology covered by the patent are the *claims* — and your patent attorney needs to write the claims.

# Disclosing Your Invention in the Specification

Writing a good patent specification requires your participation and candid communication with your attorney or agent. You're the only one who knows all the ins and outs of your invention and can point her in the right direction when its embodiments, applications, functions, and great advantages have to be explained. Primarily, the specification must provide full support for the claims in respect to the substance (technology) and the form (words used in the claims). In addition, the specification must meet two basic requirements:

✔ **The enabling rule:** The specification must clearly and concisely disclose enough for a person skilled in the field of the invention to practice the invention without a lot of experimentation.

✔ **The best mode rule:** The disclosure must state what you consider to be the best manner of carrying out the invention.

Complying with one rule but missing the other can make your patent invalid. For example, you may clearly explain how to practice your invention, but this may not be your best mode. On the other hand, your description of the best way to apply your invention may be too sketchy to meet the enabling requirement. These guidelines should keep you on the path to compliance:

✔ **Select the best mode:** In the _Description of the Preferred Embodiment of the Invention_ section of the specification, you must reveal what you believe is the most efficient way to practice your invention, which may not necessarily be the manner you build your own prototype. If you've thought of other ways to exploit the invention, you can add them as alternate embodiments. Don't be shy about mentioning various ways to construct a particular structure or perform a specific process step.

✔ **Teach enough but no more than required:** When you try to meet the enabling requirement, you're writing for a person skilled in your field. So you can use technical jargon and skip obvious details. Don't waste time explaining how to use every little component or tool. Your skilled readers can figure out which tasks are necessary on their own. Just make sure that they don't need to do a great deal of experimentation before they can use your invention. You can require their time, but not their head-scratching. For example, if you're disclosing a computer program, draw a flowchart and briefly describe the step represented by each box on the chart. You don't need to provide a program code listing.

Don't treat the specification like a promotion or marketing tool. It's not the place for puffery about your product or for disparaging comments about your competitors. Your attorney or agent should stick to legal requirements.

# *Arguing Your Case for Patentability*

According to the law, your patent application only has to include a description of the preferred embodiment of the invention and one claim. But you need a lot more to make a case for the patentability of your invention. Convincing the examiner or the appeal judges (if you have to appeal a rejection by the examiner) that you deserve a patent usually requires a little extra. You need to provide your IP professional with as much information as he needs to establish the utility, novelty, and non-obviousness of your invention (for the basic conditions of patentability, see Chapter 5).

How do you convince a patent examiner that your invention is the greatest thing since the corkscrew? You must persuasively demonstrate that

- ✔ A technological problem has existed for some time.
- ✔ Others have tried to resolve this problem with questionable success.
- ✔ You have taken a fresh and different approach.

And the places to demonstrate these things are the *Background of the Invention* and *Summary of the Invention* sections of the patent application.

## *Defining the problem*

Here's a simple approach to the background section:

1. **Define the general application of the invention.**

   *Strap-tightening ratchet mechanisms, commonly called strap ratchets, are used in connection with cargo-securing harnesses. . . .*

2. **Note the shortcomings of the current devices.**

   *The ratchet mechanisms are usually provided with short tightening levers that yield very little torque force. Accordingly, the harness cannot be tightened to the fullest extent possible. . . .*

3. **Describe the prior approaches for resolving the problem, including their shortcomings.** You can refer to prior patents, publications, or well-known devices already on the market.

   *Some mechanisms of the prior art have been provided with extended levers as disclosed in U.S. Patent No. . . .*

   *. . . The length and bulk of these extended levers often interfere with the placement of the ratcheting device near a corner of the cargo. . . .*

4. **Close the section by stating that your invention is an attempt to resolve the outlined deficiencies in the prior mechanism.**

## Laying out your solution

Provide a very condensed explanation of the primary features of the invention and their utility in addressing the problems described in the background, but don't merely recite advantages. Patent attorneys and agents used to boast about all the wonderful things the invention could achieve, until a court invalidated a patent when it found that the invention didn't in fact perform as was trumpeted in the application. Contemporary practice limits the *Summary of the Invention* to a sober, to-the-point statement of what is recited in the claims without mention of advantageous results. Some practitioners simply restate the abstract and the claims. This has the advantage of guaranteeing that all words used in the claims are also found in the description.

If you anticipate an obviousness fight with the examiner and can't help yourself from describing some of the advantages, at least make them easily attainable and open for interpretation. Also, it's good to refer to the invention as "some embodiments." For example it's better to say, "Some embodiments provide an improved way to trap a mouse" rather than, "The invention can trap more than ten mice in an hour."

Except in connection with chemical inventions, which usually can be fully described by formulae, a drawing must illustrate the invention with as many figures as might be required to understand the invention. The critical rule is that each element or feature recited in the claims be shown on the drawing.

## Giving a good example

This is where you describe in detail the best embodiment of your invention you can think of, including alternate or supplemental embodiments. You must use reference characters to point out where each described element is shown on the drawing. Your description must be sufficient to support both the wording and the substance of the following claims.

# Staking Your Claims

Your patent claims define the area of technology covered by the patent and, in the end, are the only parts of the patent that really count because they legally define your rights to the invention. The specification has only one primary purpose — to support the wording of the claims. Notice that the claims don't *define* your new device or process, which is a tangible or concrete thing, but an area of technology *represented by* it. Your actual invention is an abstract construct that can't be easily or precisely defined; the specific device or process is only one of many possible applications. Your patent attorney needs to take care of the claims, but here's a crash course on what she'll be doing.

## *Mastering the mechanics of claims*

The wording of a claim is like the description of a piece of real property in a deed. Just as a deed description defines only the limits of the lot and not anything on it, a claim recites only the minimum elements that must be present for a device or process to be covered by the patent. Anything that falls within these limits belongs to the title owner — the landlord or patent owner.

A claim usually covers a lot more than the limits it spells out. And the shorter the claim, the broader its coverage. For an example of this less-is-more rule, take a look at Figure 8-1 — the first horseless carriage, invented by Nicolas Cugnot around 1769. If Cugnot had asked us to draft a patent application for his invention, we would have worded the first claim as follows:

*A vehicle comprising:*

*a cargo-carrying member,*

*at least two wheels supporting said member, and*

*an engine driving at least one of said wheels.*

**Figure 8-1:**
Nicolas Cugnot's horseless wagon.

Cugnot's carriage had a back axle supporting a pair of wheels. The steam engine was coupled to a front wheel. But being very astute (and extremely modest) patent attorneys, we could also imagine motored vehicles riding with only two wheels because 80 years earlier, another Frenchman, Mede de Sivrac, had developed a crude bicycle. We therefore listed the minimum components necessary for a workable device. And it's a good thing we did. If the patent were still in effect today, it would cover locomotives, cars, trucks, and motorcycles. But someone could get around this claim by using only one wheel (possibly a long roller) or by detaching the engine from the wheels (by using a jet engine). Plug these loopholes by rewriting the claim as follows:

*A vehicle comprising:*

*a cargo-carrying member,*

*at least one wheel supporting said member; and*

*an engine positioned to propel said vehicle.*

Because the second claim lists only three elements instead of four like the first, more devices out there are likely to fall within its limits. So the more concise second claim has a broader scope than the first and can catch more infringers. Just for fun, try to redraft this claim to cover a boat or an aircraft.

## Checking the various types of claims

Not all inventions can be described by a concise list of components, also called *limitations,* as in the Cugnot example in the preceding section. That's why the law provides more than one way to describe them.

### Listing elements in a claim

The kind of component-listing claims we illustrate in the Cugnot example are commonly used with machine, device, and composition of matter inventions. Here are variations on the theme that lend themselves to other inventions:

✔ **Using functional limitations:** If you have to list a component that has many equivalents capable of performing the same job, you can describe that component in a *means-plus-function* form. For instance, a wheel can be attached to a vehicle frame by means of an axle or a pin or with a complex articulated structure, like the one used on the front wheel of a car. You can effectively describe the component or limitation like this:

*. . . means for rotatively securing the wheel to the vehicle frame . . .*

Can't find *rotatively* in your dictionary? It doesn't matter. When you write claims, you can create your own vocabulary, as long as you clearly define the new term in the specification section of the application.

As we point out in Chapter 21, in an infringement action, the judge will interpret the scope of a means-plus-function claim to cover the component described in the specification, plus any *equivalent structure* that achieves the same results (with insubstantial differences) as the one described in the specification, so long as that equivalent structure is available when the patent is granted. You may enhance your patent by describing as many equivalent structures as possible in the specification. For example, the means for securing the wheel only recited in a general form in the claim must be specifically described in the specification as an axle, pin, or complex car front wheel mounting structure.

✔ **Grouping similarly effective components:** Another way to cover a large gamut of similar components in a single claim is to list a group of applicable elements. This style of claim, called the *Markush claim,* after the first inventor to use it, is narrower than the means-plus-function mode but is often used to define chemical inventions. The only requirement is that the group of alternate components must be introduced by the all-inclusive phrase *consisting essentially of.* Elements not listed as part of the group are excluded from coverage. For example:

> *. . . a dry lubricant taken from a group consisting essentially of graphite, molybdenum sulphide, and boron nitride . . . excludes talcum powder.*

The specification must mention the utility and effectiveness of all listed components. For example, you may explain that tests were conducted with each type of lubricant with substantially the same effective results.

### Claiming a method or process

An invention component can also be defined in a claim by its unique manufacturing method:

> *. . . spacer made by bending a length of steel wire into a closed loop . . .*

If your invention is a method or process, you can describe it as steps:

> *An online method for confirming receipt of an electronic purchase order contained in an email message, said method comprising the steps of:*
>
> *assigning to said order an account number and a job number;*
>
> *clicking a reply button on a toolbar of said e-mail message;*
>
> *typing said account and job number; and*
>
> *clicking a send button on said toolbar.*

This is just an example. We doubt you could get a patent on that method.

### Focusing on an improvement

When the invention consists of a refinement to an existing structure, you can use a *Jepson claim,* named after another creative inventor. First recite the basic structure in the opening phrase, called the *preamble.* Then follow the preamble with a linking term such as *an improvement comprising.* And finally, list the limitations of the invention:

> *In the manufacture of a body armor in which metal plates are piled into a plurality of stacks and each of said stacks is spread in a substantially flat pattern of overlapping plates on the bed of a riveting machine, an improvement for facilitating said spreading, said improvement comprising the steps of:*

*sprinkling a light coat of a dry lubricant over each metal plate before piling into one of said stacks;*

*after riveting, placing said metal plates into a vertical position; and*

*shaking said vertically positioned plates to slough off said coat of dry lubricant.*

### Combining structures

A claim can recite a combination of two or more objects — particularly handy when the inventive gadget's utility and novelty are only evident as applied to an existing device. However, the combined structures must have interaction between them. For example, a phone mounted on a washing machine for the convenience of the housekeeper isn't a patentable combination because the two devices don't work together, but are only located together. However, the combination of a cylindrical eraser mounted at the end of a pencil might be patentable because the pencil acts as a handle for the eraser.

### Playing a medley

An astute IP professional will cleverly use a cocktail of various claiming styles to obtain the broadest coverage possible. He or she can also claim the same invention in a series of differently phrased claims. Take a look at the claims in the utility patent for an imitation wax seal, document B1 on the CD. Notice that Claim 1 lists a component and a means-plus-function limitation. Claim 8 has the same elements as Claim 1 but is phrased as a combination.

### Building a claim pyramid

Your name may not be Ramses or Nefertiti, but you can erect a mighty monument for posterity — by building one claim upon another. A claim may be *dependent* upon one or more earlier *parent* claims that it incorporates. For example, if a Claim 2 begins with *The method of Claim 1 which further comprises . . .* or *The device of Claim 1 wherein . . .*, Claim 2 includes all the limitations recited in Claim 1, plus some. In the utility patent, document B1 on the CD, Claims 1 and 8 are independent, but Claims 2–5 and 7 are dependent on Claim 1, which is a parent claim. Claim 6 is dependent on its parent, Claim 4, and its grandparent, Claim 1. Accordingly, Claim 6 incorporates all the limitations listed in Claims 1 and 4.

Claims can be spread in a radial pattern (Figure 8-2), where all dependent claims directly connect to a single parent claim. This technique allows you to add just one more element to the basic and most concise independent claim.

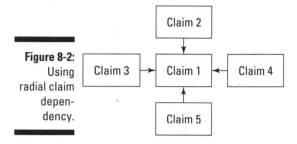

**Figure 8-2:**
Using
radial claim
depen-
dency.

Claims can also be lined up in a cascading or daisy-chain pattern where a claim can be both parent and child (Figure 8-3) — to avoid continuously repeating the same series element where you keep adding one more element in each additional claim while keeping the elements entered in the previous one.

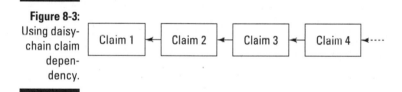

**Figure 8-3:**
Using daisy-
chain claim
depen-
dency.

Finally, claims can be scattered in a mixed pattern of radial and linear single and multiple dependency, as Figure 8-4 shows. This may be the most common way to cover an invention with many complex variations.

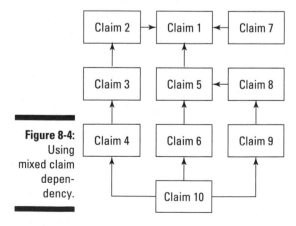

**Figure 8-4:**
Using
mixed claim
depen-
dency.

*Note:* Claim 10 in Figure 8-4 is known as a Multiple Dependent Claim because it depends from more than one claim. This type of claim can present special indefiniteness problems and costs you an extra fee ($185 for a small business) just to get an examiner to look at it. If you are a greenhorn claim drafter, your time is better spent avoiding this type of claim. How the claim drafter phrases and organizes the claims depends on the number and types of invention variations to be covered. Her skill and experience are critical. Here's the basic claim-drafting strategy:

✔ Cover the fundamental aspect of the invention in one or two independent claims that recite just enough elements to distinguish it from prior art.

✔ Cover each variation in a dependent claim that adds one or more elements to one of the independent claims. In the course of an infringement action, it's very common to declare the independent claims overbroad and invalid because of newly discovered prior art that the examiner overlooked during the prosecution of the application. You then have to rely on the narrower dependent claims.

✔ Start the whole process again with a new family of claims based on a different style, such as means-plus-function, Markush, combination, or Jepson types, rather than a simple recitation of components.

This shotgun approach to claiming is the only way to cover all potentially infringing technology, including future developments that you can't predict.

## Playing soothsayer

There are compelling signs that the USPTO, in an effort to relieve its overburdened patent examiners, is about to ask the U.S. Congress to limit the number of claims addressed to a single invention within a family of applications. The USPTO has proposed that number to be no more than 25, of which only 5 may be independent claims. When this comes to pass, claim architecture will become an even more Byzantine art than it already is.

## Following the grammatical rules

Claim drafting is more than a science — it's an art at which any patent attorney worth his "whereas" should excel and which requires every semantic and legal trick possible. Don't feel bad if you can't comprehend the full scope of each claim in your application. Rules for interpreting claims are even more complex than those that control drafting them. In a patent infringement proceeding, only the judge can interpret the claims of the patent. It's assumed that jurors can't competently make these types of determinations themselves.

Claims must comply with very peculiar grammatical rules. With apologies to your grade-school English teachers, get used to the following oddities, which are just a few of the crazy grammatical twists and turns you'll run into:

- ✔ A claim must be written in a single sentence, even if that sentence extends over three or more pages. So, run-on sentences are now okay.

- ✔ A claim must begin with a preamble that briefly states the framework of the invention, followed by a linking phrase such as *which comprise(s), including,* or *which essentially consist(s) of,* followed by the limitations (elements) of the invention. If necessary, you can tack on a *whereby* clause after a limitation in order to clear up any potential confusion as to the nature, application, or function of the invention. The whereby clause doesn't define a necessary limitation of the invention and is often discarded by the judge interpreting the claim. See the "Focusing on an improvement" section earlier in the chapter for a preamble example.

- ✔ You can't use a definite article in front of an element unless you've already introduced that element in the body of the current claim or in a parent claim. For example, you can't start a claim like this:

    *A video camera which comprises a shutter behind the lens . . .*

    The word lens hasn't been defined yet, so you have to write:

    *A video camera which comprises a lens and a shutter behind the lens . . .*

- ✔ You can use the terms *which comprise(s), comprising, including, having,* and so on, without excluding other elements in the claimed invention. However, the phrase *consisting of* or *which consists of* excludes any other element. So a claim that recites *a table which comprises a flat top and three legs* also covers tables with four or five legs. However, a claim stating *a table which consists of a flat top and three legs* wouldn't cover a four-legged table. You can use *consisting essentially of* to slightly expand coverage beyond the specific elements to known equivalents.

- ✔ You can reference previously introduced elements with the term *said* without repeating the qualifying terms, for example:

    *A camera comprising a zoom lens;*

    *a shutter positioned behind said lens*

- ✔ Don't use the conjunctions *or* and *nor* or the phrase *such as* if they make the definition ambiguous. For example, *a camera having a lens made of a material such as glass or plastic . . .* won't cut the mustard. Instead, use multiple claims, each reciting one type of lens or better yet use a Markush claim (see previous section), which covers a number of substitutable components: *A camera having a lens made of a material taken from a group consisting essentially of glass, plastic, and silicone.*

✔ Words have the meanings that you give them in the specification, even if they are different from the ones found in dictionaries. You can't go so far as calling a cat a *dog*, but you can call a joint an *accouplement*.

✔ You can't list voids, holes, and cavities in structures as primary elements, but can use them to qualify an element. For example, *a wooden beam and a transversal hole in a mid-section thereof* is a no-no. Write *a wooden beam having a transversal hole in a mid-section thereof.*

✔ Any descriptive words you use in a claim must first be mentioned and if necessary defined in the specification.

Here's a claim for the structure in Figure 8-5, with all the language rules applied. Can you pick them out for extra credit?

**Figure 8-5:**
Ratchet-
operating
tool and
strap-
tightening
mechanism.

*The combination of a ratcheted, strap-tightening mechanism having a hand-operable cranking lever and a resiliently biased ratchet-locking member, and*

*a manipulating tool, said tool comprising:*

*a rod;*

*a socket having a proximal end attached at a first end of said rod and a distal end opposite said proximal end, said socket comprising four flat joined sides defining a channel shaped and dimensioned to axially engage over said lever; and a tongue projecting from a second end of said rod opposite said first end, said tongue being shaped and dimensioned to leveredly bear against said resiliently biased member and pry it away from a locking position to release said mechanism;*

*wherein at least two opposing ones of said sides taper inwardly down axially from an opening at said distal end toward said first end of the rod,*

*whereby said socket can be securely engaged over a plurality of levers of different sizes.*

## Compiling the record

What do you need to help your legal eagle draft your patent application?

If you kept a good notebook while you were developing your invention, as we recommend doing in Chapter 6, dig it out now — it contains a lot of what your IP professional needs. Otherwise, here's a helpful list:

- ✔ Short definition of general fields of technology to which the invention relates. Include any device or process your invention applies to.

- ✔ Reasons that led you to develop the invention.

- ✔ Explanation of how the invention came about (unexpected discovery, trial-and-error approach, a flash of genius, in a dream . . .).

- ✔ Where you developed the invention (for example, as part of your employment or contracted job, or using someone else's resources or facilities).

- ✔ Outline of the existing problems the invention resolves.

- ✔ Account of how these problems were handled in the past.

- ✔ Your opinion about what the invention does that couldn't be done before, or why it's an improvement over past devices or methods.

- ✔ Depiction of the closest thing to your invention.

- ✔ Documents or references that best describe the most recent advances in the field of the invention.

- ✔ Lists and copies of all patents, publications, treatises, articles, and other written material at your disposal that may be relevant to your invention. You are not required to conduct any particular research. If you've done a search (described in Chapter 7), you'll have this info at your fingertips.

- ✔ Anticipation search results and any professional patentability opinion.

- ✔ All records of your development efforts.

✔ Dates of conception of the invention, first sketch or description, first prototype construction, first public showing, first published description, first public use, first offer to sell, first advertisement, and first sale.

✔ Explanation of the circumstances if the invention was first implemented in a foreign country.

✔ Identification of all persons (including children) who contributed to the conception and a brief description of each co-inventor's contribution. Include full names, addresses, residences, and citizenships.

✔ Copies of any prior filings, such as a Disclosure Document (see Chapter 6) or prior patent applications, whether still active or abandoned.

✔ Copies of any assignment, license, or business agreement related to the invention. Chapter 20 talks about assignments and licenses.

✔ Copies of identifying documents, such as Articles of Incorporation, Partnership Certificates, and fictitious name registrations, for any business that is (or may become) owner of the patent or the invention.

✔ Complete description of the invention, including drawings, photographs, prototypes, test results, newspaper accounts, testimonials, and anything else that could help your IP pro understand and appreciate the invention.

✔ Concise description (a single paragraph of 10–15 lines) of the basic structure of your invention that can serve as a model for the *abstract* portion of the application. Don't get into the invention's advantages here. (See the earlier section "Deconstructing the Patent Application.")

✔ Brief account of how you plan to exploit your invention, either through your own manufacturing, by licensing others, or by outright sale.

See the handy specification questionnaire (document F1) on the CD.

## Looking over the pro's shoulder

You just received the first draft of your patent application and are about to review it alone or in a tête-à-tête with your attorney. Remember to ask your IP attorney or agent to clarify anything you don't understand or change anything that doesn't adequately describe your invention.

### Scrutinizing the claims

Because the claims are the most important part of the application, you should go over them with a fine-toothed comb. Be sure that you and the claim drafter are on the same wavelength. Verify that the part of the technology that's recited is exactly the one that needs to be protected.

You may discover that the most critical aspect of your invention is recited in a dependent claim. Because you can claim only one invention in a patent, ask your attorney to reverse the organization of the claims to recite the most important portion of the invention in an independent claim. It can't hurt to include both separate independent claims drawn to each aspect. Although this inclusion will likely provoke a restriction requirement, it will also establish your right to eventually get a patent for each "invention."

If a claim lists every detail of the structure, down to the kitchen sink, stove, and oven, talk with your attorney about eliminating or rewriting it. A narrow claim doesn't provide much of a net to catch an infringer, it takes up too much space, and it adds to the filing fee (see the upcoming section "Paying the piper"). Do make sure that every inventive feature is listed in one or more claims. Don't worry too much yet about whether you're claiming more than one invention in a single application. Later, you can answer the patent examiner's objection by reshuffling the claim pyramid or by withdrawing some claims to be resubmitted in a continuing application (see Chapter 9).

### Focusing the abstract

Verify that the abstract describes the gist of your invention in plain language, without using legalistic terms such as *means for* and *whereas*. Typically, the abstract reflects the principal claim (usually Claim 1).

### Checking the drawing

The drawing must be done in accordance with USPTO guidelines. Patent attorneys and agents use professional patent draftspersons, who work from sketches prepared by the professional based on your description. The drawing must illustrate every item recited in the claims. It can be as simple as a block diagram or a flowchart. Don't include more figures than absolutely necessary to describe the preferred embodiment of the invention. Don't draw every nut and bolt. A patent drawing is an illustration, not a manufacturing blueprint.

### Reviewing the disclosure

When you look at some patents, you may think that the drafter was paid by the page. There's too much information, including verbiage that's not legally required and doesn't advance the case for patentability.

Brevity gives you a practical advantage. When you file abroad, you're charged by the word or page for translation and filing. You can save hundreds of dollars with a little literary restraint. For example, the *Background of the Invention* section is no place for a lengthy listing and discussion of prior patents and publications. You can do this when you file the *Information Disclosure Statement by Applicant* (Form PTO/SB08A) — see Chapter 9. To make your application short and effective, cross out anything that doesn't support the language of the claims or any detailed description of things well known to a person skilled in the field of the invention.

### Paying the piper

Now is the time to painfully reach for your wallet. Most IP professionals insist that you pay their fees before they file the application. After an IP professional enters the papers in the USPTO under her Joan Hancock, she is obligated (whether or not she's been paid) to do everything reasonably necessary to advance your case (unless relieved of her duty by petitioning the Commissioner of Patents). You also have to pay the application filing fee, which is based, in part, on the number and types of claims you present.

# Chapter 9

# Filing Your Patent Application

. . . . . . . . . . . . . . . . . . . . . . . . . . . . . . . . . . . . . . . . . . .

. . . . . . . . . . . . . . . . . . . . . . . . . . . . . . . . . . . . . . . . . . .

*Y*ou probably think that the hardest part is over after the patent application is prepared. It's true that a lot of the detail work is done, but you still have a lot of things to keep in mind when getting ready to file your application, and even more things to keep track of after your application hits the United States Patent and Trademark Office (USPTO). Your patent attorney takes care of most of these details, but you need to have a clear view of the filing process, so we describe that here in some detail. We also refer you to more extensive source material in case you want to find out more on the subject.

The contents of this chapter mainly address the filing of utility patent applications. We add some additional special comments about provisional applications and applications for design and plant patents.

## Packaging the Application

If you plan to file and prosecute your patent application yourself (which we don't recommend, even if you're dealing with a relatively simple provisional or a design patent application), you need to obtain a *customer number,* which acts as a password in accessing your application file. Because it's linked to your name and address, the customer number also acts as a mailing code for all correspondence from the USPTO. Instructions about applying for and using a customer number can be found on the USPTO Web site www.uspto. gov/ebc/digitalcert.htm.

Whether you're using a patent attorney or agent or going it alone, get the applicable one of the following pamphlets from the "Guidance, Tools & Manuals" page at the USPTO Web site www.uspto.gov/web/patents/guides.htm. You can also order a pamphlet by calling the USPTO General Information Service at 800-786-9199.

✔ *Provisional Application for Patent* brochure

✔ *Guide to Filing a Utility Patent Application*

✔ *Guide to Filing a Design Patent Application*

✔ *General Information about 35 U.S.C. 161 Plant Patents*

In this section, we supplement the information in these pamphlets with a handy checklist of the most common documents that accompany the application, we discuss additional material you may want to submit, and we tell you how to get discounts on fees during the application process.

## Application checklist

In addition to the patent application specification and claims (see Chapter 8 for preparing the application itself), you should fill out and send the following forms, with some exceptions if you're filing online. You can download the forms from www.uspto.gov by clicking on Patents and then on Forms. The USPTO is forever adding, splitting, or canceling forms. Make sure you pick up the latest ones for your particular needs and type of patent application.

✔ An application transmittal form (one for each type of application).

✔ A declaration form (for all formal applications).

✔ A fee transmittal form (online, this form is generated automatically).

✔ A Non-publication Request form when applicable (see "Keeping Your Application under Wraps," later in the chapter).

✔ An Information Disclosure Statement by Applicant form. This form is optional at this time (see "Showing all your cards," later in the chapter).

✔ And don't forget the filing fee itself, by check or money order (if you're filing online its easiest to pay by credit card).

When filing by mail, include a self-addressed, stamped postcard (like the one shown in Figure 9-1) identifying your application if you want to get an early confirmation that the USPTO received your application. The USPTO takes weeks to issue an official receipt. With early confirmation, you won't have to wonder if your application ended up in the dead-letter office.

```
PATENT APPLICATION            Case No.

Applicant:

Title:

Design: ( )   Dwg Sheets _____
Utility ( )   Pages: _____   # of Claims
Declaration ( )  Small Entity ( )
Check enclosed in the amount of $_____

Please acknowledge receipt of the enclosed PATENT APPLICATION
by returning this card stamped with the date received and the
Serial Number to the addressee on the reverse side.

THANK YOU
```

**Figure 9-1:** Early return card format.

Fill in the card by indicating whether you are filing a design or utility application; entering the number of drawing sheets, total pages of specification and claims, number of claims, whether the signed declaration form is enclosed, whether you qualified for a "small entity" fee reduction (see "Asking for a break," later in this chapter), and the amount of your payment.

## Showing all your cards

The law requires that you submit copies of documents disclosing information related to your invention that you found during your patent search and any other matter that may be relevant to the examination of your application. You need to reveal every document that you're aware of that relates to your invention and that isn't generally known by the public, before your application is examined. So do this now when you file the application. List all the documents on the Information Disclosure Statement by Applicant form.

You may (don't feel obligated) also attach a statement explaining what distinguishes your invention from each piece of *prior art* — everything relating to your invention that's already been created — disclosed in the submitted material. (We discuss prior art in Chapters 5–8.) This statement necessitates some legal conclusions about the patentability of your invention over the disclosed material. Don't try to do it yourself or you may overstate the relevance of a piece of prior art. If you can't get a patent attorney to draft it, you'd better skip the statement altogether.

If you're not sure that a particular piece of published information is relevant, send it anyway. If you don't disclose known prior art, your patent is doomed.

## *Asking for a break*

If you're an individual, nonprofit organization, or small business, you may get half off the patent application filing fee and most other USPTO charges. Indicate your *small entity* status by checking the appropriate box on the application transmittal form. To qualify for the small entity break, no part of your invention can be owned by, licensed to, or assigned to an entity that's not an individual, a nonprofit organization, or small business as defined by the Small Business Administration, typically with no more than 500 employees (see document A6 on the CD).

# *Sending Your Application to the USPTO*

The current mailing address for your patent application is: Commissioner of Patents, P.O. Box 1450, Alexandria, VA 22313-1450. But check the USPTO Web site for any changes.

The USPTO considers your mailing date as the official filing date, no matter when it actually receives your application, providing you use the following Express Mail procedure — something that's highly recommended if you choose to not file online. An application sent via any other delivery service is given the date of receipt as its filing date. Send your application via U.S. Express Mail service and paste the Express Mail label in the box provided on the Transmittal Form. You can also deliver your application during business hours. Check the Web site for the correct Alexandria, Virginia, address.

If you're familiar with the terms *browser*, *PDF*, and *upload*, you should consider filing your utility patent application online. Apart from the added peace of mind of getting immediate feedback that your application has been successfully filed, you currently save $80 on the filing fee.

In a few years, electronic filing will likely be the norm for all applications — if not the only accepted method. But for now, the procedure is still being adjusted. You first need to make sure that your computer is capable of creating electronic files in the proper format. Currently, the USPTO accepts PDF (Adobe Acrobat documents), plain old ASCII text, and PCT-Easy Zip files (a program offered for download by the USPTO) only. Check the USPTO Web site for the latest scoop on the subject. From the Patents main page click on File Online (EFS-Web) and EFS-Web Help & Tutorial. Applications filed electronically are immediately dated and the receipt is generated on the spot.

The online filing system is not exactly user-friendly, especially when it comes time to select the type of document you are uploading. So make sure you leave yourself plenty of time to navigate your way through the system. While filing your application, keep a browser window open on the filing wizard and another one open on the EFS-Web FAQ for quick reference.

# Meeting Your Filing Deadlines

Dates are everything, and we're not talking about what you're doing this weekend. In the United States, a patent application, whether formal or provisional, must be filed before all the following time deadlines:

- ✔ A reasonable time from the date of invention. Any unjustified delay may be legally construed as an abandonment of your invention, which can allow a later inventor to get the patent.

- ✔ Within one year from

  - Your offer to sell the invention.

  - A public use or showing of the invention.

  - A description of the invention in a publication.

  - The filing date of a foreign application upon which you want to claim priority (this period is only six months for a design patent application).

- ✔ As soon as possible after you've developed a viable invention. If you know you're going to apply for a patent, why wait?

At the time of this writing, a new patent law being considered by Congress would give priority to the first person who files his application over another inventor's application for the same invention. Under the current law, simultaneous or closely timed applications usually trigger an *interference* (a lengthy and expensive legal procedure, conducted in the USPTO, between claimants to the same invention — see Chapter 10). Of course, you don't know whether somebody else has come up with the same invention and is about to file a patent application. That's why we added this last entry to this list.

Most foreign countries require that you file your first domestic patent application before *any* public disclosure of the invention and that you file your application abroad within one year of the first filing (six months for a design application). Early filing of a provisional patent application can satisfy this requirement, providing that the application fully discloses the invention.

# Keeping Your Application under Wraps

Unless you file a non-publication request, which has some drawbacks, utility and plant patent applications are automatically published about 18 months after the filing date (or from any earlier priority date you may have claimed based on a prior domestic or foreign application). Until an application is published on the USPTO Web site, only you and your patent attorney can access the application file, commonly called the *file wrapper*. Log on to `www.uspto.gov/web/patents/access.html` to look at published applications.

To avoid publication of your application, when you initially file your patent application you should fill out and enclose a Non-publication Request form. There's no extra fee for that request, and it can't be denied. It's now or never: You can't stop publication later. If you request non-publication, the file wrapper remains confidential until the patent is granted (and it remains hidden away forever if the patent isn't granted).

If you previously filed a provisional patent application and are filing your formal application just short of one year later (see Chapter 8 for a discussion on provisional and formal applications), your application could be published within seven months. If you're filing a continuation application (see "Entering a Continuation Application," later in the chapter) on an application filed more than 18 months earlier, your new application may be up for publication within a few weeks.

Don't let your application be published by default, especially if you're concerned about loss of your trade secret. If you're confused, talk to your IP professional and let her help you make the right decision.

## Advantages of publication

Before you decide whether to have your application published, consider the advantages and disadvantages. First, the advantages:

- ✔ Anyone who infringes on any published claim of your patent application is liable from the publication date, provided that the claim is part of the patent when it's granted. You can't sue the infringer until you get the patent. But, after you do, you can request compensation for all losses resulting from the infringer's activities since the date of publication. Your patent may not be granted for more than a year after publication, so these losses may translate into a lot of moolah in damages. Taking advantage of these so-called *provisional patent rights* (don't ask us why the USPTO confusingly uses the word *provisional* here because this has nothing to do with provisional patent applications) may require mailing a copy of the publication to the infringer, something which is best handled by your IP professional.

- ✔ The publication of your application acts as a public notice of your impending patent, which is particularly important if you have practiced your invention publicly or sold items manufactured according to your invention before you get your patent. The law gives immunity to anyone who copies a product that does not have a patent number, unless that person is duly notified of the existence of the patent either personally or by the publication of your application. Because the items you sold before getting your patent can't carry a patent number, the chance of one of these items being copied is fairly high. Before your application is published, your right to compensation for infringement doesn't apply until the infringer is duly notified.

The presence of the patent number (see Chapter 11 for the appropriate notice) on all items ever sold constitutes proper notice to the entire world. The legend "Patent Pending" on a product has no legal value. If you sold patented items before the patent was issued, the infringer may not be liable for copying those items until you notify him by letter or otherwise.

✔ You can file an application abroad claiming the priority date, based on the filing date of the U.S. application, provided you do so within one year of that filing date.

The request for non-publication bars you from filing abroad with a claim of priority. There is a way out though. If you initially requested no publication and then decide, within one year, to file a foreign application claiming priority based on your U.S. application, you must petition that the U.S. application be published no later than 45 days from the foreign filing date — and pay a petition fee of about $130.

To get the most benefit from publication, request that your application be published anytime prior to the statutory 18-month scheduled date. You can also change your mind and request early publication even if you initially petitioned for no publication. The petition fee applies to both a request for early publication and a rescission of a previous non-publication request. Get the appropriate forms from the USPTO.

## Disadvantages of publication

And on the other hand, you need to factor in the disadvantages:

✔ Publication may punch a big hole in your trade-secret protection strategy. As we point out in Chapters 1, 2, and 4, you may want to keep your invention confidential for as long as you can. This is particularly true if you intend to rely on your trade-secret strategy and are just filing a patent application as back-up protection (we talk about this strategy in Chapter 5).

✔ If your invention isn't quite ready for the market, the publication gives an early opportunity to some sneaky folks to start working around your patent claims, and beat you in the race to the market place.

✔ You must pay a fee of about $300 in addition to the regular issue charges to get your patent issued if the application was published either automatically or at your specific request.

## Back in the good old days

In the 1960s and 1970s, the federal government subsidized the USPTO, and applicants' fees were negligible. However, these days, inventors and patent owners pay hefty sums to the USPTO almost every time they file a document or ask for special treatment. At the end of every budget year, the USPTO kicks back millions of unspent dollars into the "General Fund." Yet fees increase every year, sometimes by huge percentages, while examiners remain underpaid — with no relief in sight. These increases exist because a few years ago, Congress decided that inventors and patent owners were sheep that could be mercilessly shorn. Now individuals and companies like you have to finance the whole USPTO operation and also pay for unspecified federal expenditures. When you get tired of being shorn and milked dry, as we predict you'll soon be, don't complain to your IP professional. It's not her fault. Instead, write your congressperson and ask why you are being unfairly taxed.

# Asking for Special Status: Speeding Up Your Application

In general, patent applications are examined in the order of their *effective filing dates,* typically their actual filing dates or their priority dates (see Chapter 8), whichever came first. We have to qualify this statement with words such as *in general* and *typically* because this rule is subject to many exceptions. What else is new? We won't get into irritating details, but because of the lack of proper staffing and other such excuses, your application may not rise to the top of the pile for one to two years. However, if your trigger finger is itchy enough, you may petition the Commissioner of Patents to give your application "special" status so that it will be examined more quickly. There are basically two ways to qualify. The first is where the applicant is 65 or older or has health problems. The second is filing under the Accelerated Examination Program. We also discuss a backdoor approach at the end of this section for those who have friends in high places.

Not long ago a pilot program was in place to grant special status to applications having a corresponding Japanese application where claims have been allowed. In the future, this may be reimplemented and even expanded to include European applications and perhaps other countries. Check the USPTO Web site for the latest.

## Special status based on age or health

Here are a couple of easy ways to make your application "special." You don't even have to pay a petition fee.

✔ **Alleging old age:** If you're 65 years or older and can provide supporting documentation such as a birth certificate, you're in the pink, even if you have only a few gray hairs.

✔ **Standing on your last leg:** No matter how young you are, if you're critically sick and may not be around long enough to assist in the examination of your patent application, you have our deep sympathy. We can cheer you up a bit by assuring you that attaching a statement from your attending physician to your petition will get you that special status.

If your petition based on the applicant's age or health is granted, it's moved ahead of all the non-special applications, but still sits behind the special applications that qualified before yours.

Depending on how many applications are ahead of yours, the benefit to special status could be minimal, saving you only a few months. If you're lucky, you may gain six months to a year. Unfortunately, you can't predict the effect of the petition. The only sure thing (apart from death and taxes) is that your application will be pushed to the bottom of the barrel if you don't file the petition.

A petition to make your application special based on age or health should be filed with the application or shortly after. The USPTO takes two to six months, depending on your supporting reason, to review and approve the petition, so filing the petition months after your application filing date may delay your application instead of expediting it! Note that you must present your petition on a document separate from the specification and claims.

## The Accelerated Examination Program

An alternate, if harder, way to obtain special status is to file under the Accelerated Examination Program (AEP). A petition based on this program must be accompanied by the results of an anticipation search and a patentability analysis (see Chapter 7) along with a fee, currently $130. The search and analysis should be done by an IP pro and must report the classes and subclasses of prior patents searched. The Office will waive the petition fee if you can show that your claimed invention is related to:

✔ **Joining the green crowd:** If your invention benefits the environment by contributing to the restoration of basic life-sustaining natural elements, such as air, water, and soil, you keep your green.

✔ **Conserving energy:** If your invention leads to a new power source or more efficient energy use (a better appliance), you save $130.

✔ **Counter-terrorism:** Countering international terrorism has become a national priority. The USPTO will waive the petition fee for patent applications related to technology for countering terrorism — such as systems for detecting or identifying explosives, aircraft sensor or security devices, vehicular barricades, and vehicle-disabling systems.

Under the AEP, have your patent attorney conduct a preliminary examination of your application in the same manner as a patent examiner's. You must supply a complete report of the examination, including the results and analysis of an anticipation search, a list of classes and subclasses searched, copies of all the prior art documents uncovered, and a professional analysis of their impact upon the patentability of the invention. If the USPTO is satisfied by all this, it'll put your application on the fast track.

The AEP has drawbacks. Even if the fee is waived, the additional time and money spent conducting the anticipation search, performing the preliminary examination analysis, and writing up the results is significant, especially if your IP professional does the work. The amount of prosecution time saved doesn't always justify the cost (in time and money) of the procedure. And keep in mind that this preliminary examination analysis requires you to discuss the differences and often admit the similarities between your invention and the prior art discovered in the search. If you're not careful about what you admit, you could narrow the scope of your claims.

The law provides that if your invention is important to some branch of public service, your application can be given priority at the request of the head of a governmental department. Of course, to get your invention noticed, you'll need some friends in high places, a lot of chutzpah, and a dose of good luck.

# Preparing and Filing Patent Applications

Chapter 8 deals primarily with the preparation of formal utility patent applications. Preparing a provisional, design, or plant patent application is often a little less complicated. Due to their relative simplicity and lack of specific claims, they don't require as much legal expertise. With the help of one of the pamphlets listed earlier and the following guidelines, you should be able to prepare and file one of these applications on your own, although the assistance of an IP professional is recommended.

## Provisional applications

A provisional application doesn't need to be in any particular format. It only needs to fully describe the invention to support the formal patent application filed within a year. A patent attorney writes the specification in the same way with the same topics as in a formal application because that's the best, most common way to describe an invention. You may try to do the same or create your own format, but don't leave out any substantial aspect of the invention that could be separately claimed in the subsequent formal application. Needless to say, a patent attorney may do a better job of identifying all patentable aspects of your invention. The filing of a provisional application doesn't require the declaration and fee transmittal forms, just a Provisional Application for Patent cover sheet and a modest fee of about $105.

Your patent is only as good as its claims, and the rest of the application is primarily there to support the language used in those claims. When you file a provisional application without claims, you run the risk of not providing enough support for the claims in the later formal application.

## Design patent applications

A design patent application, which is relatively simple and inexpensive, addresses the ornamental aspect of an article of manufacture, not its function (see Chapters 5 and 6 for more info). In most aspects, filing an application for a design patent is the same as for a utility patent, except the filing fee is only about $230 for a small entity (no discount for filing electronically). But the specification and claim are simpler. Here's where design patents differ:

✔ The description of the invention is limited to a drawing or set of photographs that illustrate the article from all angles and a brief description of each view (see documents B11 and B12 on the CD).

✔ The description must start with a formal preamble giving the name of the applicant, the title of the design, and a brief description of the nature and intended use of the article in which the design is embodied as follows:

> *Be It Known That I, Jane Dee, a citizen of the United States of America, resident of Dade County, State of Florida, have invented a new and ornamental design for a TEA KETTLE of which the following is a specification.*

✔ You only need one formally written claim (see the last pages of the design patents, documents B11 and B12 on the CD).

✔ The drawing must strictly be in accordance with the rules spelled out in Section 1503 of the *Manual of Patent Examining Procedure* (MPEP) (see document A4 on the CD).

## Plant patent applications

An application for a plant patent (see Chapter 5), follows the same format as a utility patent application, except that the illustration is usually one or more photographs. Only one formal claim is allowed (see the last page of the plant patent, document B13 on the CD). Use a plant patent application transmittal form, and pay a standard fee of about $36 for a small entity.

# Wise Things to Do While You Wait

Years may pass before a patent is issued — if it's issued. We've seen utility patents issued within six months from their application date (extremely rare), and others that required up to ten years. The average pending time is about 32 months, but don't count on that estimate for any serious business planning. While you wait, you can exploit your invention in the same ways you'll use to make some cash after you get your patent. We discuss the following avenues in detail in Chapter 20: manufacturing and selling products embodying the invention, licensing your invention and patent to others for royalties, and selling the invention and patent rights.

Do *not* disclose the contents, serial number, or filing date of your patent application to anyone, except under strict conditions of confidentiality, before it is published by the USPTO. Even if the receiving party has signed a confidentiality agreement, don't disclose the wording of the pending claims.

While your patent is pending, someone who's filed an application for the same invention may challenge your application. This process, called an *interference,* determines which of two inventors claiming the same invention deserves the patent (see Chapter 10). Someone privy to your patent application can file his own application, copy some of your claims, and trigger an interference proceeding. If the person knows the date of your patent application filing, he can claim an earlier date of invention. Just the expenses and delay associated with the interference are enough to give you nightmares. Further, the usurper might walk away with the patent.

Don't forget to mark your products "Patent Pending" and make your licensees do the same. Although it can't support an infringement claim, the notice deters potential copycats. They'll hesitate to invest in manufacturing your product, for fear they may be shut down within months. But if you let it be known that you *just* filed your patent application, a copycat may speculate that he has two or three years to compete without consequences — a good reason to keep your filing date secret until your application is published.

# Entering a Continuation Application

Often, something comes up after you file your formal patent application, and you need to file a *continuation application.* This allows you to

✔ Enter a more complete application that includes some recent improvements to the invention in place of the original application.

✔ Claim a second invention embodied in that original device or process. A filtering mechanism for a coffeemaker might be the invention claimed in the original application, but a continuation application could claim an improvement in the heating element. You can claim them together in one application, but the examiner will ask you to select one of the inventions because a patent only covers one. An inventor usually finds it necessary to file a series of applications in order to fully cover his or her creations.

If you go the continuation route, remember these peculiarities:

✔ A continuation application must have at least one inventor in common with its parent application.

✔ If the continuation application contains *new matter* (anything not described in the original application), the new application is called a *continuation in part application.*

✔ If the continuation application doesn't disclose anything new, and simply claims something previously disclosed but not currently claimed in the pending original application, the new application is called a *divisional continuation application* or simply a *divisional application.*

A divisional application often results from an examiner's request that certain claims in an original application be withdrawn because they refer to a separate invention. In such a case, claims cancelled in the original application and now presented in the continuation application are immune to certain grounds for rejection. Divisional applications are like teachers' pets — they get preferential treatment by the patent examiner (because they're mere extensions of their parent applications).

✔ After filing a continuation application, you can abandon the original application, let it expire, or keep it alive until the first patent is issued.

## Too much of a good thing?

The USPTO has come up with new rules limiting the number of related continuation applications that a person can file. On October 1, 2007, one day before the new rules were to be effective, a federal district judge declared that they went beyond the authority of the Commissioner and stopped the USPTO from implementing them. At the time of this writing, we can't predict whether any part of these restrictive regulations will be reinstated. We recommend that you include as much as you can in your application by disclosing and claiming every aspect and all features of your invention. This should preserve your right to file as many continuation applications (in the form of divisional applications) as necessary to fully cover and protect your creations.

To claim priority on an application filed earlier, the previous application must still be in good standing. Don't let the original application expire because you forgot to answer a communication from the examiner. Also, continuation practice is often very different in foreign countries. Many countries don't provide for a continuation-in-part application. This means the improvement in the more recently filed application must be patentable all on its own, and your own parent application can be used as prior art against you.

# Chapter 10

# Wrestling with the Patent Examiner

*T*he process of pushing your application through the USPTO (called the prosecution) isn't that bad if you're patient. Like the great Wheel of Justice, the gears and cogs of the USPTO turn very slowly — and all at your expense, because the 20-year life of your patent is computed from the date you file the application. Only the time you spend successfully appealing adverse decisions of the patent examiner isn't held against you. Because utility patents are the most complex, we focus on their examination in this chapter.

You probably can't answer the examiner's requests, objections, or rejections after reading this chapter. We know this book is good, but it isn't law school. You have to rely on your IP attorney. All communications from the patent examiner are written in a formal style and are often accompanied by citations of statutes, rules, or controlling court decisions. They should be answered the same way, point by point, with opposing citations supporting your position when appropriate. For an example see Document E1 on the CD.

We can only give you a basic outline of the rules and regulations that govern the prosecution of patent applications. Many nuances, exceptions, and provisions are too complex and numerous to address.

# *Touring the USPTO*

Before tackling the substantive issues that the patent examiner will raise after looking at your application, you really should get more intimately acquainted with the USPTO, an agency of the U.S. Government that manages

- ✔ Accepting and examining patent applications.
- ✔ Granting patents.
- ✔ Resolving conflicts between applicants claiming the same invention.
- ✔ Maintaining a library of issued patents.
- ✔ Correcting defective patents.
- ✔ Registering and keeping copies of documents related to patents and patent applications.
- ✔ Qualifying and disciplining patent attorneys and agents.
- ✔ Collecting hefty fees from applicants and patent owners.

Notably absent from this list is helping you obtain your patent. In fact, the USPTO examiners act contrary to your best interests. They will prevent you from getting a patent that goes beyond the merits of your invention. Don't expect much help from a patent examiner except to guide you through minor administrative procedures. Also notice: The USPTO has absolutely nothing to do with patent infringement — that's the exclusive domain of federal courts.

## *Consulting the golden book*

All the USPTO's activities related to patents and patent applications are governed by the rules and legislations in the *Manual of Patent Examining Procedure* (MPEP). This manual lists the patent laws, the federal regulations applicable to patents, patent applications, and all related administrative procedures, and very detailed instructions and guidelines for use by patent examiners and USPTO personnel. To order the manual or consult the MPEP, check out the USPTO Web site or see document A5 on the CD.

## *Meeting your examiner and the art unit*

The patent examining section of the USPTO is divided into art units. Each *art unit* specializes in a specific field of technology identified by reference to one or more groups. A *group* is a subdivision of the patent classification system that includes several technological classes and subclasses (see Chapter 9). And within each art unit are the patent examiners who work their legal voodoo on your application. The *patent examiner* performs the down-in-the-trenches work of reviewing hundreds of patent applications a week, conducting anticipation searches, and drafting examination reports. Over many years of personal dealings with the USPTO, we've found that the examiners are well-trained, dedicated professionals.

Whenever you communicate with the USPTO about a pending application, include the number of the relevant art unit in the top-right corner of your first page. You can find that number on the original application receipt and on all papers from the examiner. If you know the name of the examiner assigned to the case, you must add it to the art unit number.

## Crying and other appeal routes

The big kahuna at the USPTO is the *Commissioner of Patents,* who oversees all patent-related activities. You may have to kiss his ring occasionally while applying for your patent, if you know what we mean. If you get a decision you don't like, your appeal options are illustrated in Figure 10-1.

- ✔ **Regulatory matters:** Petition the commissioner directly to reverse a decision by the examiner of a procedural rather than legal nature, such as a refusal to accept a filed document on technical grounds or an objection to the contents of your patent application. (See "Getting In on the Office Action," later in the chapter.)

- ✔ **Legal decisions:** Rulings of a legal nature, such as rejection of claims in your application for lack of novelty or obviousness, are taken to the Board of Patent Appeals and Interferences (BPAI), on which the commissioner sits. Proceedings there are conducted in accordance with the *Federal Rules of Civil Procedure* (www.law.cornell.edu/rules/frcp) — the kind of stuff that gives law students nightmares.

  If your appeal to the commissioner or to the BPAI is unsuccessful, your attorney can take your case to the Court of Appeals for the Federal Circuit (CAFC ) and, if necessary, all the way to the U.S. Supreme Court. You can also sue the commissioner in the U.S. District Court for the District of Columbia to force him to grant you a patent. Talk with your attorney about which is the best route to follow.

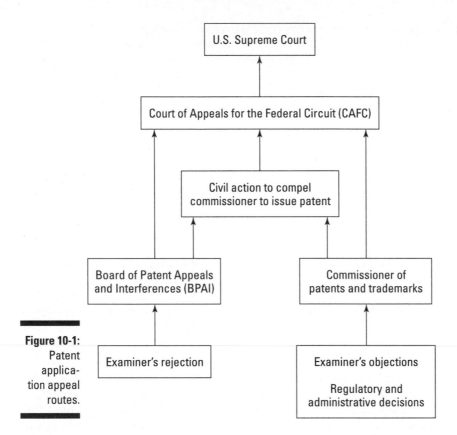

**Figure 10-1:**
Patent
applica-
tion appeal
routes.

# Clearing Initial Administrative Hurdles

The USPTO only corresponds with one person. If you're flying solo, that's you. But if you take our advice, that person is your patent attorney or agent.

## Meeting the minimum requirements

When you file your patent application online, you're immediately given a filing date and serial number. If you mail or hand-deliver it to the USPTO (see Chapter 9), it's forwarded by the mailroom to the Office of Initial Patent Examination (OIPE). The OIPE quickly mails you back the early return card (that we suggest you submit with your application in Chapter 9) stamped with a temporary and conditional application filing date and serial number.

If you don't get the return card within a week or two of mailing your application, you may assume that something went awry in its mailing. And don't disclose the filing date or serial number to anyone, except under strict conditions of confidentiality. See Chapter 9 and the sidebar, "Avoiding a third-party protest," later in this chapter).

The OIPE then checks your application to see whether it meets the minimum filing requirements — just a specification and one claim. If so, the application's temporary and conditional filing date and serial number are confirmed for the record of the USPTO. Meeting these minimum requirements only puts your application in the USPTO's hopper. It doesn't guarantee you'll get a patent. Your application needs a lot more, as we explain in Chapters 8 and 9, to survive the examination.

If the application doesn't include a complying specification and at least one claim, the OIPE sends you a *notice of incomplete application,* asking for the missing part, and cancels your temporary filing date and serial number. You're given two months to complete the application before it's returned to you. When you mail in the complying part, you must include a declaration that identifies the supplied material, indicating that it accurately describes, illustrates, or claims your invention. Use the supplemental declaration form.

## *Dealing with additional issues*

When your application meets the minimum requirements, it takes about six weeks before you receive an official *notice of receipt* of your application, and sometimes a *notice of defective application.* You get the latter if, for instance, you didn't enclose the filing fee or a signed declaration form. In such a case, you have a few weeks to send the missing part and pay a fine of about $65.

The OIPE may also object to some components of your application. For example, if you printed your specifications on both sides of a sheet, used the wrong size of paper, or sent a drawing of such a poor quality that it can't be reproduced, the OIPE sends you a *Notice to File Corrected Application Papers* (document E11 on the CD). You must respond within two months.

The OIPE, or later the examiner, sometimes wants a little more information about the invention. They may request information about the field of technology to which the application pertains or ask for existing documentation or reference material about the general area of the invention. This information helps them determine the application's relevant art unit. A reply is usually required within two months of the request.

## Foreign filing licenses and secrecy orders

For most applications, a *foreign filing license* accompanies the official notice of receipt (Document E1k on the CD). You can't file in a foreign patent office until you get this foreign filing license from the USPTO.

Disclosing your invention or filing for a patent in a foreign country before filing in the United States or before receiving the foreign filing license may prevent you from getting a U.S. patent. Depending on the subject of your application, you could be prosecuted for violating export regulations, which means that your next communication to the USPTO could be on federal penitentiary letterhead. The main purpose of the foreign license requirement is to prevent U.S. residents from disclosing to other countries critical inventions that have military applications. See Chapter 19 and Section 140 of the MPEP if you want to know more about this license business.

If your invention relates to atomic energy or space, you must certify that it wasn't developed under a government-sponsored program or grant, which includes acting as a subcontractor to a company under a government contract. A sample of the required certification is in Section 150 of the MPEP.

More significantly, all patent applications that have military applications are subject to review by the U.S. Department of Defense or a law enforcement agency. Depending upon the sensitivity of the technology, a foreign filing license may be denied and your application placed under a secrecy order.

A *secrecy order* forbids you and anybody else from disclosing your invention to anyone and prevents the USPTO from publishing your application or allowing it to mature into a patent. You can petition to have the order rescinded by proving that secrecy is fruitless — for example someone has already let the cat out of the bag. But, if the secrecy order is maintained, you can request monetary compensation from the agency that issued the order.

Failure to comply with a secrecy order makes you criminally liable, subject to a fine of up to $10,000 and two years in the federal pokey.

# Splitting Up Is Hard to Do: Restricting the Application

A few months later, when your patent application makes its way to the top of the pile on the examiner's desk, she may issue a request for restriction. A *request for restriction* demands that you limit the scope of your present application. A request for restriction occurs only if you claim more than one invention — or several *species* (variations) of a single invention — that could be patented independently from one another.

Say you invented an electric toothbrush with bristles that have different directions and ranges of motion. You claim several species of the brush — one with a straight handle, one with a curved handle, one with a metal handle, and one with a plastic handle. The metal and plastic handle species aren't patentably distinguishable from each other because substituting a plastic handle for a metal one would be obvious and not deserve a separate patent. But using a curved handle instead of a straight one may provide some significant and not necessarily obvious advantages (making it easier to reach back teeth) that could be the object of a separate patent. You'd have to restrict your application to one of these last two species of brushes.

If a claim applies to all species of the invention, that claim is said to be *generic.* A generic claim defines the *genus* that has the basic characteristic of all claimed inventions. In the toothbrush example, a claim that recites the bristle arrangement and simply "a handle" would be generic because it covers all the various handle species.

The examiner expresses the restriction request by singling out one or more generic claims, and listing all the independently patentable species she can identify. She then asks you to elect claims addressed to a single species and withdraw the claims that recite non-elected species.

If you comply with the request, the claims you withdraw are set aside. If, at the end of the examination process, one of the generic claims is allowed, all the withdrawn species claims covered by that allowed generic one are automatically brought back and allowed. If no generic claim is allowed, you end up with the group of claims addressed to a single species that you've elected. In that case, in order to cover the inventions recited in the claims you have withdrawn, you must include them in one or more divisional continuation applications (see Chapter 9) that you must file before the issue or abandonment of your original application.

You have to respond to a request for restriction by electing one of the inventions. You can't refuse to restrict the invention and elect a species. But, you have options: You can choose the one invention with or without a protest.

If you make your claim election without filing an objection to the request for restriction (called filing *without traverse*), the restriction is final and can't be contested later. If you *traverse* (contest) the request, the examiner will probably find your argument unconvincing, reject it, and fire back a final request that can be appealed. You can then petition the Commissioner to reverse the examiner's decision, and wait about four to eight months for a ruling. In the meantime, you have to make an election, and it better be the right one because you may have to live with it if your petition is denied. So deciding which aspect of the invention to patent first is very important.

The best choice is the aspect of the invention that gives you the most legal rights against your eventual competitors, not necessarily the one that you think is the most clever or innovative. When in doubt, let your IP counselor help you make the most sensible decision.

The main reason for contesting a request for restriction is to force the examiner to reconsider. Another reason is to reserve the right to appeal the examiner's decision to the Commissioner, or later, the BPAI if you're not satisfied with the final outcome of your application. But there's a problem: When you try to argue that the request for restriction isn't warranted, you may have to point out that the various embodiments and species claimed aren't patently distinguishable. This could be dangerous, if not fatal, for your application. If you maintain that all embodiments and species are patentably equivalent, and later the examiner finds that one embodiment is anticipated by the prior art, all species of your invention are in jeopardy. Most patent professionals prefer not to take the risk and file a restriction without traverse.

Before answering a request for restriction, take a good look at the way your claims are drafted. You may want to amend them to eliminate some of the grounds for restrictions. For example, you may enter one or more means-plus-function claims that cover several or all of the embodiments of your invention. You could also reshuffle the claim hierarchy to place the most valuable invention in the generic claim, or at least in an elected one. We explain the various kinds of claims in Chapter 8.

You can modify the claims in a *preliminary amendment* to your application. The amendment must be submitted before any substantive examination by the examiner, but no later than your response to the request for restriction. In addition, if you file a preliminary amendment after you receive a request for restriction, you must elect the embodiment and species in relation to the amended claims and not the claims as originally filed.

# Getting In on the Office Action

After you have the whole request for restriction thing straightened out (see the "Splitting Up Is Hard to Do: Restricting the Application" section, earlier in this chapter), you're ready for the next test. If you avoided that fun because the claims of your application address a single invention (or through some other stroke of good fortune), your story continues here as well.

At this point you may refer to Documents E1a through E1mm on the CD as examples of some of the things to come.

The examiner conducts an anticipation search (see Chapter 7) and issues an *office action* (OA) — the first report on the merits of your claims. If you're the exception, all is well. You receive a *notice of allowance* of all your claims, and you can go straight to Chapter 11. However, if the OA contains an adverse ruling, you have to attempt to refute it. Most likely, you'll amend (change) the specification or claims to make them more acceptable. Then the examiner fires back with another, but final, OA, giving you a last opportunity to argue or amend. Additional procedures allow the exchanges to continue until you and the examiner reach a meeting of the minds as we explain later. Unfortunately, these procedures also include additional fee payments.

Although receiving a notice of allowance right off the bat will rightfully make you wanna kiss your mailman, it should also raise a bright-red warning flag. Perhaps the claims of your application are too narrow. Carefully look over any new prior art found by the examiner and reread your broadest claim(s) to make sure your patent will extend to the limits of the prior art.

The OA may contain two types of actions.

✔ **Objections:** Objections usually mean you didn't comply with the *definite ness requirement* in drafting the specifications or claims. Typographic and grammatical errors (including the peculiar grammatical rules of claim drafting in Chapter 8), vague or long-winded descriptions, discrepancies between the written description and the drawing, and otherwise defective drawings are examples of indefiniteness.

These mistakes are fairly easy to correct and should be addressed in the first portion of the amendment filed in response to the OA. An objection is subject to review by the commissioner. (Refer to Figure 10-1 for a refresher course on the appeals routes.)

✔ **Rejection:** If the examiner rejects some or all of your claims, you have a more troublesome matter that may require vigorous arguments on your part. You may also need to make extensive amendments to a claim or cancel it altogether. A rejection applies to a claim and more specifically to the invention recited in that claim. It can only be appealed, preferably by a competent lawyer, to the Board of Patent Appeals, and then a qualified federal court (refer to Figure 10-1).

The examiner can reject claims on a number of grounds. In the following sections, we cover each kind of rejection and how you can overcome it.

## Overcoming a rejection for indefiniteness

A rejection of one or more claims for indefiniteness usually parallels an objection on the same ground. Or it can state that your wording is incomprehensible or too vague. This last ground can present a serious problem for you. As we cover in Chapter 8, having claims that are as broad as possible is to your advantage, and broadness can be achieved by not being too precise. Here lies a tug of war between you and the examiner. You want a claim that can cover as many machines, compositions, or processes as possible even at the risk of being ambiguous. But the examiner wants to make sure that one can readily assess the coverage of the claim from its wording.

You can overcome the rejection of a claim for indefiniteness by cleaning up the informalities and tightening its wording. But you have to be very careful not to unduly narrow its coverage. That's when your patent attorney's experience and expertise become invaluable.

## *Fighting a lack-of-utility rejection*

Being rejected because of a lack of utility basically means the invention has no demonstrable practical use. (Utility, along with novelty and obviousness, is one of the tests of patentability, as we discuss in Chapter 5.) See section 101 of the patent law for a complete explanation of the utility requirement.

The courts have interpreted this to mean that a person with some skill in the area can immediately appreciate that the invention is useful, and that its utility is specific, substantial, and credible. The following are examples of questionable claims content and the statements you'd see in the first OA:

- **Compound for softening fingernails:** *The claimed invention lacks patentable utility. There is no conceivable application for a nail-softening compound. The role of a nail is to strengthen a fingertip. Softening a nail would be counter-productive.*

- **Perpetual motion machine:** *The claimed invention is inoperative and therefore lacks utility. The invention is a perpetual motion machine that defies the laws of physics and cannot be credible.*

- **Method for growing hair by exposure to a magnetic field:** *The claimed invention has no demonstrable utility. The effect of a magnetic field on the physiology of hair growth is neither demonstrated in the specification nor credible in view of current medical knowledge.*

If you get a rejection for lack of utility because the invention is absolutely nutty, you can't do much about it, so we won't waste time trying to show you how to salvage a claim to an absurd invention. But an invention with merit can be rejected if you didn't do your homework when preparing the application. Your application should've mentioned any actual or potential utility of your invention in the specification. But you can easily counter a lack-of-utility rejection with a reasonable answer that demonstrates whichever one of the following attributes the examiner says your invention lacks:

- **Substantial utility:** You must demonstrate a use or application of the invention that's reasonably related to the invention itself and isn't insubstantial or frivolous. For instance, you can't argue that a nail-softening solution can also be used to fill the glass tube of a bubble level because any liquid can do that. However, arguing that fingernails softened with your solution can be reshaped for a more aesthetic appearance would be sufficient to overcome the rejection.

✔ **Specific utility:** You must indicate at least one plausible, specific application for the invention. Claims rejected for lack of specific utility are usually for chemical products and therapeutic preparations or treatments because the specification doesn't include examples and test results that sufficiently support the invention. For example, indicating that a compound may be useful in the treatment of a specific disorder isn't specific enough to overcome a rejection, without also submitting clinical test results that prove that the compound works as claimed.

✔ **Credible utility:** An invention, such as a perpetual motion machine, that's deemed totally incapable of achieving a useful result will be rejected for lack of credible utility. However, even a minimum of utility can salvage the invention. Just because an invention lacks sophistication, performs poorly, or operates only under very specific conditions doesn't mean it should be rejected. Demonstrating partial success in achieving a useful result is enough to avoid the rejection.

One catchall form of utility that we've found to be very useful in salvaging inventions of questionable credibility is to claim utility as an educational device or toy. Even a harebrained perpetual motion machine can be a great toy for educating young minds about the law of conservation of energy.

## Contesting a lack-of-novelty rejection

Lack-of-novelty rejections happen when the invention is already known or is disclosed in a prior document. Ah, but if it were only that easy. Section 35 U.S.C. § 102 of the patent law contains several subsections that outline the circumstances for rejecting a patent. Any lack-of-novelty rejection that you get will cite one or more of these subsections as the grounds for the rejection. For a plain-English explanation of these circumstances, see the patentability checklist in Chapter 5.

It may help you to follow us through the next section to take a look at the seven subsections — (a) through (g) — of Section 35 U.S.C. § 102 in all their glory that you'll find in document D1 on the CD.

Like any other legal concept, lack of novelty isn't easy to delineate. A piece of prior art cited against one of your claims may look black or white, but there's always a large gray area that leaves room for argument and interpretation. Enter the skill, experience, and advice of an IP pro. But you're here for some answers. So in the sections that follow, we outline the two most common paths for rebutting lack-of-novelty rejections.

### Using the different invention defense

A claimed invention can be rejected for lack of novelty if the examiner believes that it's *anticipated* by the prior art because every element in the claim is explicitly or implicitly described in an alleged prior art reference. In other words, the earlier device or process must be *exactly* identical in *all* details. This rule gives you two options:

- ✔ Demonstrate that your claimed invention is different from the disclosures in the prior art reference.

- ✔ Amend your claim to show a difference between your invention and the cited prior art. (See "Presenting a timely, professional answer," later in this chapter, about how to amend a claim and present an argument.)

Even if you think your existing claim language should be allowable, it may be worthwhile to consider making a minor modification to show your willingness to work together with the examiner and maintain an amicable relationship, at least for the time being. Most would prefer the bureaucrat who works with you over the one who works against you.

Be careful though, any change to the claims could provide the basis for a prosecution history estoppel defense to your competitors A *prosecution history estoppel* prevents you from asserting something contrary to what you stated in your earlier amendment. It's best to proceed under the advice of your IP professional.

In most cases, differentiating your invention from prior art is relatively easy, although examiners have a few tricks up their sleeves to counter your defense. Be on the lookout for these common examiner comebacks:

- ✔ If you argue that the prior art reference, although it may be similar to your invention, doesn't disclose a characteristic listed in your claim, the examiner may cite another earlier or contemporary patent or reference. Inevitably, that citation will mention that the characteristic in question is well known, and thus inherently disclosed in the first cited prior art reference.

- ✔ If you claim a generic compound, the examiner can use a reference disclosing a single species of that generic compound, even if the earlier species is only a partial example of the broad generic compound (see "Splitting Up Is Hard to Do: Restricting the Application," earlier, for the difference between generic and species).

- ✔ If you claim a species, the examiner can use a previously known genus as well as other evidence to show that a person with ordinary skill in the art would envision your species.

- ✔ If your claim specifies a range or a list of equivalent elements, the examiner need only find a prior reference partially within that range or list to make a case of anticipation.

### Setting the date: Swearing back of a reference

A patent usually doesn't give the date an invention happened. So, lacking any other evidence, the law presumes that the invention took place just around the application-filing date or the publication date of a non-patent document.

Depending on the specific subsection (namely the second paragraph of 102(a) or 102(b)), if your claim is rejected for lack of novelty, you can take advantage of this presumption. You can use the *swearing back defense* — demonstrating that you developed your invention before the filing date of the patent or the publication date of the document cited against your claim. You have to declare, under penalty of perjury, that you were the first to develop the invention. The declaration must:

✔ Establish that you developed your invention before the effective filing date (see Chapter 9) of the patent or the publication date of the document used against your claim.

✔ State the dates of your invention conception, its first written description, first construction, and other pertinent acts.

You must also support the declaration with evidence, such as copies of an engineering notebook, correspondence, photographs, and whatever else is available to prove your case. We recommend in Chapter 6 that you keep detailed notes about your invention development in a bound notebook, periodically witnessed by someone you trust. Such a record can provide convincing evidence of your date of invention.

We realize this is complicated stuff, but we've tried to condense and simplify the convoluted rules that govern the swearing back defense. First, the swearing-back-of-reference defense can only be used if the rejection falls under one of two subsections:

✔ Under subsection 102(a), you can't get a patent if the invention was known or used in the U.S. before you came up with it (what was done abroad doesn't count). You also face rejection if your invention was patented or described in a printed publication anywhere (yes, even the writings of Confucius, printed on woodblocks circa AD 750 in China, are printed publications).

✔ Under subsection 102(e), you're out of the game if your invention was described (it doesn't have to be claimed) in a published U.S. patent application or in a U.S. patent before you developed your invention.

Also, keep in mind that you can't use the swearing back defense if:

✔ Your invention was already known or used by someone in the U.S. when you developed it as stated in the first part of subsection 102(a).

✔ You abandoned your invention, expressly or by prolonged inactivity.

✔ You goofed — you applied for and obtained a foreign patent more than 12 months before filing in the U.S.

✔ Someone else published a U.S. patent application or obtained a U.S. patent claiming the same invention as yours.

✔ The document cited against your claim came out more than one year before you filed your patent application.

### Nabbing the invention thief

What can you do if the person responsible for the reference cited against your claim actually stole your invention? What if Cousin Ernie, who was always milling around your garage, asked too many questions, got too many answers, fired off a quick application, and beat you to the patent office? Patent law allows you to use the swearing back defense to prove that Ernie copied your invention. You need to file a declaration, with supporting evidence, showing that you're the real McCoy. In your declaration, you also have to explain how that sneaky Ernie found out about your invention.

Be totally honest in your statements — you're under penalty of perjury. You'll go to jail or pay a heavy fine if you're caught lying.

### Applying the defenses

We'll try to bring all these defense tactics into focus with a hypothetical example that describes the sequence of inventing something, filing a patent application, getting rejected, and forming your responses.

You've noticed that the circular pads on your rotating polishing machine wear out more quickly around the edge than in the center. This happens because with each rotation, the bristles on the outer edges of the pad travel a longer distance in contact with the work surface than the bristles in the center.

So, you've developed a new buffing pad with a graduated thickness of pile. The tufting gets tighter as it moves away from the center, even though the length or height of the pile is the same on the entire pad, as shown under "Applicant" in Figure 10-2.

**Figure 10-2:**
Claimed
inventions.

You've filed a patent application including the following claim:

> *Claim 1. A rotary polishing pad which comprises an arrangement of strands of equal length and thickness, tufted in a gradually increasing number of strands per square centimeter from a central region to a peripheral region of said pad.*

You can't believe your eyes when you read this statement in the first OA:

> *Claim 1 is rejected under 35 U.S.C.§ 102(a) as being anticipated by Abbott Publication of U.S. Application No.0,000.*
>
> *Abbott discloses a rotary polishing pad comprising strands of equal length but gradually increasing thickness from a central region to a peripheral region of said pad.*
>
> *It is well known in the art and therefore inherent in the disclosure of Abbott that increase in density of a pile can be achieved by either increasing the thickness of the strands or tufting the strands in a tighter pattern.*

Looking at Abbott, you notice that the application was filed just six months before yours and has just been published. You could try the "different invention defense," but you'll have to overcome the examiner's opinion that thicker strands are inherently equivalent to more strands and are therefore a substitutable method for increasing pile density. Your best bet is to apply the *swearing-back-of-the-reference* defense by filing a declaration, supported by a copy of your development notebook, showing that you conceived and tested your invention before Mr. Abbott filed his patent application.

## Challenging an obviousness rejection

An obviousness rejection says the invention doesn't rise beyond ordinary skill in the field. Subsection 35 U.S.C. § 103(a) of the patent law provides that:

> *A patent may not be granted though the invention is not identically disclosed or described as set forth in section 102 . . ., if the differences between the subject matter sought to be patented and the prior art are such that the subject matter as a whole would have been obvious at the time the invention was made to a person having ordinary skill in the art to which said subject matter pertains.*

This short paragraph has inspired shelves full of books and caused thousands of court battles. If you review the patentability criteria sections in Chapter 5, you know as much technical info as you need to know about obviousness. So here we explain the strategy you and your IP counselor must follow to challenge a rejection of a claim for obviousness. Put on your thinking cap and send the kids to Grandma. This is going to require your undivided attention.

The examiner may cite one or more prior art references in his rejection. A reference may be a patent, a published patent application, or a document published anywhere in the world, including on the Internet. The examiner may also refer to "well-known" facts, practices, or information without providing evidence. Each reference must have existed at the time of the invention.

You can overcome a rejection for obviousness with defensive approaches:

- ✔ Contesting the applicability of the references on the grounds that either they're disqualified as prior art or don't meet the conditions necessary to support a lack of novelty rejection under one of the 102 subsections.

- ✔ Arguing that the references belong to a *non-analogous* (unrelated) *art* into which an inventor would not look to resolve the problem addressed by your patent, and don't teach anything relevant to your invention.

- ✔ Challenging the examiner's combining two or more references to support her rejection, on the grounds that there is no basis for the combination, either in the references themselves or in the common knowledge.

- ✔ Specifying that the differences between the claimed invention and the prior art are beyond the ability of a person with ordinary skill in the art.

- ✔ Demonstrating secondary factors of non-obviousness: acceptance of the invention, commercial success, or unexpected advantages.

For convenience, we stick to your handy-dandy buffing pad from the previous section in which the tufting gets tighter as it moves away from the center, even though the length or height of the pile is the same on the entire pad.

To your great disappointment, you read this statement in the first OA:

> *Claim 1 is rejected under 35 U.S.C. § 103(a) over Abbott Publication of Application No.0,000, and also over Abel British Patent No. 11,111,111, in view of Babele Italian Patent No. 22,222,222 or Chizu Japanese Patent No. 33,333,333.*
>
> *Abbott discloses a rotary polishing pad comprising strands of equal length but gradually increasing thickness from a central region to a peripheral region of said pad.*
>
> *Abel discloses a rotary polishing pad having strands arranged in gradually greater length from the center to the periphery.*
>
> *Babele discloses a car floor mat having a more densely tufted area in the center where the heels of the driver are resting.*
>
> *It would have been obvious to a person with ordinary skill in the art to use the variable tufting of Babele in the manufacture of the Abbott pad instead of using thicker strands, or in the manufacture of the Abel pad instead of using strands of different lengths.*

*Chizu discloses a sanding belt having a coarser grade along the center of the belt than along its longitudinal edges. It would have been obvious to a person with ordinary skill in the art to use a coarser (thicker) tufting on the Abbott or Abel pad in areas subject to greatest friction than in other areas as taught by Chizu.*

The diagrams in Figure 10-2 illustrate the various pile configurations.

When you examine these references, you discover that Abbott and Abel address the same problem you identified, but with progressively thicker or longer strands. You also observe that the different sanding grades of Chizu are intended to create contrasting finishes on polished metal surfaces for purely aesthetic reasons, not to reduce edge wear. Abel, Babele, and Chizu were filed several years before your application. To overcome the obviousness rejection, you could try these defensive approaches, in this order:

1. **Not part of prior art:** Get rid of Abbott by showing that this reference isn't applicable: It was already disqualified as prior art because it wasn't patented or published before your application. But the other references are too old to be polished off (pun absolutely intended) that way.

2. **Non-analogous art:** Try to disqualify Babele and Chizu on the grounds that they belong to non-analogous arts by arguing that your buffing pads are in different and unrelated fields from automobile floor mats or sanding belts. Citing Babele's mat is a good point. But the Chizu argument is very weak because buffing pads and sanding belts are commonly found in workshops and are often used on the same piece.

   Even if you win the argument, you still have to meet the second part of the test by demonstrating that the non-analogous art reference doesn't teach anything about the invention. Babele does teach a very relevant technique of using a tighter tufting of the pile in areas of maximum wear. One could point out that Chizu suggests the use of different grades of grinding, sanding, or polishing agents on the same tool. So, non-analogous art isn't a very strong defense. Look at the other defenses.

3. **Improper combination of references:** You may have better luck here. To combine one reference with another, that combination must be suggested in the references themselves, or be part of the general knowledge of one with ordinary skill in the art. Moreover, the combination can't change the principle of operation of the primary reference or render the primary reference inoperable for its intended purpose. For example, if the sanding belt of Chizu was mounted on Abel's rotary machine, the combination wouldn't function as a buffer.

   The remaining primary reference is Abel. The secondary references are Babele with the floor mat and Chizu with the sanding belt. Abel and Babele are designed to resolve the same problem of excessive wear in the most worked areas of the pad or mat. It'd be difficult to convince the examiner that the Babele approach couldn't be practically used on Abel's pad. However, the coarser sanding grade in the center portion of

Chizu's belt can't be carried over into Abel's without completely changing the operation of the buffing pad; there's no motivation to combine the references. You can eliminate Chizu. You'll win that round and get rid of the last ground for rejection.

4. **Non-obvious differences:** You're left now with Abel and Babele. You can try to discredit the examiner's application of the obviousness test spelled out in the statute.

   The difference between the teachings of the combined references (what you can find out from them) and the invention is extremely small. Abel recognized the problem of excessive peripheral wear in the pad and Babele teaches how to minimize that type of wear in a floor mat. The issue remaining is whether a person with ordinary skill in the field of buffing pads who is fully aware of the two references would be inclined to combine their teachings and develop your invention.

   You can argue that Abel's use of longer strands to solve the wear problem was a poor solution because the pad's now uneven working surface puts more pressure on the edges than in the center. The shorter strands in the center of the pad won't wear out until the peripheral strands wear down to the same length as those in the center. At which point the initial problem reappears. So Abel's invention is a nice try but is an unsuccessful way to solve the problem. I can predict the examiner answering: "Yeah, Abel didn't know about Babele, but a theoretical person with ordinary skill in the art would have." You still have a chance to win the argument by pointing out the following. Buffing pad design isn't rocket science and the "level of ordinary skill" in the field is relatively low. Abel is a good representative of the person with ordinary skill. So if Abel didn't know about Babele, neither would that skilled person. That last argument might just carry enough water to win the case.

5. **Secondary factors:** Another opportunity to salvage the claim is to demonstrate some unexpected advantages of your invention called *secondary factors,* such as commercial success or important contribution to the industry, by presenting sales records, testimonials from people in the field, and magazine articles praising your achievements.

Defeating an obviousness rejection requires modesty. Use the Internet to find support for a relatively low level of ordinary skill in your field of technology. If you can find examples of problems faced by others in your field by using earlier prior art approaches, this helps indicate a lack of a spirit of innovation.

## Proving your invention is patentable

Section 35 U.S.C. § 101 of the patent law provides the granting of a patent to *whoever invents or discovers any new and useful process, machine, manufacture, or composition of matter or any new and useful improvement thereof.* Those things are called *statutory subject matters.*

You may have a hard time imagining an invention that doesn't fit into one of these categories. Yet there's always someone who tries to patent (and therefore monopolize) a law of nature, natural phenomenon, algorithm, abstract idea, simple manipulation of abstract ideas, or purely descriptive material. These subject matters are patently non-patentable. Einstein couldn't patent $E=mc^2$ because it's an algorithm expressing a law of nature.

The rejection of a claim on the ground that it recites *non-statutory* (non-patentable) subject matter is rather unusual, except in the area of computer programs and software inventions that involve a method of doing business. Such a rejection is often tacked on to a rejection for lack of utility. Indeed, if the invention is useless, it is a non-statutory invention.

To answer a lack of statutory subject matter rejection, you must convince the examiner that your claim recites a physical structure, composition, or process that produces a tangible result. For example, a database or compilation of information, even in an electronic form, fulfills neither of these requirements. However, the structure of a computer database that is organized and indexed to facilitate access to specific information constitutes statutory subject matter.

A pure manipulation of data to obtain a final dimension or other parameter is not statutory subject matter. However, when this calculation is done by a computer coupled to an industrial process machine, such as a computer that drives a machine to regulate rubber vulcanization, the regulation method, including the algorithm used by the computer program, becomes patentable.

Make sure you go the extra step in your patent application, at least by way of example, in applying your newly mined data to solving a specific problem, or better yet, use the data output to run a specific device.

## Showing your disclosure is enabling

A rejection for lack of enabling disclosure claims the specification doesn't teach how to make and use the invention. It is based on the first paragraph of section 35 U.S.C. §112 of the statute that states:

> *The specification shall contain a written description of the invention, and the manner and process of making and using it, in such clear, concise, and exact terms as to enable any person skilled in the art to which it pertains, or with which it is most nearly connected, to make and use the same. . .*

In Chapter 8, we discuss how to meet this requirement. If you try to claim something that isn't adequately disclosed in the specification, you'll get a rejection that's hard to overcome. Basically, if you don't spell out the enabling material somewhere in the specification, you must either:

✔ Convince the examiner that what is missing is common knowledge to people skilled in the art, using supporting documents such as treatises, encyclopedia excerpts, or magazine articles. If possible, also provide declarations by experts in your field to support your argument.

✔ Cancel the rejected claim and file a continuation-in-part application (see Chapter 9) that fully supports the claim to the invention. This solution is nearly foolproof, but costly and time consuming. Plus it gives your competitors the defense that you admit that your initial application was defective with regard to enablement and doesn't carry any priority right. Therefore, use it only as a last resort, after the first approach has failed.

## Dodging a double-patenting decision

Section 35 U.S.C. § 101 of the patent law specifies that *whoever invents . . . may obtain a patent* — that's one patent for each invention, not two or more. This rejection can come in one of two flavors:

✔ **Same invention double patenting:** If you already have a patent or an application pending claiming the same invention in similar language, your claim will be rejected because of *same invention double patenting.* You can overcome this rejection by slightly rewording your claim so that the two claimed inventions aren't identical. The objective is to make sure that a structure or process can't infringe on both the original patent and the one you're applying for. After you overcome a same-invention-double-patenting rejection, the examiner will probably fire another rejection for non-statutory *obviousness double patenting.*

✔ **Obviousness double patenting:** If you claim an invention that's not identical to one claimed in your earlier patent or other pending application, but is not distinct from it either, your claim will be rejected because of a judge-made rule of *obviousness double patenting.* Courts have decided that it would be wrong to let you obtain multiple patents for inventions that are obvious modifications of one another. You can overcome a rejection for obviousness double patenting by filing a *terminal disclaimer,* dedicating any portion of the pending patent beyond the life of your earlier patent to the public. Even if both applications have the same effective filing date (thus the same expiration date), you should file the disclaimer (the USPTO has a handy form).

A double-patenting rejection can't be issued in a divisional application that's filed after a request for restriction in the parent application (see "Splitting Up Is Hard to Do: Restricting the Application," earlier in this chapter).

# *Presenting a timely, professional answer*

You have to answer an OA in a format specified by the commissioner. This format is subject to periodical changes as published in the *Gazette of the Patent Office* and the MPEP. Consult either on online at www.uspto.gov. Amendments to the specification, claims, drawings, or remarks (including any arguments) must each begin on a new page. Like all communications with the Patent Office, there are specific ways to present each amendment:

✔ **Specification:** Type a marked-up replacement paragraph that shows all the additions underlined and the deleted words crossed out. You can conveniently show deletions and insertions by using the track changes feature of most word-processing programs.

✔ **Claims:** Use the same deletion and insertion method as for the specification. If you're deleting less than six characters, you may frame the deleted part between double brackets. That's the only way you can delete certain characters such as the numeral 4 standing alone.

You must list the claims with one of seven status indications: (original), (currently amended), (canceled), (withdrawn), (new), (previously presented), and (not entered) after the claim number as shown here:

*Claim 1 (currently amended) A rotary polishing pad which comprises . . .*

*Claims 2-5 (canceled)*

*Claims 6 (original) The polishing pad of Claim 1 wherein . . .*

*Claim 7 (currently amended) The polishing pad of Claim [[4]] 6 wherein . . .*

*Claim 8 (previously presented) The polishing pad . . .*

*Claim 9 (withdrawn) The polishing pad . . .*

*Claim 10 (previously added) The polishing pad of Claim 6 . . .*

*Claim 11 (not entered)*

*Claim 12 (new) The pad of Claim 10 which further comprises, et. . . .*

The text of the cancelled and not entered claims need not be typed out.

✔ **Drawings:** Submit each drawing on a replacement sheet, explaining the change in the Arguments section of the amendment. Structural changes to the figures must also be shown in red on a marked-up copy.

✔ **Arguments:** Under the title REMARKS, answer point by point every statement in the OA, following the same format and paragraph sequence. Make sure you point out every correction or addition you made in answer to each examiner's objection and rejection.

If the amendment introduces a new word or phrase in the specification, make sure that it doesn't introduce *new matter* — something that wasn't present or obviously implied in the original text. If you add a new word or phrase to a claim, you must point out where support for the added material can be found in the original specification text or drawing either expressly or implicitly. The argument must be based on the law with appropriate citations of statutes and prior legal decisions (see document E1ee on the CD). A faulty argument may not support a subsequent appeal. Trust your attorney to draft that part in a professional style.

You have a month or two to answer a notice or request, such as a notice of defective application or a request for restriction, and three months to answer an examination report on the merit of your invention. In most cases, this period can be extended by up to three months by filing a *request for extension,* accompanied by the applicable late fee. The OA will specify the period to answer. There's no need to file the request for extension before or on the deadline; just include it with your delayed answer.

## Reviving an abandoned application

If you don't answer an OA or pay a fee within the initial time allocated or during the extension period, your application will be declared abandoned. If your application is declared abandoned, you can petition the commissioner at any time to revive an abandoned application on one of two grounds:

✔ **Unavoidable abandonment:** This is very hard to prove, but has a low filing fee of about $255 for a small entity. A destructive fire at your local post office may constitute good cause, but the fact that you moved without leaving a forwarding address or notifying your attorney isn't enough. You can petition to revive an application on grounds of unavoidable abandonment if you provide the following:

   • A reply to the last OA or requested fee unless previously filed.

   • An explanation, with supporting evidence, showing that the delay in filing an answer or paying a fee was totally beyond your control.

   • A *terminal disclaimer,* which states that you agree to forfeit any time that the delay could add to the life of your patent. Use form PTO/SB/63 to file the disclaimer.

   • The applicable fee payment with form PTO/SB/61.

✔ **Unintentional abandonment:** This is easier to establish but costs about $770 for a small entity. On a petition for revival because of involuntary abandonment (such as you forgot to enter the deadline on your calendar), state that the delay was unintentional (it must in fact be), without stating the reasons for the delay. Use form PTO/SB/64.

Don't miss a filing date or intentionally abandon your application and rely on these petitions to save your hide. The undue delay may cast some doubt on your credibility. The commissioner may ask you to explain the cause of the unintentional abandonment. Any misstatement can be used against you later on when you try to enforce your patent against an infringer.

# Reacting to a Final Rejection

You've replied to the first OA with a clever amendment and what you thought was an ironclad argument proving that all your claims are allowable. Yet you get another rejection of some claims or an objection to the specification. The examiner declares that this last decision is final. Don't panic.

A final OA is as definitive as a stand-up comic's retirement or a rock band's "farewell tour." You still have some alternatives:

- ✔ Try to comply with the examiner's requirement in the final OA.
- ✔ Try to change the examiner's mind with logical and persuasive argument.
- ✔ Amend your claims one more time.
- ✔ Answer as soon as possible to give the examiner an opportunity to review it before the answer deadline. You may get a break if he reviews your application and is persuaded by your brilliant argument to pass all your pending claims. If there are unresolved issues, as a matter of professional courtesy, he may call your attorney and attempt to iron out the remaining problems. Don't count on that if you're flying solo.

Any argument or amendment filed after the final OA should bear the following legend in red ink in the upper right-hand corner of the first page:

AMENDMENT UNDER 37 C.F.R. 1.116 AFTER FINAL REJECTION.

This guarantees that your reply is handled promptly by the USPTO receiving office. However, examiners have no obligation to do anything after the final OA. But being the gentlepersons that they are, we've never been refused the courtesy of an answer to a promptly filed post-final reply.

If you reply within two months, the USPTO will try to respond with an *Advisory Action* by the third month, or at least let you measure further extensions for the date of the Advisory Action.

## Asking for an examination rerun

After a final rejection, you may ask to restart the examination by filing a *Request for Continued Examination* (RCE). Fill out and mail form PTO/SB/30 to the USPTO (with the applicable filing fee of course). This is particularly appropriate when the examiner has rejected all your claims or allowed some but rejected the ones you really need or want (see document E1dd on the CD). If the examiner refuses to consider your last amended claims, it's usually on the grounds that the claims require a new search. The new examination will start where the original left off. You get two reviews. If the examiner refused to enter some claims presented after the final OA, include them in a preliminary amendment filed with or right after your RCE.

You can't enter an amendment to a specification that introduces new matter as part of a RCE. Instead, you should file a *continuation-in-part* (CIP) application (see Chapter 9). Include all the new material. Make sure the original application is still pending when you file your CIP. Your original application will lapse if you don't timely answer or appeal the final OA.

## Meeting the examiner face to face

At any time during the examination of your application, you can request a face-to-face interview with the examiner to try and resolve pending objections and rejections. Make the request directly to the examiner in writing or by fax, e-mail, or telephone. The request must specify the topics to be discussed.

We can't overemphasize the advantages of a heart-to-heart conversation with the examiner, especially when the outstanding patentability issue or the invention itself is very complex. Occasionally, with a few minutes of live conversation, we've been able to resolve rejection problems that would have consumed months of written communications. If you request in advance, the USPTO will make audio-visual equipment available to you so you can play a video showing your invention in action. You can even bring your computer or a small prototype to your meeting to demonstrate a piece of software.

With at least three days notice, you can arrange a long-distance interview through the USPTO Video Conference Center. You can also request e-mail exchanges with the examiner after filing an authorization worded as follows:

> *Recognizing that Internet communications are not secure, I hereby authorize the USPTO to communicate with me concerning any subject matter of this application by electronic mail. I understand that a copy of these communications will be made of record in the application file.*

We don't suggest that you personally engage in a live or audio-visual interview with an examiner. Let your patent attorney act on your behalf. Examiners aren't particularly keen on dealing with a nonprofessional who isn't versed in patent law and doesn't speak the language. More significantly, on your own, you're more likely to agree to a concession offered by the examiner even if that concession is detrimental to your case. Your attorney can help you interpret and consider any written concessions.

# Getting Flagged for Interference

An *interference* is a USPTO procedure to decide who gets the patent if two or more inventors claim (not just describe) the same invention. It fulfills the mandate of subsection 35 U.S.C. § 102(g) that basically says the first to invent gets the patent. There's no telling what impact the new patent law now pending before Congress will have on interference practice. If priority disputes between inventors are resolved in favor of the first to file rather than the first to invent, an interference might be declared only when their respective applications are filed at the same time. We can only explain the current procedure. As of this writing, an interference may be declared

- ✔ When one or more claims in two or more pending applications are addressed to substantially the same subject matter.

- ✔ When an application contains a claim that's been copied from, or is almost identical to, a claim found in an issued patent.

Because of their complexity and cost, try to avoid interferences. Your best bet is to try to settle the issue of inventorship amicably.

## Initiating an interference

You or the examiner may initiate an interference under one of these scenarios:

- ✔ The USPTO asks your examiner to trigger an interference if your application conflicts with another pending application.

- ✔ Your neighbor, Johnny Come Lately, lets you read his patent application (bad move). To your amazement, you find that he claims your invention. Seeking justice, you file an amendment to your own application that copies one or more of Johnny's claims, and then ask the examiner to declare an interference, citing the other application's serial number.

✔ Your examiner notices that your invention is already covered by an issued patent or claimed in a pending published application. He orders you to copy one or more claims of the issued patent or published application in your own application to remove any issue of dissimilarity between the two applications. Then he declares an interference.

✔ You discover a patent or published application on your own that covers your invention. You copy one or more of its claims into your application and ask for an interference.

Note that it's none of the USPTO's business if two issued patents address the same invention. This kind of conflict can only be resolved in a federal court where the complexity, time, and lawyers' fees are much higher. Still confused? Here's some useful information and rules about interferences:

✔ An interference can't be declared until the claim in your application is found allowable.

✔ You can't justify an interference by copying claims from a patent or published application that was issued or published more than one year earlier, unless you've already claimed substantially the same invention in your application before that one-year deadline.

✔ An interference can't be declared between applications or patents that have the same owner.

✔ An application under a secrecy order can't be part of an interference.

## Determining priority of invention

An interference is conducted like a trial, according to standard Federal Rules of Civil Procedures. Therefore, you need the services of a knowledgeable IP attorney. Interferences are held before the Board of Patent Appeals and Interferences (BPAI), which we also mention in the "Crying and other appeal routes" section, earlier in this chapter. To determine priority of invention, the BPAI looks at two phases of the invention process:

✔ **Conception:** The mental process through which you, the inventor, first imagines and devises a clear definition of your invention.

✔ **Reduction to practice:** The physical embodiment of the invention into a structure or process that can be shown with a prototype or computer model (actual reduction to practice) or by filing a patent application (constructive reduction to practice).

Here's the legal rule for deciding priority of inventorship in an interference: *Pay attention*. This rule confirms the importance of what we've been preaching all along — diligence and good record keeping.

The first inventor who reduces the invention to practice gets the patent *unless* another inventor conceived the invention earlier *and* was diligent in doing his own reduction to practice. Say, in January, you get the idea for a turbo-charged air-cooled lawn mower engine. You finish a working prototype in late September. In June, Johnny conceives the same engine and gets a model running by late August. Because he was the first to reduce the invention to practice by building a working model, he'd get the patent — except between June and September you worked diligently on your prototype. If you'd waited a year to build a prototype or file your patent application, Johnny would win the interference and get the patent. But you win because you can demonstrate diligent work before June, when he had his brainstorm.

Keeping detailed records of your entire invention development process so that you can prove your diligence if needed is *very* important. If you haven't kept a periodically witnessed notebook, as we suggest in Chapter 6, you may not be able to prove your dates of conception and reduction to practice.

Don't waste time fiddling with your invention for months before filing a patent application. Prepare and file it as soon as you think you have a valuable invention. It's better to file a provisional application early (Chapter 8) and supplement it later with a more complete application. Otherwise, if someone files ahead of you, you could lose your right to the patent.

# Requesting a SIR

If you get frustrated with the lack of progress in the prosecution of your formal patent application, you may decide to give up and drop it. But now you have to worry that someone else could get a patent covering your invention and prevent you from practicing your own discovery in the future.

You can avoid this situation by requesting a *Statutory Invention Registration* (SIR) on Form PTO/SB/94 that dedicates your invention to the public. The filing of a SIR request waives your right to obtain a patent for your invention. You can't claim anything that's disclosed in the SIR in a future or pending application, but you can still manufacture, use, or sell your invention. If you request a SIR while your application is pending and pay the applicable fee, the specification and drawing (but not the claims) will be published without further examination of the merits of your claims.

Your SIR is like any other patent or publication — it becomes prior art that can be cited against any other application. A SIR is considered a constructive reduction to practice when determining the issue of priority between you and another inventor who is trying to get a patent. But the SIR has no effect on the rights of another inventor who manages to get a patent, even if the subject matter of your SIR and that of another inventor's application are identical.

The effects of a SIR are drastic and final, so you may prefer to have your application published and then, if you still want to waive your rights, let it lapse for failure to answer an office action or pay the issue fee. This may be a more convenient and less risky way to waive your rights to the invention because you still have the possibility of reviving an abandoned application.

## Avoiding a third-party protest

If you disclose your application serial number, you may have given someone the key to your application file. They can file a protest against the grant of your patent on a number of reasons: an allegation that you're not the first or only inventor, prior art, public disclosure, or an offer to sell the invention made more than a year before you filed your application. The USPTO doesn't entertain a protest if it doesn't include the serial number, or, even when it does, if the USPTO receives the protest after the publication of your application or the issue of a notice of allowance, whichever comes first. You'll be notified of the protest and be able to contest all of its allegations. The protestor won't see your filings or participate in the prosecution of the patent.

# Chapter 11

# Reeling In the Prize: Getting Your Patent Issued

. . . . . . . . . . . . . . . . . . . . . . . . . . . . . . . . . . . . . . . . . . . . .

*In This Chapter*

▶ Reviewing your patent strategy

▶ Taking care of typos

▶ Applying for a reissue patent

▶ Requesting a reexamination

▶ Taking care of maintenance fees

▶ Slapping down your patent number

. . . . . . . . . . . . . . . . . . . . . . . . . . . . . . . . . . . . . . . . . . . . .

*B*elieve it or not, and you may not if you've read Chapters 5 through 10, the day will very likely come when you or your attorney go to the mailbox and find a communication from the United States Patent and Trademark Office (USPTO) telling you that your patent application (not necessarily the first one you filed in a series of continuation applications) is squared away, and all you have left to do is pay a few more fees to get your patent.

It's 5 o'clock somewhere in the world, but it's not quite happy hour for you just yet. You have a few more issues to consider before you get that snazzy patent. In this chapter, we walk you through one last reconsideration of your patent strategy and how to finally secure your patent. But problems can occur and corrections may be necessary even after you get the piece of paper, so we also help you tie up loose ends after a patent is issued. Finally, we take you to the finish line with a few comments on correctly affixing your patent number to your now-patented invention. The topics in this chapter apply to utility, design, and plant patents. Forms we mention that aren't sent to you automatically by the USPTO are available on its Web site (www.uspto.gov).

# Getting the Green Light

When you, your attorney, and the patent examiner are finally through slugging it out in the prosecution phase (see Chapter 10), the USPTO issues a notice of allowance. The *notice of allowance* is a letter telling you that all the pending claims in your patent application are allowed. The patent press is warming up and all you have to do is grease the wheels with a bit more cash.

Which brings us to the more somber news: With your notice of allowance, you also get a *fee transmittal form.* Yes, just when you thought you were through shelling out fistfuls of dollars (and we don't mean singles) to the USPTO, here comes the least expected bill of them all. At this time, you have to pay a hefty patent issue fee and a publication fee (if you didn't petition for non-publication as we explain in Chapter 9). Plus, the USPTO will nickel and dime you to death for extra copies of your patent. By the time you add your attorney's last bill, you'll need more than a thousand bucks to close the deal.

So before you shell out the cash for these last expenses, you may want to take a hard look at how much your upcoming patent really contributes to your intellectual property (IP) protection strategy.

## Reviewing your patent strategy one last time

In Chapters 5 and 6, we detail alternatives to acquiring a patent for protecting your IP assets. Now, two or three years down the line, you're staring a possible patent in the face. But you're also probably looking at a new set of circumstances, which now may not justify taking the last step of getting the patent issued.

 Thoroughly reevaluating your patent strategy with the help of your IP professional, even at this late date, isn't a bad idea. Take a good look at the allowed claims, the part of the patent that spells out the extent of your protection, and with a cool head, ask yourself:

- ✔ Do the allowed claims give you the scope of protection you originally expected? If not, is the protection they do give sufficient to enhance your market position? If the answer is negative, you don't need this patent.

- ✔ Could you reasonably obtain broader coverage by filing a continuation or a continuation-in-part application (which we go over in Chapter 9)? If so, consider abandoning your current application after you file a new one. Not only will you save the issue charges for a patent of questionable value, but also the maintenance fees that are due three and a half years from the date of issue and every four years thereafter (see the

"Remembering to Pay Maintenance Fees" section, later in this chapter). Your money will be better used on the new application. If you think your about-to-issue patent has some value and could be used immediately against some infringer, get it. But don't overlook the possibility of getting a better one by filing a new application.

✔ Can you get the same degree of protection under one or more alternate forms of IP rights? You can still rely on a trade-secret strategy to protect your invention if your application hasn't been published. If it has been published, take another look at copyrights, trade dress, and some effective commercial identifiers. They may offer you as much protection as the upcoming patent.

✔ Could you benefit from adding a few broader claims to those already allowed and asking for a continuing prosecution (see Chapter 9)?

These are tough business and legal decisions that every inventor has to make. You can benefit from some advice from an IP professional.

## Signing the check and requesting copies

You're convinced that you need that patent after all. All you need to do is fill out the fee transmittal form and mail it back to the USPTO with your check or money order made out to the Commissioner of Patents. And don't forget to pay your last patent agent or attorney invoice.

Don't miss the payment deadline. If you miss the date or your check bounces on the last day, your application will lapse and need to be revived (see Chapter 10). Don't forget to indicate how many extra copies of the patent (at about $3 a piece) you want. Actually, they aren't copies, but unadorned duplicate originals. Order at least ten for your files. You don't want to send that one-and-only beribboned original to a court when you sue an infringer.

If you've assigned your invention to another person or your company, and you want the assignee's name on the patent, fill out Item 3 on the form.

# Put Down the Champagne: Taking Corrective Action

That's right. Don't touch that cork just yet. Slowly back away from the bottle. Even though you've just received that long-awaited, blue-ribboned, fancily-bound patent, don't celebrate until you've carefully gone over every line of the document. If you spot a glitch, you need to see your IP professional about fixing it up. And to determine if it's a bit more than a glitch, see the "Dealing with Defective Patents" section, later in the chapter.

You can easily fix typographic or grammatical errors and omissions in one of two ways. If your intended meaning is obvious from the context despite minor errors or omissions, you can simply point the errors out in a letter to the commissioner. The letter will be made part of the patent file. And here's a pleasant surprise — there's no filing fee for this service.

If, however, the errors or omissions aren't obvious or require some additional information, you need to file a *certificate of correction* (Form PTO/SB/44). Here's an example of how to word your corrections on the form:

> *In column 3, line 33, "the bands of the" should read: –the strands of the–.*
>
> *In column 4, formula XX, the part of the formula reading "H2CO4" should read –H2SO4–.*
>
> *On Figure 2 of the drawing, reference "25" should be –35–.*
>
> *On Figure 3 of the drawing, reference numeral "40" should be applied to the nut engaged on threaded shaft –39–.*

Common practice is to put deleted material between quotation marks and frame added material with double hyphens.

A couple of months later, after the USPTO accepts the certificate of correction, you'll receive a copy, and the certificate becomes an integral part of your patent in the USPTO's library. If you were responsible for the error, you must include a filing fee (currently $100) with the certificate. If the USPTO personnel caused it, filing the certificate of correction is free. But you need to indicate in a cover letter why the error isn't yours.

*Note:* The two procedures we just described are only available if the corrections don't affect the scope of the patent, don't introduce new material that could affect the nature of the disclosed or claimed invention, and don't require a reexamination. If they do, you've got yourself a defective patent that requires a more drastic and expensive corrective action.

# Dealing with Defective Patents

A *defective patent* is one that, through errors or omissions but without deceptive intention, provides you with more or less coverage than your invention deserves. Maybe you failed to claim a prior application as the priority date or you claimed the invention too narrowly. The only way to correct a defective patent is by filing a *reissue application* (your defective patent is cancelled and replaced by a corrected one). Reissues are subject to the following rules:

✔ Only the patent owner, or the inventor with the consent of the patent owners, can file an application for reissue.

✔ An application that seeks to enlarge the coverage of the patent must be filed within two years from the issue date of the original patent and bear the signature of the inventor.

✔ A reissue application filed more than two years after the issue date of the original patent may be rejected for lack of diligence if you can't provide a reasonable excuse for the delay.

With a reissue application, you offer to surrender the patent you just received, alleging that it's wholly or partly inoperative, and ask for a new one. All the claims in the reissue application, including those copied from the original patent, are examined and may be rejected on new grounds. You also risk a third party submitting info that affects the patentability of your claims. In the worst case, you could end up with an extremely weak reissued patent.

The surrender of your original patent doesn't take effect until the grant of the reissue. So if you don't like the way the reissue application is going, you can abandon it and keep your original, uncorrected patent.

Reissue applications tend to be trickier than original applications because of the additional complications of having to admit errors and possibly needing to recapture a previously overlooked patent coverage. Let a good IP professional be your pilot — and navigator.

## Combing over common errors

You must allege at least one error of conduct to justify your application for reissue. An *error of conduct* must meet three conditions:

✔ The error occurred during the preparation or prosecution of the original patent application.

✔ The error was made without deceptive intention.

✔ The error directly causes your patent to be wholly or partially ineffective.

The following sections outline the most common errors alleged in applications for reissue.

### Correcting the inventors' names

If the inventorship is incorrectly stated (the wrong inventor is named or inventors need to be added or deleted) *and* one of the original inventors doesn't consent to the correction, use a reissue to correct the inventors' names. The disagreement will be disputed and settled as part of the reissue examination. If all inventors agree that changes need to be made, you simply need to petition the commissioner, as we detail in the "Changing the Names of the Inventors or Assignees" section, later in this chapter.

### Broadening the claims

The most common reason for a reissue is that the original patent claims less than the invention deserves. Here's a typical scenario:

About 23 months ago, you obtained a patent on a turbo-charged, five-cycle engine for lawn mowers. All of your claims recite a combination of a lawn mower with the improved engine. In a recent issue of the *Garden Gopher* magazine, you discover that the Kopikatt Company has just come out with a leaf blower that uses the same type of engine as your lawn mower. Your attorney says that a leaf-blower engine doesn't infringe on any of the claims in your patent. You must file an application for reissue that amends and broadens at least one of your claims to recite the improved engine independent of the lawn mower.

You have to file the reissue application no later than the second anniversary of your original patent.

Broadening a claim can be complicated stuff. You may have to restrict one of its elements while enlarging another in order to achieve your coverage goal. Such legal maneuvers may make it difficult to determine, at first look, if the amended claim now has a broader coverage than before. You can resolve the ambiguity by applying the following rule:

An amended claim is considered broadened if it can be read upon any conceivable thing that wasn't covered by that claim in its original form. A claim is said to *read on* a device or process if, as you read each element of the claim, you can find a corresponding element in that device or process.

Another way to determine that the claim has been broadened: Check whether you can now sue somebody for infringement that you couldn't sue before.

Don't think for a minute that, in the reissue process, you can reclaim patent coverage that you willingly abandoned during the prosecution of your original application. If, by mistake, you added a limitation to the claim trying to get around some prior art when in fact overcoming that prior art didn't require that particular limitation, you're stuck.

### Narrowing the claims

You might wonder why you'd ever want to narrow the scope of your patent — you just got a lucky break, right? Wrong. Your deceptively broad patent can be declared invalid by a judge when you try to sue an infringer.

Allow us to return to the lawn mower example from the preceding section. This time, we assume that all the claims are addressed to the engine without mentioning its application to lawn mowers. You just discovered that in the past, the same type of engine was used on small hand-held power tools, such as leaf blowers and string grass trimmers. However, you were the first to draw enough power from this kind of engine to drive a lawn mower or any other device requiring more than one horsepower. Your invention uses a weighted lawn mower cutting blade as a flywheel to smooth out intermittent power gaps inherent to your five-stroke engine.

Because your current claims *read on* (recite elements found in) prior art machines, they shouldn't have been allowed (see patentability requirements in Chapter 5). However, because no prior patent or documentation existed for that kind of engine, you couldn't have discovered it through a comprehensive anticipation search. And, of course, you didn't hear about this use of the engine until recently, so the error isn't due to any deception on your part.

You need to promptly file an application for reissue that amends your claims to a narrower scope by reciting the lawn mower or any other tool that requires more than one horsepower. You may also for good measure add some claims that simply mention the flywheel.

### Correcting the disclosure

As we explain in Chapter 8, the disclosure consists of the specification supported by a drawing of the invention. If you unintentionally misstated some facts in the specification or inaccurately drew a particular structure, you can set the record straight with a reissue application — as long as the error didn't prevent someone from practicing the invention and your proposed corrections don't introduce *new matter* (information necessary to use the invention that wasn't present in the original application).

For example, you didn't appreciate the regulating effect of the flywheel blade in the new lawn mower engine you've patented, so you gave some other incorrect explanation for the engine's exceptional performance. No sweat. That error didn't prevent someone with skill in the mechanical field from building your lawn mower. You can correct the problem with a reissue.

Another example: A structural detail, such as the distribution of the weight around the blade, may have been adequately described in the specification, but not illustrated in the drawing. Because the rules require that everything recited in a claim be shown in the drawing, your omission may cast doubt on the validity of some of your claims. You can dissipate this cloud of doubt by offering an amended drawing in your application for reissue.

### Referencing a previously omitted prior application

Establishing the earliest priority date (see Chapter 8) for your invention is critical to eliminate any interim prior art that could be cited against your claims. To do so, you may need to refer to an earlier filed application in the U.S. or abroad. You can use the reissue process to remedy these situations:

- You forgot to claim priority of a prior domestic or foreign application.

- You claimed foreign priority, but forgot to submit a certified copy of the foreign application.

- You forgot to make reference to a prior co-pending non-provisional application.

- You forgot to claim priority on a provisional application filed before November 29, 2000. If the provisional application was filed after this date, you can't claim priority upon it after the formal application that followed it is no longer pending.

## Preparing the reissue application

The contents of the application and the accompanying documents are basically the same as for a formal utility, design, or plant patent application (see Chapters 8 and 9). However, the formatting of the disclosure and a utility application claims and the declaration is different. Some additional enclosures are required.

### The specification, drawing, and claims

The specification and claims must be a clean, reproducible photocopy of the original patent, mounted in a two-columns-per-page format on a single-sided sheet. The specification and claims must reflect the status of the patent as of the filing date of the reissue application and must include all the changes previously made by certificates of correction. The drawing must also be a clean and reproducible copy of the original.

### The proposed amendments

Proposed amendments to the specification and claims can be presented in one of the following two ways:

- By cutting and pasting a photocopy of the original patent specification and claims. The amended part must be typed and inserted between pasted sections of the photocopied text, showing the deleted material between brackets and underlining the added material. We don't recommend this method.

✔ By providing a separate amendment paper, formatted in the same manner as a patent application amendment, which we discuss in Chapter 10. This is a more practical and cleaner way to format the reissue application.

You must submit an amendment to the drawing as a sketch on a separate paper, showing the proposed changes in red. When the examiner approves the changes, you file a new formal drawing that incorporates the changes.

### The declarations

A reissue application must include a declaration, under penalty of perjury, signed by the inventor. In a reissue application for a patent that's wholly owned by an assignee and doesn't seek to broaden the scope of any claim, only the assignee has to sign the declaration. Because of the precision and completeness required in the reissue declarations, we strongly suggest that you use Form PTO/SB/51 for the inventor and Form PTO/SB/52 for the assignee. The declaration form is pretty straightforward.

You can indicate that the original patent was wholly or partly inoperative or invalid because of a defective specification or drawing or because you claimed more than you had the right to by checking the appropriate box. However, if you're filing for a reissue for any other reason, such as you claimed less than the invention merited in your original application and you want to broaden the patent coverage, you must provide an explanation in the space provided at the bottom of the declaration.

If you're trying to broaden a claim, you may state the following (pulled from the earlier engine example):

> *Applicant seeks to broaden Claims 1, 5, and 6 by removing limitations relative to the type of machinery upon which the engine can be used.*

If you forgot to claim priority on a prior application, you may state:

> *Applicant failed to claim the priority of a parent application, Serial Number XX/X,XXX, that was still pending when the application for the patent in reissue was filed.*

### Other documents

Your reissue application must also include the following material:

✔ **Written consent from each assignee (Form PTO/SB53).** If any interest in the patent has been assigned, you must submit a written consent to the reissue from each assignee, accompanied by documentary evidence of the assignee's interest. To establish the assignee's ownership of the invention and patent, you can specify the reel and frame numbers of all the documents recorded in the USPTO regarding the transfer of the invention and patent. For example, if you assigned the invention and patent to your corporation, Big Deal, Inc., and the corporation then assigned the whole thing to the Bunco Bank as security for a loan, you must identify the two recorded assignments, even though only the bank (the current owner) needs to sign a written consent to the reissue.

✔ **Information disclosure statement.** You must submit any information that may be relevant to the patentability of the reissue claims, including prior art. Use Form PTO/SB/08A to list patents and Form PTO/SB/08B to list non-patent documents.

✔ **Copies of any litigation or reexamination documents related to your patent.**

✔ **Offer to surrender patent.** You may include an offer to surrender the original patent, or you can wait until the examiner makes a specific request. If you have lost that original patent document, use Form PTO/SB/55 to report the loss.

✔ **Return receipt postcard.** Suggested when mailing anything to the USPTO, as explained in Chapter 9.

✔ **Fee transmittal form (PTO/SB/56).** And, of course, a check or money order to cover the filing fee.

✔ **Reissue patent application transmittal form (PTO/SB/50).** Make sure that you list on this form all the documents you're submitting.

After you file your application for reissue, the USPTO will publish a notice of your application in the *Official Gazette*. The examiner will wait at least two months after publication before taking your case, which gives any interested party an opportunity to file a protest against your application. Reissue applications are given priority over regular applications. However, a hard-fought case may take two or three years before the patent is reissued.

# *Submitting to Reexamination*

Your patent is subject to reexamination throughout its life. Reexamination must be based on prior patents or printed publications that the examiner didn't properly consider during the prosecution of your application, if this omission casts doubt on the validity of some or all of your claims. Anyone — you, the guy down the street, or the examiner— can initiate a reexamination.

## Distinguishing reexamination from reissue

Although a reissue and a reexamination overlap a bit, a reexamination is usually preferable, as the following list demonstrates:

✔ A reissue application brings the whole patent into question, but you can limit a request for reexamination to one or more claims.

✔ A reissue application must be filed quickly, preferably within two years of the original patent issue date. A request for reexamination can be filed any time during the life of the patent.

✔ An examiner can take an undetermined number of months to review an application for reissue. However, a request for reexamination must be acted upon immediately. The examiner must determine within three months of the filing date whether the prior art submitted raises a question of patentability sufficient to warrant a reexamination.

✔ In an application for reissue, you have to establish why the patent is ineffective yourself, including the materiality of the error. You must sign an affidavit, under oath, or a declaration under penalty of perjury to that effect. That puts you at risk if what you stated is later proven false. In a request for reexamination, you only need to cite the new prior art and point out each substantial new question of patentability. It's the examiner's responsibility to determine the validity and relevance of your allegations.

There are a couple of drawbacks: At the end of a patent reissue process, you may end up with narrower or broader coverage than you had under the original patent — whereas a reexamination never enlarges the scope of a patent, but can result in a narrower patent. Moreover, the filing fee for a reexamination request is about seven times more than for a reissue application.

## Kicking things off

Anyone can initiate a reexamination, and for a multitude of reasons:

✔ You or someone interested in buying your patent or licensing your technology wants to confirm the validity of all your claims in view of a newly discovered prior art. Call it peace of mind.

✔ A potential or actual infringer of your patent wants to eliminate some of your claims that cover his own activities.

✔ Another inventor who filed a patent application covering the same subject matter as your patent elects the less expensive approach of requesting reexamination to challenge you, instead of asking for a declaration of interference (see Chapter 10 for more on interference).

If you're not the inventor or owner of the patent, you can petition for either one of two types of reexamination: ex parte or inter partes. No need to reach for the Kazakh dictionary — we explain.

In an *ex parte* proceeding, the petitioner's participation is limited to filing the initial petition for reexamination. Issues are jostled between the patent owner and the patent examiner. In an *inter partes* type, the proceeding is run like a three-ring circus; sorry, we mean like a trial where the representatives of the parties slug it out with arguments and counterarguments. As you might expect, the former might cost you $3,000 or $4,000; the latter, $20,000 or $30,000.

You can initiate a reexamination of a patent by filing Form PTO/SB/57 (ex parte) or Form PTO/SB/58 (inter partes). Attach copies of the new prior art material and a statement that includes the following information:

- A list of claims to be reexamined and the prior art documents that apply to them.

- An explanation of how the cited prior art relates to each claim at issue. This is best done in a two-column format. Quote each element of a claim in the first column and place the matching quotation from the relevant prior art next to it in the second column, as shown below by using the polishing pad example from Chapter 10.

| Patent | Prior Art |
| --- | --- |
| Claim 1: A rotary polishing pad . . . | Abbott and Abel disclose rotary polishing pads. |
| that comprises an arrangement of strands of equal length and thickness . . . | Abbott's strands are of equal length. Abel's strands are of equal thickness. |
| tufted in a gradually increasing number of strands per square centimeter from a central region to a peripheral region of said pad. | Babele discloses a car floor mat wherein strands are tufted in a larger number of strands per square centimeter in the center than in the peripheral region. |

- A statement pointing out the substantial new question of patentability and stating that the cited prior art wasn't considered by the examiner during the prosecution of the patent application.

- The required filing fee of about $2,500, of course.

If you file a request for reexamination of your own patent, you may include a proposed amendment of the claims and specification if warranted. However, you can't offer an amendment when filing a request for reexamination of someone else's patent. Instead, you must serve a copy of the request to the patent owner according to standard legal procedure and certify, on the request you file with the USPTO, that you have done so.

## Selecting the relevant prior art material

You can't base a reexamination on a prior art patent or printed publication that was used by the examiner in the original examination against the claims at issue.

Even a reference listed on the front page (see Chapter 5) of the patent may be the basis of the reexamination if the examiner didn't specifically cite it as grounds for rejecting the claim in question.

In requesting reexamination of your own patent, cite only prior art that could reasonably be used to attack your patent's validity in future litigation against an infringer. Don't complicate and prolong the reexamination by bringing up all the potential but tenuous prior art that could be frivolously cited by an adverse party. However, if your patent has already been litigated, make sure that you submit all the prior art that the accused infringer brought up in attacking your patent. If the patent survives the reexamination, it'll prevent other future infringers from presenting the same prior art.

## Prosecuting the reexamination

About three months after filing for reexamination, you'll receive the examiner's answer to your request. If reexamination of your patent is denied, you can pop the champagne cork. Your patent has withstood an attack at very little cost to you. If the request for reexamination of your own patent is approved, you're back to square one and must again deal with the examiner, as you did during the prosecution of your original application. Do not pass Go. Do not collect $200. Go directly to Chapter 10.

If your request to reexamine a potential opponent's patent is rejected, you may petition the Commissioner of Patents to review the examiner's decision. If your petition is denied, you can appeal to the Court of Appeals for the Federal Circuit.

### Deferring to others' intervening rights

A reissue has no effect on the rights of anyone who made, purchased, offered to sell, used, or imported anything that's covered by the new or amended claims before the reissue is complete.

Only activities covered by the original patent can be prohibited. A court may even allow activities that should constitute an infringement when substantial preparation was made prior to the reexamination. It's an issue of fairness and equity, and, of course, a source of costly litigations we wouldn't wish on our worst enemy.

## Changing the Names of the Inventors or Assignees

A patent that misstates the names of the inventors may be declared invalid and unenforceable, which is pretty serious, especially when an infringer's attorney discovers the error in the middle of an infringement case. If all parties agree that an inventor was omitted or listed by mistake on your patent, you can use the *petition and certificate of correction* procedure to clear up the issue. (If everyone doesn't agree, we're sorry, but you have to take the reissue route; see the "Correcting the inventors' names" section, earlier in this chapter.)

You simply petition the commissioner to correct the names of the inventors listed (or omitted) on the patent or to correct the names of the assignees. When the petition is granted, the commissioner issues a certificate of correction, saving you the trouble and expenses of applying for a reissue.

The petition, with the applicable fee, must include statements by the following:

- ✔ Each person whose name is being deleted, stating that he or she has no disagreement regarding the requested change.
- ✔ Each person whose name is to be added, stating that the omission occurred without any deceptive intention on his or her part.
- ✔ Each assignee consenting to the change, accompanied by documentary evidence of that assignee's interest in the patent.

If the patent is involved in an interference, you must also address a motion requesting permission for the change to the Board of Patent Appeals and Interferences, the tribunal handling that procedure.

# Remembering to Pay Maintenance Fees

Utility patents are subject to periodic maintenance fees during the first 12 years following their issue dates (but not design or plant patents; you got the easier row to hoe in this regard, too).

Failure to pay a maintenance fee on time (or late with penalties) results in the cancellation of the patent. About half of all issued patents are cancelled early because maintenance fees weren't paid. You can revive a cancelled patent, however, if you petition the commissioner within two years.

At the time of this writing, the patent maintenance fees due at the $3^1/_2$, $7^1/_2$, and $11^1/_2$ anniversaries of the issue date are $465, $1,180, and $1,955, respectively, for an individual or small business entity. Double these figures for a large business entity. The surcharge for late payment during the six month grace period is $65 and $130, respectively. Unintentional late payment and revival of the expired patent is $1,640 for a small or large entity. Not chicken feed, as you can see.

We strongly recommend that you register your patent with a maintenance and annuity fee service. The service gives you plenty of notice before any forthcoming payment and can even pay the fees on your behalf, for a small charge. You can get information on one of the oldest and most reliable maintenance and annuity fee services by going to www.cpaglobal.com or emailing your questions to enquiries@cpaglobal.com.

Most important, keep the USPTO and your maintenance fee handler informed of any long-term change of address.

When you look at a patent that's more than four years old, don't automatically assume that it's still effective. It may have been canceled for failure to pay the maintenance fee. You can check its status by emailing MaintenanceFeeInquiries@uspto.gov or by calling 703-308-5036 or -5037.

# Marking Your Widgets with the Patent Number

The law requires you to put your patent number on all products covered by your patent or made according to your patented process. The requirement applies to all products made under your authority by your associates or licensees.

A person isn't liable for patent infringement unless that person is notified of the existence of the patent. A proper notice may be laid out as follows: *U.S. Patent No. 19,999,999*. If appropriate, you may add: *Other domestic and foreign patents pending.*

Don't place a false patent or patent pending notice on your product. You may be subject to a fine and you may lose the right to enforce your patent through certain proceedings. Note that a patent pending notice has no recognized legal value. It just acts as a deterrent to potential infringers by warning them that a patent could be issued at any time. It can only be used when, and only as long as, an application is pending.

# Part III
# Asserting Your Copyrights

The 5th Wave          By Rich Tennant

"Well, that's all very colorful, but in order to register your mark in this country you also have to fill out these forms."

## In this part . . .

*W*hether you're writing a novel, creating an architectural drawing, developing new software, or filming an instructional video on the care and feeding of pet ferrets, you own an original work of authorship that deserves protection. In this part, we categorize, dissect, and otherwise pick apart the wide variety of creative works that you can protect with a copyright.

But you have to make sure that you actually own the creative work, so we give you some tests, tips, and tricks to help you make sure that it belongs to you and not your employer, employee, or someone else who had a hand in the creation. And even though you have some automatic copyright protection (who said there's no such thing as a free lunch?), we explain how to register your copyright and put some teeth into your protection.

# Chapter 12

# If It's Got Style, You've Got Copyrights

## In This Chapter

▶ Looking at the nature and scope of copyrights

▶ Acquiring copyrights

▶ Understanding copyrights and their limitations

*O*f all the types of intellectual property rights, copyrights are probably the easiest to understand. Certainly they're the easiest to acquire. However, for all its apparent simplicity, the concept of copyright is like a fish underwater. It's easy to see, but it's hard to get a good grip on it. You first have to get a handle on what an original work of authorship (OWA) is and what it is not, understand which part of an OWA is covered by the copyright, and finally, appreciate the scope of protection that the copyright law provides. In this chapter, we define the various kinds of works protected by copyright and then analyze the rights held by a copyright owner. We end the chapter by going over some copyright acquisition and ownership issues.

Of course, this chapter covers only the basic nature and limitations of copyrights. In Chapters 13 and 14, we show you how to avoid major problems with copyright acquisition and transfer and also how to bulletproof your rights against copycats. However, there's even more. Check out Chapter 20 to find out how to make money from copyrights, and Chapter 21 to get the scoop on enforcing your copyright through litigation.

## Getting to Know the Copyright

A *copyright* is primarily an exclusive right to reproduce an original work. That right falls to the person who created the work or to her employer. But because it's a legal matter, it's somewhat more involved and complicated.

Copyrights and patents spring from the same constitutional clause mandating that Congress *"promote the progress of science and useful arts, by securing for limited times to authors and inventors the exclusive right to their respective writings and discoveries."* And like patents, copyrights are exclusively regulated by federal law. State courts have no jurisdiction over copyright issues.

But, unlike patents, copyrights aren't granted by the government after a complex and expensive application process. Instead, and here comes the good news, a copyright automatically attaches to an original work as soon as it's created. That's right: As soon as you write that next book-club selection or record the next chart-topping song, it's already copyrighted. You can even mark copies of your work with a legal notice including the © symbol, as shown in Chapter 14. And for extra added protection, you can register your copyright with the U. S. Copyright Office, as we also explain in that chapter.

The U.S. Copyright Office, a division of the Library of Congress in Washington, D.C., administers copyright matters under the direction of the *Register of Copyrights*. Title 17 of the U.S. Code (*The Copyright Act*) contains the fundamental laws regulating copyright matters, which can be found in section D on the CD. The Copyright Office Web site, `www.copyright.gov`, is full of well-organized information.

# Defining an Original Work of Authorship

So, now that your interest is piqued, here's the official definition: An *original work of authorship* (OWA) is a substantial and fixed creative work of a non-technical character originated by its author. Clear as mud? Hang on. This definition can be broken down into four basic parts, which we cover in the following sections. Each section outlines one of the requirements that an OWA must meet to be copyrightable.

---

## Even an E.T. can create an OWA — with some help

A few years ago, a court was asked to decide whether a "sacred" text that had been "authored" by celestial beings qualified as an original work of authorship — which is a bit like asking whether Moses could have obtained a copyright on the Ten Commandments. In a thoughtful exercise of common sense, sprinkled with a pinch of skepticism, the court declared that, so long as the text was transcribed, compiled, and collected by mortals, it was protected by copyright.

---

# Fixed creation of the mind

An OWA must be the result of creativity, originating in the author's mind and not merely a discovery of something that already exists. Furthermore, the work isn't considered "created" until it's fixed, tangible, permanent, or stable, and reproducible or otherwise communicable. Here are some examples:

✔ Making a natural-looking plaster-cast replica of a tree trunk to serve as a pedestal doesn't require any mental creativity. But, composing a symphony that suggests wildlife sounds of a virgin forest requires many mental steps to select and arrange sounds in a pleasant composition.

✔ Giving an ad-libbed speech or improvising a musical composition doesn't result in a fixed creation and doesn't qualify as an OWA unless it is recorded simultaneously.

✔ Once upon a time, video games were denied copyright protection on the grounds that the moving images only occurred in response to the players' commands and were therefore not fixed and reproducible. Eventually, the courts recognized that coded instructions stored on a computer chip dictate everything on the screen. By manipulating a joystick, the player selects a series of prerecorded or predetermined program sequences. Thus, the screen images aren't only recorded, but are also reproducible at will.

For your own protection, you must fix your work as early as possible. If you're developing a teaching method or an aerobic dance routine, have somebody record it as you go. If you created an original knitting design, take pictures of it. Keep track of the date you first fixed and distributed your OWA. You'll need that information later, as we explain in Chapter 14.

Observing something and carefully listing its characteristics isn't an OWA; it's a mere representation of pre-existing conditions. For example, the diagnostic of a psychologist that details the personality profile of a patient can't be protected by copyright.

# Substantive and nontrivial mental activity

To qualify as an OWA, the work must have significant complexity, scope, length, or duration. To test compliance with this requirement, you have to use different measuring sticks, according to the nature of the work.

Written, pictorial, and nonmusical works must have a certain degree of complexity or length.

> ✔ Titles, slogans, maxims, two-verse poems, and reproductions of common geometrical figures don't meet the test. On those grounds, the slogan, *"You got the right one, uh-huh,"* used to promote the Pepsi brand of soda, was denied copyright protection. That was also the fate of the folder icon by Apple Computer, Inc., that depicts a common cardboard folder together with the term *Waste Basket* to identify a discarded folder.
>
> ✔ A limerick barely passes the threshold of substantiality.
>
> ✔ A simple line drawing of a dove by the hand of Pablo Picasso, however, is certainly complex (and original) enough to get copyright protection.

Sounds are measured with a shorter yardstick than words are. In a musical composition, a single distinctive bar or even one original measure may be sufficient to deserve protection. The four opening notes of Beethoven's Symphony No. 5 that are used throughout the symphony are a case in point. They would have enough substance to deserve copyright protection if they were composed today. Of a more recent vintage is the one-measure "hook" of a commercial song used in connection with Pepsi products. Although it consists of only four repetitions of the phrase "Uh-oh" in hip-hop rhythm, that jingle was declared protected by copyright.

## A non-functional creation

To qualify as an OWA, the work must not be primarily functional, such as a belt buckle or other useful article. However a degree of functionality in a work isn't necessarily fatal to its protection.

An architectural drawing has a function — to guide the construction of a building. But its functionality resides in the use of the drawing and isn't inherent in the drawing itself. The drawing embodies an imaginative rendition of a nonexisting structure, including a representation of its shapes, proportions, arrangements of openings, and other characteristics that reflect the architect's talented vision, and so is copyrightable.

The rules of a board game are unprotected because they're purely functional steps. However, the decorative graphics on a game board, or the design of a chess piece that represents a whimsical character are nonutilitarian, protected creations. Indeed, the *ornamental design* of a useful article, as distinguished from the article itself, may be considered a visual OWA.

However, that rule applies only if the design can be identified separately from, and exist independently of, the article's function. For example, the shape of a belt buckle — no matter how creative — can't be separated from the buckle and isn't protected by copyright. But a medallion depicting a bucking bronco affixed to the face of a western-style buckle is protected because it isn't a primarily functional element.

## An original work

The originality of an OWA doesn't imply that it's new, unusual, or innovative. The work is original if it isn't copied from a pre-existing source, but is independently created. It doesn't matter that the exact same work was created in another place or time by someone else, so long as the author wasn't exposed to and didn't copy the earlier work.

If you create an OWA that's based on or incorporates one or more pre-existing works, the copyright attaches only to that part of the OWA that's exclusively yours. For instance, if you write a cookbook, you may select recipes from various sources, including previously published cookbooks. You then arrange those recipes in a sequence and format of your choice, describe them in your own words, and add comments and illustrations — all mental steps that together constitute an OWA protected by copyright. If you transcribe the recipes as you find them in a cookbook (with the authors' permission) you get no copyright in the copied text. The recipes themselves are mere functional processes that aren't protected by copyright.

# Determining What Is Copyrighted and What Isn't

In order for a copyright to attach to your work, it must be an OWA meeting all the previously listed basic requirements and a few more spelled out in the Copyright Act. The concept of OWAs is very elastic and can occasionally be extended to cover newfangled things that the law hasn't anticipated. For example, video games, inconceivable a few decades ago, are now considered OWAs. But even if you're creating something in a genre that's been around for a while, it's good to know if it's protected by copyright.

## Copyrighting categories

The law classifies OWAs into the following categories:

- **Literary works:** Any written or recorded sequence of words, numbers, or symbols, including the instructions that constitute a computer program.
- **Musical works:** All musical compositions and their accompanying lyrics, from commercial jingles to epic operas.
- **Dramatic works:** Any work that incorporates the spoken word, including accompanying music, to be performed by one or more characters.

- ✔ **Pantomimes and choreographic works:** Any nonvocal performance from classical ballet to "bump-and-grind" gyrations, from a trapeze act to a clown's silent routine.

- ✔ **Pictorial, graphic, and sculptural works:** Two- and three-dimensional works of fine, graphic, and applied art, including paintings, photographs, prints, art reproductions, maps, globes, charts, diagrams, models, and technical drawings.

- ✔ **Motion pictures and other audio-visual works:** Works that consist of a series of related images together with any accompanying sounds that are designed to be shown on a machine or device such as a projector, cassette or disc player, or other electronic contraption.

- ✔ **Sound recording works:** Works that result from the fixation of a series of musical, spoken, or other sounds on phonograph records, tapes, digital memory chips, or any other embodying device. This category doesn't include the sounds themselves, only the result of preparing, directing, recording, mixing, editing, and other steps in the recording process. (*Note:* This category excludes movies and other audio-visual works.)

- ✔ **Architectural works:** Building designs that are embodied in any tangible medium of expression, including buildings and architectural plans or drawings. Each architectural work includes the overall form, as well as the arrangement and composition of spaces and elements in the design. However, it excludes individual standard features such as doors, windows, and balconies.

These classifications were devised for practical administrative purposes and must be construed very loosely. A work may fit into several categories or incorporate several works falling in different categories. For example, a puppet show can be a dramatic work and a choreographic one. A motion picture is an audio-visual work that may include literary, musical, dramatic, choreographic, and pictorial works.

In addition, the Copyright Act also covers two types of hybrid works, although they don't meet all the required characteristics of an OWA:

- ✔ **Original mask works for semiconductor chip products:** Mask works look like photonegative films and are used to manufacture multilayered microchip circuits. They're used in photosensitive processes to form the intricate semiconductor layers and metallic connecting traces that constitute an integrated circuit.

- ✔ **Original designs of useful articles:** Protection applies to the original design of a useful article that makes the article attractive or distinctive in appearance to the public. So far, only ship hulls and their molds that have a utilitarian function (and not drawings, blueprints, or the mere portrayal of a hull) qualify as "useful articles" pertaining to ships.

Recently, Europe has greatly expanded and improved the protection of original designs of useful articles to all manufactured practical objects from safety pins to locomotives. The United States is expected to someday follow suit and increase its coverage of the designs of useful articles under this section of the Copyright Act.

## Works without copyright protection

Categories of works that don't benefit from copyright protection include:

- **Works generated by the U.S. Government:** Congressional records, census data, maps issued by the Department of the Interior, and so on.

- **Information in the public domain and containing no original presentation:** Calendars, scientific charts or displays, or statistical charts.

- **Clothing designs:** Fashion designers must resort to design patents to protect their creations.

- **Typeface designs (fonts):** However, computer programs used to generate unprotectable typeface designs can be protected by copyright. See the section on "Separating facts from expressions in computer programs" for more information.

- **Unsubstantial works:** Titles, names, short phrases, slogans, common symbols and designs, mere listings of ingredients or contents, bumper stickers, and traffic signs.

- **Transitory works:** Unrecorded improvised speeches, radio and television broadcasts, and dramatic or choreographic performances.

Whether a particular work falls into one of these exceptions isn't easily resolved because you can't apply any defined rule of thumb. Prior court decisions are narrowly drawn on the particularities of each case. Lawyers and judges must rely on common sense and a continuing familiarity with legal precedents when they give opinions or rulings on these issues.

## The Scope of Copyright Protection

With this section, we get into one of the most subtle and critical aspects of copyright protection, which is the source of a great deal of misunderstanding and endless litigation. If you partied until early this morning or are worried about the plastic toy your 3-year-old dumped into the toilet bowl, go take a nap or call the plumber and wait for a better time to read what follows.

The *golden rule* of copyright is simple to define, but it's not always easy to interpret. Copyright doesn't protect the *idea* behind an OWA. It only protects the *original expression* of the idea. There, we said it. Note that the idea may be a fact, and to further explain what is meant by idea, we quote subsection 102(b) of the Copyright Act:

> *In no case does copyright protection for an original work of authorship extend to any idea, procedure, process, system, method of operation, concept, principle or discovery, regardless of the form in which it is described, explained, illustrated, or embodied in such work.*

Distinguishing between the fact or idea embodied in a work and the manner in which the author expresses that fact or idea isn't always easy. We try to illustrate this kind of analysis in the following sections.

## Just the facts, ma'am

Maggie, a reporter for the *Daily Humdrum*, witnesses a major traffic accident involving a famous rock singer. She writes her piece at the scene on her notebook computer and sends it to her editor, via unsecured email. However, before Maggie's editor has a chance to read her message, KNAV, a local TV station, intercepts the message and broadcasts a special announcement relating the accident — using only the facts in Maggie's pilfered message.

Does the *Daily Humdrum* have a cause of action for copyright infringement against KNAV? The answer, like the proper answer to every legal question, is, "It depends." It depends upon whether KNAV reported just the facts of the accident, which aren't protected by copyright, or copied Maggie's exact words and phrases — the manner in which she expressed those facts — in which case there may be infringement. However, if Maggie used a telegraphic style to draft her report, as in the following paragraph, the message doesn't have a substantial amount of original expression and no copyright protection can attach to it.

> Mond. - 4pm – Accident at 4th and Brdway – Rock band Wigglebutt's limo broadsides milk truck – Singer taken unconscious to Squickygurney hosp. – suspected neck injury.

That was an easy one to resolve. Let's raise the ante in the next section.

## Unlocking the flow of ideas

The purpose of the copyright golden rule is to permit the free flow of ideas, as the following example shows.

Sam writes a very successful novel about John Applebrown, a U.S. resident who traces his ancestry to a famous British lord and goes to England to look for remaining relatives. When he reaches England, he locates and eventually falls in love with a distant cousin who's heir to a great fortune.

Maxine, inspired by John Applebrown's story, decides to write the saga of Suho Chizu, a Japanese American who discovers that her great-grandfather was a powerful shogun. She travels to the Land of the Rising Sun and finds a cousin in a high government position who offers her marriage.

Do you think there's a copyright infringement here? If you said, It depends," you're catching on. The concept of someone looking into his or her ancestry, discovering an illustrious foreign lineage, and then locating and eventually marrying a rich or powerful relative in his or her country of origin is what some judges would call a *scène à faire*, which is Latvian for "wow, I'm smart; I can use foreign phrases." Actually, the phrase is French and loosely means "a story to be told," which is one of those basic ideas or concepts that are excluded from protection. However, if Maxine copied some of Sam's flowery sentences or used some of the same colorful characters that lend life and interest to Sam's book, Sam has a good cause of action against Maxine and her publisher.

As the details of a scène à faire are developed, protected expression begins to emerge. One can't copy a very complex plot with impunity, even if the imitator's writing style is quite different from the original author's. Determining when one crosses the line from idea to expression isn't always obvious. In a nutshell, basic plots such as "boy meets girl, boy loses girl, boy gets girl" are unprotected, unless the author adds distinctive twists to the basic scenario.

## Separating facts from expressions in computer programs

In this section, we delve into the intricacies of copyrights and computer programs. If you haven't picked up this book with such issues in mind, feel free to skip to another section.

In what most people call a creative and welcome expansion of copyright protection, a few years ago the Copyright Act extended coverage to computer programs as literary works, in spite of the rumbling sounds detected in Emily Dickinson's and T. S. Eliot's graves.

A *computer program* is a set of statements or instructions used to bring about a certain result, regardless of the form in which the program is embodied. Therefore, the program source code and the object code burned as ones and zeros into a read-only memory chip are protected by copyright. However, the process performed by the computer program isn't protected. Therefore, you can write a program to perform the same functions as someone else's, as long as you don't copy their code. For example, there are many accounting programs out there, and as long as each is written without copying the code from another program, all the programs are protected.

You can draw an analogy with the plot of a novel, like the one discussed earlier, to determine how much of the original program is protected. The process run by the computer corresponds to the scène à faire of the book. If the program is very simple and there's only one practical way to code the instructions, the expression of the process has no substance — it's merely an idea or concept — and therefore can't be protected. However, as the program becomes more elaborate, it acquires distinctive characteristics that reflect a unique way to code the program. Because this particular approach isn't the only way to "express" the program, the one selected by the original programmer is protected.

## Protected or not?

Some courts have returned to a concept called the *abstraction-filtration-comparison test*, which was first applied circa 1930 in a Universal Pictures Corp. case about the alleged copying of a play. According to this test, a work is dissected into a series of increasing generalities. At the bottom are detailed renditions of characters, situations, and activities, and at the top is the title of the work. The court then examines each level of abstraction, from the bottom up, in order to filter out those elements of the work that constitute unprotectable elements of ideas, processes, public domain information, merger material, and scènes à faire. Then the protected elements are compared to those in the accused work. As soon as a match is found, that work is said to infringe on the rights of the copyright owner.

In one particular case, the test was applied to a set of 64-digit numerical command codes used by Mitel, Inc., to instruct a telephone call controller, a device that enhances the operation of a telephone system. Using the abstraction-filtration-comparison test, the court eliminated every element of the device, after determining that the selection of the codes was merely sequential or didn't evince any originality.

A contrary conclusion was reached in a case involving the copying of a font-shaping program by Adobe Systems, Inc. The program selects several curve reference points on a typeface and uses these points to alter its outline. The court found that the selection of the points was a matter of judgment, about which two programmers may disagree. Accordingly, the mere choice of reference point exhibited sufficient creativity to warrant copyright protection.

These two examples illustrate how closely the courts articulate their decisions and how complex their reasoning can be.

The issue of which components of a computer program are protected goes to the core of the idea/expression conundrum. This issue is extremely important because copyright has, by far, become the preferred method for protecting software. In a multitude of software infringement cases, the courts have refined the criteria used to separate protectable expression from unprotectable ideas and concepts. The last chapter on the subject probably hasn't been written yet, so if you're dealing with similar issues, check with a computer law specialist and peruse the nearby "Protected or not?" sidebar.

# So What Does a Copyright Do for Me?

As the author of an OWA, you have some exclusive rights to control how your creation is used. For historical and practical reasons, these rights are collectively referred to as copyrights. However, they extend far beyond the right to prevent others from copying your work. Copyrights aren't absolute. Like patent rights, they're subject to a time limitation. Also, some exceptions allow others fair use of your work without your permission, in specific circumstances.

## Reading your rights

The owner of an OWA holds a number of *exclusive rights* or powers that he or she alone can exercise. The following sections discuss the nature and scope of these exclusive rights as they apply to the various categories of works.

### Thou shalt not copy

The primary and most important right held by the creator or owner of an OWA, regardless of its category, is to exclude others from duplicating the work. The mere copying is what's forbidden, even if the copy is never used:

- ✔ You can't make a copy of your own portrait bought from a photographer without infringing on the photographer's copyright. The fact that you paid good money for the original and some copies of the portrait doesn't automatically transfer the copyright to you.

- ✔ The minute you download a pirated copy of a song or computer program onto your hard drive, you commit an act of copyright infringement.

- ✔ You can't download or install a legitimate copy of software without a license to do so.

- ✔ Using copyrighted popular music as background for your home video production is a clear violation of the composer or songwriter's rights.

### Prohibiting preparation of derivative works

Based on one or more pre-existing works, a *derivative work* can be a translation, musical arrangement, dramatization, fictionalization, motion picture, sound recording, art reproduction, abridgment, or other form in which a previous work is recast, transformed, or adapted. That last phrase covers many activities, such as making editorial revisions, annotations, elaborations, or any other modification that by itself is original and substantive enough to qualify as an OWA. Nobody has the right to make a derivative work of your OWA without your permission. Here are some examples of derivative works:

- ✔ A statue or puppet drawn from a cartoon character
- ✔ A TV sitcom based on a novel
- ✔ A photograph of a statue
- ✔ The modification of a computer program to make it compatible with a different hardware or software product

A young man wrote a script for a sequel to a popular motion picture. He sent it, unsolicited, to the movie's producer, asking for compensation if his script was used. When a film based on his script was released, and the producer didn't respond to requests for payment, he sued claiming infringement of copyright. The producer counterclaimed for copyright infringement and won the case. The script was an unauthorized derivative work that infringed on the copyright of the original film.

In order to spice up the sauce, let us mention a couple exceptions to the right that prevents making derivative works.

- ✔ The owner of the copyright of a sound recording can't legally prevent someone from making a recording that faithfully simulates the sounds of the original recording, so long as the new work records a different performance. However the owner of the copyright of the underlying song or other recorded OWA can.
- ✔ A derivative work consisting of photographs or paintings of a building or other architectural work is permitted.

### No handouts allowed

Distributing copies or adaptations of a work, whether by public sale, free distribution, rental, lease, or loan, is an infringement, even if you didn't actually make the copies. For example, copying a clipping from a newspaper or magazine about the impact of secondhand tobacco smoke and giving copies to all your chain-smoking relatives is a no-no. So is passing a copy of a spreadsheet program, licensed only to you, to one of your associates.

### Barring public performances

You can prevent the public performance of a copyrighted work that falls under one of the following categories (see the "Copyrighting categories" section, earlier in this chapter): literary, musical, dramatic, pantomimes and choreographic, and motion picture and other audio-visual work.

If you own a copyright on a piece of popular music, you can prevent anyone else from playing a recording of it in public, such as background to an exercise class or a processional at a high-school graduation pageant (see Chapter 20 about performing licenses).

A radio or TV station can't broadcast any copyrighted music or video program without a license from the copyright owner. In Chapter 20, we explain how public broadcasters obtain such licenses.

### Proscribing public display

Not only the performance, but also the mere public display of a literary, musical, dramatic, pantomime or choreographic work, pictorial, graphic, or sculptural work, or an individual image from a motion picture or other audio-visual work can be prohibited by its copyright owner. For example, an unauthorized display of a protected statue in an art gallery is a copyright infringement. In addition, public display of sheet music, textual documents, or photographs of a ballet performance are controlled by copyrights.

### Quashing digital audio transmissions

The digital transmission of words or music from a copyrighted sound recording is forbidden without a license from the copyright owner. This restriction is key in the music industry's attempt to control the peer-to-peer music sharing practices that are so common between Internet users.

### Protecting your artistic reputation

A *work of visual art* is defined as a painting, drawing, print, still photograph, or sculpture existing in a single copy or in a series of signed and consecutively numbered limited edition copies not exceeding 200. If you've created a work of visual art during your lifetime, you have certain rights designed to give you credit for your work and protect your reputation even if you transfer your copyright in the work to someone else. You can

✔ Claim authorship of the work.

✔ Prevent your name from being used as the author of a work that you didn't create.

  ✔ Prevent any intentional distortion, mutilation, or modification of one of your works that is detrimental to your honor or reputation, as well as prevent your name from being used as the author of such a work.

  ✔ Prevent the intentional or grossly negligent destruction of any OWA of recognized stature, such as a piece of public art or the work of a renowned artist.

## Knowing your limitations

So, did the last section make you a bit nervous about how many times you've infringed on a copyright? If all these copyright owners' rights were always enforced, we'd all be in jail. But those rights have numerous limitations, restrictions, exceptions, and exemptions.

### Nothing lasts forever

In a major overhaul of the Copyright Act in 1978, the duration of copyright protection was considerably extended, but copyright renewal was abolished. (Before 1978, a copyright could be renewed for an additional 28-year term.) Because of numerous amendments to the Copyright Act since that date, the duration of any particular copyright depends on the date of creation and the nature of the authorship. Without getting into all the sordid details, here are some general guidelines to determine the duration of copyright protection:

  ✔ **Works created on or after January 1, 1978:**

  • **By one or more identified authors:** Life of the last surviving author plus an additional 70 years.

  • **By one or more anonymous or pseudonymous authors:** 95 years from publication or 120 years from creation of work, whichever is shorter.

  • **In the employment of or under the control of another (also called *works made for hire*):** 95 years from publication or 120 years from creation of work, whichever is shorter. (See Chapter 13 for more on works for hire.)

  ✔ **Works created, but not published, by January 1, 1978:** Same duration as those created on or after January 1, 1978, but with no expiration before December 31, 2002.

  ✔ **Works published after December 31, 1977, but before January 1, 2003:** Same duration as those created on or after January 1, 1978, but with no expiration before December 31, 2047.

  ✔ **Works created and published with notice (see Chapter 14) or registered between January 1, 1964, and December 31, 1977:** 95 years from publication or registration, whichever comes first.

✔ **Works created and published with notice or registered between January 1, 1950, and December 31, 1963:**

- **If renewed during their 28th year:** 95 years from publication or registration, whichever comes first.

- **If not renewed:** 28 years from publication or registration, whichever comes first.

A copyright always extends through December 31 of its year of expiration.

## Losing control

Under the *first sale doctrine,* after you sell or otherwise transfer a copy or recording of your copyrighted work (see Chapter 13 for ownership issues info), you can't prevent the resale or transfer of that copy and you can't continue to collect a fee or royalty every time it changes hands either.

However, even the legitimate owner of a copy of a sound recording or computer program doesn't have the right to commercially exploit that copy by lease or rental, except to benefit a nonprofit library or educational institution. This prohibition doesn't apply to computer programs built into a machine or device, such as the program that controls the operation of a video game or your automobile ignition system. By the way, a computer program is rarely actually sold, but only licensed to you exclusively, as stated on the CD jacket or in the license you approve before downloading it: You can't sell it or give it away.

## Playing fair

The concept of *fair use* allows others to use your copyrighted work (published or unpublished) without your permission. Of course, fairness is one of those subjective criteria about which you and the user of your work may disagree — so the law spells out what's fair use of copyrighted material.

✔ Reviews or criticism of the work

✔ News reporting

✔ Teaching (including making multiple copies for classroom use)

✔ Scholarship

✔ Research

Four factors determine whether the use of the original work is fair:

✔ The purpose and character of the use, including whether it is used for a commercial or a nonprofit educational purpose: A commercial, for profit activity is rarely characterized as fair use.

✔ The nature of the work: A work that represents a lot of talent or considerable labor is less subject to fair use than a cheap or trivial one. For instance, a dime novel carries less weight than a public monument or sculpture, and a homemade video production less than a sophisticated ballet performance.

✔ The amount and substantiality of the portion used in relation to the entire work: Lifting 3 or 4 pages from a 300-page novel is more likely to be tolerated than reproducing an entire short poem.

✔ The effect upon the market or the value of the copyrighted work: A teacher can't routinely make and distribute copies of an entire textbook in order to save the students the cost of buying the textbook.

### Licensing your work whether you like it or not

After you distribute a recording of a nondramatic musical work, such as a song, you're forced to grant a *compulsory license* (involuntary permission) to anyone else in the U.S. who wants to make and distribute new recordings of that work, either with physical copies or through digital transmission. The "gotcha" is that, each month, the person who takes advantage of the compulsory license has to pay you a royalty at a rate set by a permanent institution called the *royalty panel,* enthroned by the Copyright Office.

The person who takes advantage of the compulsory license can't just copy your recording, but must record his own. He may make a new arrangement of the music, so long as the new arrangement doesn't change the basic melody or the fundamental character of the work. The new recording isn't considered a derivative of your own work unless you consent to it. Keep in mind that you have a certain degree of control over a derivative work. In Chapter 20, we explain how the music industry deals with this provision of the law, and how you, as a songwriter, can benefit from it.

Also, in an effort to make radio and TV programs more accessible to people living beyond the broadcasting ranges of network stations, the law allows radio and TV stations to rebroadcast programs, under another kind of compulsory license and payment of a royalty, specified by the royalty panel, to the original broadcaster.

We could fill another book discussing the rules governing the compulsory licensing process, royalty rates, and arbitrating royalty-related disputes. We'll spare you for now — just know that these rules exist and usually require circumstantial interpretation by an IP lawyer.

### Claiming exemptions and privileges

Some activities that would otherwise infringe on a copyright are allowed for specific nonprofit, charitable, or educational purposes.

✔ **Copies for the blind:** Nondramatic literary works reproduced or distributed as copies or recordings in specialized formats exclusively for use by blind or other disabled persons are copyright exempt. Braille copies of a text are an obvious example of this type of exemption.

- ✓ **Libraries and archives:** Public librarians and archivists may reproduce and distribute one copy or phonorecord of a copyrighted work for a noncommercial purpose, providing that a notice of copyright appears on the reproduced copy or recording. They may also make up to three copies for preservation, security deposit, or research in another library or archive center.

- ✓ **Teachers:** Teachers can perform or display a copyrighted work for their students in a face-to-face teaching activity in the classroom of a non-profit educational institution.

  Don't confuse this with the fair use exception that allows teachers to make multiple copies of a reasonable portion of a protected work for distribution in the classroom, regardless of the status of the educational institution.

- ✓ **Nonprofit education:** Government agencies and nonprofit educational institutions may transmit, such as by broadcasting, by cable, and over the Internet or any other network, the performance of a nondramatic literary or musical work and the display of literary, pictorial, or any other type of work under these circumstances:

    - In a classroom or other teaching location

    - To persons whose disabilities or other circumstances prevent their attendance in a classroom

    - By officers and employees of a governmental body as part of their duties

- ✓ **Religious activities:** In places of worship and religious assemblies, you can perform or display a nondramatic literary work, a musical work, or a dramatic-musical work of a religious character without consent of the copyright owner.

- ✓ **Charitable purposes:** With advance notice to the copyright owner, you can perform (although not transmit) a nondramatic literary or musical work for nonprofit, educational, religious, or charitable purposes, unless the copyright owner objects at least seven days before the scheduled performance.

- ✓ **Private transmissions:** Retransmitting the performance or display of a work for public reception on a single receiving apparatus (such as a home theater) is exempt if the public is not charged and you don't retransmit it publicly. For example, if one of us appears on a TV show, he can receive the program on a regular TV set and then rig a cable connection to communicate it to a large plasma screen on the patio for a viewing party.

- ✓ **Commercial establishments:** A small commercial establishment may retransmit a radio or television program free of charge to its customers. The law limits the number of speakers or TV sets you can use, depending on the type and size of the business. This exemption isn't available to food service and drinking establishments.

✔ **Agricultural fairs:** In the course of an annual agricultural or horticultural fair or exhibition, a government agency or a nonprofit agricultural or horticultural organization may perform a nondramatic musical work without license from the copyright owner.

✔ **Record shops:** Music and record shops (if there are any left) can play or perform nondramatic musical works, including audio-visual works, for the benefit of their customers and to promote the sale of recordings of the works.

✔ **Transmissions to disabled persons:** You can transmit performances of literary works over ten years old to blind or other handicapped persons in nonprofit education or governmentally controlled circumstances. Don't confuse this right to transmit with the right to make copies mentioned at the head of this list.

✔ **Fraternal organization events:** Veterans' organizations and other nonprofit fraternal organizations can perform nondramatic literary or musical works during a social function to which the general public is not invited. University fraternities and sororities can't benefit from this exemption unless the social function is held solely to raise funds for a specific charitable purpose.

✔ **In-house retransmissions:** Some secondary retransmissions of the performance or display of a work may be exempt under certain circumstances and settings, such as by a hotel or apartment house to individual rooms or flats and by cable companies (under a compulsory license, as explained earlier in "Licensing your work whether you like it or not").

✔ **Ephemeral recordings:** Radio and TV studios may make temporary recordings of their programs for internal use, under certain conditions.

✔ **Computer programs:** You may make one copy of a computer program as part of your use of the program or for your archives without permission from the copyright owner. You can also adapt that copy to your hardware. It isn't an infringement to let your computer generate an extra copy of a program to use for maintenance or repair. The archival copy may be transferred with the sale of the original program, but the repair copy must be destroyed when the maintenance or repair is done.

✔ **Personal use:** Finally, an exemption familiar to everybody. You may record a radio or television program while it's played on the air for later listening or viewing by you and the members of your household. You may not, without permission from the copyright owner, copy, sell, lend, or publicly play your recording.

# Chapter 13

# Untangling Ownership Issues

. . . . . . . . . . . . . . . . . . . . . . . . . . . . . . . . . . . . . . . . .

*In This Chapter*

▶ Getting the copyright in a work made for hire

▶ Transferring your copyright

▶ Checking the copyright status of a work

. . . . . . . . . . . . . . . . . . . . . . . . . . . . . . . . . . . . . . . . .

Copyright law casts a very broad net. It's hard to imagine a human endeavor that doesn't have a copyrightable component. Whether you write a book, peddle hotdogs from a street cart, coach aerobic exercises, teach a knitting course, sell real estate, or design a sophisticated, scientific instrument, copyright issues are all over the place.

While bouncing about your exercise studio, teaching your knitting class, decorating your street cart, programming your computer, or designing a new electronic package, you use recorded music, textbooks, audio-visual teaching aids, graphics, promotional material, mask works or multiple listing compilations — all *original works of authorship* (OWAs) protected by copyrights.

Each of these OWAs raises ownership and protection issues and conceals potential legal pitfalls for the unwary. And as you create your masterpiece or hire someone to do it for you, understanding who created an OWA, and consequently, who has the rights to it, is vitally important. An oversight or mistake in this area can have disastrous consequences.

In this chapter, we talk about how to decide whether you own a copyright (and if not, who does), how to give or sell your copyright to someone else, and how to track down copyright ownership. Often, it's fairly simple and you can figure it out yourself. But if it all seems incredibly confusing, your IP attorney can help you unravel the tangle of copyright ownership.

## Making Sure You Own the Copyright

Any original creation is a potentially valuable intellectual property. And when you start throwing the word *valuable* around, you know things won't remain simple for long. If you've been locked away in your home office writing the great American novel or developing the next world-famous pantomime routine, the question of who owns the original work of authorship (OWA) is probably simple — you do. However, if you developed a script while working for a movie production studio, or wrote the background music as a freelance composer, chances are that the studio owns the copyright in your creation. But if you're reading this chapter, we're guessing your situation is a bit more complex.

Many of the difficulties and costly litigations that you can have with copyrights involve questions of ownership. The usual participants in the great ownership debate are you and your associates, your employer or employees, collaborators, and contractors. Anyone who contributed to an OWA may have a full or partial interest in the work. You need to be aware of how the legalities of ownership affect your role in the creative process.

## You and your associates

If you work (on your own and not as someone's employee) with a coauthor, you two jointly own the copyright, unless you have an agreement to the contrary. Joint ownership of the copyright, just like a business partnership or a marriage, can be messy and quickly turn nasty when a disagreement surfaces. Contrary to patent law, which allows each co-inventor to exploit the invention independently without accounting to the other, joint owners of a copyright must account to each other for any benefit realized from the licensing or sale of the work or the copyright — and share the benefit. However, a joint owner can exploit the copyright or even transfer it to a third party without permission from the other owner — which can lead to very awkward situations.

If you can't avoid joint ownership of a copyright, you and the other joint owner should sign a written comprehensive agreement that spells out all critical and potentially contentious issues, such as:

- **Respective percentages of ownership:** The interest of co-owners of a copyright can be apportioned in any percentages the parties decide. If you can't agree, the law presumes that all parties have an equal, undivided interest in the copyright.

- **Joint or separate right to exploit the copyright:** Whether or not you and the other co-owner are equal owners, you can exploit the copyright jointly or allow each other to take advantage of any opportunity separately. You must also decide whether to pool your benefits or let each party keep his or her own receipts.

✔ **Right to prepare a derivative work:** A derivative work (see Chapter 12) can become more lucrative than the original, even to a point where there's no more market for the original.

For example, John and Rob together devise an asset management computer program, tailored to Rob's tool-rental business. Both are co-authors of the program and co-owners of the copyright. Larry, Rob's friend who operates vending machines, hears about the program and asks Rob to help him write a similar program for his business.

Starting with the tool-rental management program, Rob and Larry develop a more sophisticated program to manage Larry's vending machine operation. The new program adapts easily to other businesses. Rob and Larry, finding more and more applications for the program, embark on a very lucrative licensing venture.

Rob must account to John for all proceeds collected from the exploitation of the initial program. However, knowing that the new program is far more elaborate than the original program, Rob thinks that John only deserves a very small percentage of the proceeds from the second program (if any).

If John sues Rob and Larry for a reasonable share of those proceeds, a court would most likely award half of the proceeds to Larry (the half owner of the new program) and a quarter of the proceeds to each Rob and John, the owners of equal and undivided shares of the copyright in the original program, upon which the derivative work is based.

Here's why: Although John and Rob created the original program, when the second program was developed, Larry also became a part owner. If John didn't want any more partners, in an initial agreement between Rob and John, he should've specified that each party has veto power over a joint authorship of a derivative work with a third party.

✔ **Right to transfer one's interest to a third party:** If you aren't comfortable with the idea of being in bed (joint ownership) with a stranger, you should arrange for each party to have first choice in buying the interest of the other.

✔ **Right of succession in case of death or disability of one party:** Succession laws vary from state to state. You can bypass those laws with a well-drafted agreement that guarantees an orderly transfer of the copyright to the surviving co-owner upon paying a stipulated sum to the deceased party's estate. You can fund and guarantee that payment by each taking an insurance policy on the life of the other.

All these considerations have important legal implications that deserve the attention of a competent lawyer (yes, trust us, there are incompetent ones).

# Work made for hire: When the creator isn't the author

A *work made for hire* (WMFH) is an OWA that's created by an employee within the scope of his employment, or one that is commissioned under a special agreement (see the following sections for details). In both cases the legal author of the work isn't its actual creator, but the employer, or the commissioning party is, whether that's an individual or a corporation. The copyright in a WMFH never belongs to the actual creator of the work.

## Employees' creations

Let's set the stage: An *employee* is someone regularly employed by another (the *employer* — groundbreaking stuff, huh?) and subject to payroll withdrawals. Freelance operators and independent contractors aren't considered employees in this context. (For more on those independents, see the next section.)

The law considers the employer to be the author of the work on the theory that an employee is just a robot that executes the task upon the direction of his boss: "Bob, fix me a cup of coffee. And while you're at it, write me a computer program." It's all in a day's work. ***Note:*** This aspect of copyright law is totally contrary to patent law, which requires that only the genuine inventor, not the boss, be listed on a patent application (see Chapter 11).

## Works commissioned from non-employees

A creation by a non-employee is classified as a WMFH if it falls within one of the nine qualifying works categories in the following list and the work is specifically commissioned under a written contract signed by both parties.

- ✔ **Contribution to a collective work:** A *collective work,* such as a periodical, anthology, or encyclopedia, contains a number of separate and independent contributions assembled into a collective whole. Any contribution to such a work can be classified as a WMFH.

  When two non-employee authors jointly contribute to the text of a book, and both perform tasks such as writing or editing, and in the final work their contributions are merged into inseparable or interdependent parts, they create a joint work — not a collective one (see the "You and your associates" section, earlier in this chapter). A joint work by non-employees can never qualify as a WMFH under contract or by law. But when two or more non-employees contribute separate portions of a single work under a WMFH agreement, the employer legally becomes the sole author and is presumed to have authored all its employees' separate contributions.

- ✔ **Part of a motion picture or other audiovisual work:** Composing background music or designing graphic stage sets for a film, writing a script for a teaching video cassette, or laying out a dancing act for a movie ballroom scene are examples of qualifying works.

- ✔ **A translation:** Translation of written or aural text from one language to another.

- ✔ **A supplementary work:** A work prepared for publication that is adjunct to a work by another author, such as an introduction, preface, foreword, epilogue, afterword, conclusion, illustration, explanation, revision, update, commentary, map, diagram, chart, table, editorial notes, musical arrangement, answer sheet, bibliography, appendix, glossary, index, or anything that may assist in the use of the principal work.

- ✔ **A compilation:** A work formed by collecting and assembling pre-existing materials or data. The way that this material is selected and arranged creates a work that, as a whole, can constitute an OWA. A collective work is also a compilation, but a compilation can be authored by a single person. Reference works such as dictionaries and lexicons, directories, cookbooks, and anthologies qualify as compilations.

- ✔ **An instructional text:** Any work intended for use in a systematic teaching activity, ranging from scholarly treatises to simple ABC books used by kindergarteners.

- ✔ **A test and/or its answers:** Such as the S.A.T., or any literary or graphical work that solicits a subject's written, oral, or physical answers or reactions.

- ✔ **An atlas:** Any collection of territorial maps and related textual material.

The requisite contract to create a WMFH out of a non-employee's contribution must be signed by all parties and must include a clause substantially equivalent to the following:

> *Any original work of authorship created by XXX (the "Creator") under this agreement shall be a work-made-for-hire pursuant to 17 U.S.C. 101 and the copyright in said work shall vest in YYY (the "Commissioning party"). The Creator shall assign to the Commissioning party any work that doesn't qualify as a work-made-for-hire. Both parties have signified their consent to this agreement by their respective signatures below.*

## When you have a choice

If you're the boss, you must either let the actual creator of the work acquire the copyright, which he then *assigns* (legally transfers) to you after the work is completed (see "Knowing when to assign," later in this chapter), or have him work under a WMFH agreement. In the latter situation, you get the copyright, but for a different duration than a standard non-WMFH (see Chapter 12). The best alternative depends upon the age of the creator, and other factors discussed in the next paragraph. If the creator is relatively young, the copyright life will be longer if it's kept in his or her name. If the creator is of advanced age, a WMFH may yield a longer copyright duration.

The commissioning party retains complete control over the copyright in a WMFH, even more than in a case of assignment. On the other end, if you're not in the driver's seat, but are hired to perform a task that's subject to WMFH status, you should carefully consider all the ramifications of working under a WMFH agreement instead of your simple promise to assign. You should pay particular consideration to the following right-to-cancel provision.

Besides the difference in copyright duration in a standard work versus a WMFH, the assignment of a standard work to a commissioning party can be cancelled by the assignor or by their heirs, in whole or in part, under certain circumstances such as the author's death. If you're concerned about these matters, you probably need to consult an IP attorney.

In certain states, notably California, the law classifies a person working under a WMFH agreement as a full-fledged employee, subject to all the benefits and payroll withdrawals of a regular employee. If you're in one of these jurisdictions (check your state labor and insurance codes, or ask your attorney), only use WMFH agreements when commissioning corporate entities, and not with individuals. If you don't withhold taxes and other deductions from their paychecks, you'll be breaking state and federal laws.

### Handling nonqualifying WMFH situations

Because of the advantages WMFH agreements often provide to the commissioning party, companies routinely use them to hire outside contributors. But many of these agreements are inappropriate because they are for nonqualified types of works. For example, a publisher may commission an author to write a book under a WMFH agreement, even though the work doesn't fit into any of the nine categories listed in the previous section. What happens to the copyright under these circumstances? Does the contract confer any right to the commissioning party?

As always, the answers to these questions depend on the particular circumstances of the case in question. The courts tend to treat these improper agreements as nonexclusive copyright licenses granted by the creator to the commissioning party to use the contemplated work while reserving to the creator the right to do whatever he wants with the work and copyright. In other words, he can authorize someone else to use and exploit the work and also do that himself in competition with the commissioning party.

# Changing the Owner: Transferring Interest in a Copyright

The copyright to an OWA can be sliced like salami into separate ownership portions (legally called interests) that you can then assign (transfer) to different people. You can also assign to different parties all or some of the various exclusive rights of a copyright owner that we painstakingly list in Chapter 12. For example, a movie studio can get the right to make a TV sitcom from your story, while a magazine can serialize it over a number of weeks.

## Knowing when to assign

The law is very clear that an OWA isn't created until it is *fixed* (in a tangible or reproducible state, described in Chapter 12). Furthermore, when a work is prepared over a period of time, the portion of it that is fixed at any particular point in time constitutes the work as of that time.

You can only transfer copyright ownership on what is fixed at the time of the transfer. The transfer doesn't automatically cover any part of the work that will be created and fixed in the future. Accordingly, if you ask a contractor to assign (transfer) a copyright on his contribution to a project before the work is started or fixed, the assignment document will have no legal effect.

By now, you're wondering how you can ensure, at the outset, that the copyright on a future work will be transferred to you. In your hiring agreement, have the contractor or prospective author sign an agreement to assign the copyrights of every OWA created within the scope of the job to you. Then have a formal assignment document ready for signature as soon as a work is fixed.

## Drafting a binding assignment agreement

The basic rule of transferring an entire copyright interest is to get it in writing. Any transfer, other than by court order, inheritance, or other automatic manner specified by law, is invalid unless it's in a written conveyance (the transfer of an interest from one person to another) signed by the owner.

Note that the conveyance of a partial interest, such as a nonexclusive license (see Chapter 20) need not be in writing to be legally effective. But who would be foolish enough to enter into a license agreement by oral agreement?

A written conveyance assignment effectively transfers copyright ownership. But you need to go one step farther. You must have the conveyance notarized (or sworn before an authorized person) to use it in court as *prima facie evidence* (evidence admissible without any further proof) of the transfer.

If you assign the copyright abroad, have it witnessed by a U.S. diplomatic or consular officer or by a foreign official authorized to administer oaths (much as a notary would be here). Make sure that the official certifies his or her authority, for example with a seal or stamp.

Here's a simple example of a copyright assignment:

> *For good and sufficient consideration, I, _____, the undersigned, hereby assign and transfer to _____ all my right, title and interest in the entire copyright in the United States of America and everywhere in the world for the original work entitled_____, authored by_____, a copy/ photograph of which is attached hereto, and to the Copyright Registration No._____. Dated _____*

> SIGNATURE

> NOTARIZATION or CERTIFICATION

If the work for which you want to own the copyright hasn't been created yet, the hiring agreement with your contractor should include the following promise to assign clause:

> *Contractor agrees to assign to Developer [that's you] any original work or authorship created by Contractor within the scope of this agreement and will diligently execute, at the request of Developer, any assignment or other document reasonably necessary to transfer the copyright in said work to "Developer. The phrase "original work of authorship" shall comprise any such work authored by any person under the control or direction of Contractor, including employees and subcontractors. Contractor shall make any contractual arrangement necessary, with such persons, to allow Contractor compliance with this agreement.*

This is the type of hiring agreement clause that can be used when a WMFH agreement isn't applicable or advisable as explained under "When you have a choice," earlier in this chapter.

After the work is completed, you ask the creator to execute an assignment in the form shown earlier in this section.

# Investigating the Status of a Copyright

Imagine yourself in one of these situations:

> ✔ You're writing a coffee-table book about Renaissance gardens. You found an encyclopedia containing beautiful engravings of wild roses, and you'd like to use them to illustrate your own work. You need to find the owner of the copyright covering these engravings and get permission to copy them.

✔ You're writing a short skit for a high school performance and want to use the music of a popular song with your own lyrics. You need permission to create your derivative work from the song's copyright owner.

✔ You own a small bronze statue of a Tom Sawyer character that you'd like to reproduce as part of a painting or photographic print. You can't do it without permission from the owner of the copyright in the statue.

✔ You want to incorporate a number of pre-existing OWAs in your own creation, but don't have the time or resources to obtain necessary licenses or permissions from copyright owners. So you decide to select pre-existing works are in the *public domain,* which means they were never or are no longer copyrighted.

Your course of action in any of these four situations isn't easy. In addition, the older the work, the harder identifying the current copyright owner becomes. If you're lucky enough to identify and find the copyright owner, getting a license or permission can be like pulling teeth, unless you're ready to plunk down a good amount of cash.

Before you spend time and money searching for a copyright owner, keep in mind that finding the owner is no guarantee that you'll readily get the license or permission you need. The copyright owner may be unwilling to grant you one or may be under a legal obligation to prohibit anyone from using the work. The price you can pay for the permission or license isn't worth what the copyright owner's attorney might charge to prepare the necessary paperwork.

If you can't secure the permission, don't even think of using the copyrighted material without it. As we show in Chapter 21, a copyright owner can get a relatively large damage award for a single infringement act — without having to prove any loss resulting from the infringement. Not good news for you.

Here are some general guidelines for your quest to find a copyright owner and secure permission. First, find your best good luck charm — you're gonna need it.

✔ If you're certain that a work has been on the market or that the copyright has been registered for more than 95 years, you can safely assume the work is in the public domain. However, make sure you're not copying a more recent edition or adaptation that may still have a copyright.

✔ For a book, first contact the publisher. You may get lucky and talk with a very understanding attorney or licensing agent who can answer all your questions and give you the license or permission you're after. Based on our own experience, even if you find him, he's unlikely to be that cooperative. Unless you get a final refusal by the copyright owner, you need to keep digging. To find the copyright owner, first check the copyright notice on the work.

✔ If you're interested in a musical work, start with the record company. If you have no luck there, try to contact a mechanical licensing agency — a clearing house that a songwriter or a music publishing company uses to license record companies. The most famous is The Harry Fox Agency, Inc., 711 Third Avenue, New York, NY 10017. A smaller agency is The American Mechanical Right Agency (AMRA), 333 S. Tamiami Tr., Venice, FL 34285.

✔ When dealing with a statue or other sculptural work, consult an art dealer if you can't decipher a recognizable name on the work. She may be able to identify the author and the approximate date of distribution.

✔ Search the records of the U.S. Copyright Office. Online, you can access works registered and documents, such as assignments, recorded since 1978. Older papers must be searched manually. You can do it yourself or ask the good people in the Copyright Office to do it for you for a fee of $150 per hour (last time we checked). We recommend that you download or request *Circular 22, How to Investigate the Copyright Status of a Work*.

✔ Some companies offer copyright clearance and licensing services over the Internet. For a start you can try `www.copyright.com`.

✔ As a last resort, consult a copyright attorney.

# Chapter 14

# Giving Your Copyright Fangs

## In This Chapter

▶ Registering your copyright

▶ Depositing copies of your work in the Library of Congress

▶ Putting the correct copyright notice on copies of your work

▶ Drawing on government resources

*A*s we explain in Chapter 12, you don't have to do anything to get a copyright, except create and own an original work of authorship (OWA). However, if you're a U.S. resident, before you can go to court and stop a copycat, you must first register your copyright with the Copyright Office, a part of the Library of Congress. Luckily for you, in most cases, the registration is a relatively simple and inexpensive process that you should be able to handle by yourself after you read this chapter.

If you have an unusual case and you face a complex situation that raises a legal issue (we flag them along the way throughout this chapter), consult a copyright attorney. By the way, Congress wants its library to accumulate a collection of every substantial OWA that's published in this country — without paying for it. So, you're obligated by law to deposit two copies of the best edition of your work in the Copyright Office.

In this chapter, we tell you how to comply with both registration and deposit requirements in the most practical and economical way. Then we explain the purpose, advantages, and proper manner of applying a copyright notice on copies of your creation. We also explain how to take advantage of government resources and take care of some administrative and housekeeping matters.

## *Making It Official: Registration*

Registering a copyright consists essentially of filling out an official application form provided by the Copyright Office, filing it along with a nominal fee ($45 at the time of this writing), and submitting some material that identifies your creation. When the good people in the Copyright Office get to your application in three to six months, they'll either stamp it and return it to you as a proof of registration, send you a request for more info, or heaven forbid, flatly reject it because you didn't follow our directions.

Seems pretty straightforward, doesn't it? Hold your horses. As with all legal formalities, a few tricky twists and turns await you along the way that require careful consideration about when to apply for registration: which form you should use; how to answer some of the cryptic questions on the form; and what kind of identifying material to send. Don't worry. We go over all that, but as an incentive to register your copyright, we start by telling you all the good things the registration will accomplish for you.

Registration, unlike deposit, isn't mandatory. That's what they say, but don't believe it. If there is a chance someone might copy or unlawfully use your work, you'll want it to be registered. Because discretion is the better part of valor (or of a savvy business mind), and the bad guys really are out there, we strongly recommend that you always register the copyright in your creations.

### Getting to court

The main reason for registering your copyright is to give you the right to file an action for infringement in a U.S. district court. Basically, *infringement* is the unauthorized use of a copyrighted work (see Chapter 12 for an explanation of copyright infringement and Chapter 21 for ways to stop infringers in their tracks). Unless you're a foreign resident, you can't file a complaint against a copycat if you didn't register your copyright.

Foreigners don't have to register their copyright before going to court, because on March 1, 1989, the U.S. joined an international treaty called the Berne Convention that says: "*The enjoyment and the exercise of copyright shall not be subject to any formalities.*" However, this prohibition applies only to "*countries other than the country of origin.*" This means that the U.S. can't impose any formalities upon foreign copyright claimants, but can subject *you* to any red tape Congress may devise.

The Copyright Office may take months to process your application and con-firm the registration, but don't fret — it's supposed to be effective from the day it reaches the Office. You can send your application today, and file an infringement complaint tomorrow. If the judge finds your application in good order and upholds your complaint, she may direct the U.S. marshal to seize infringing goods and issue a restraining order to suspend all infringing activi-ties. If the validity or your application is iffy, she may wait to see what the Copyright Office does with it before issuing her orders (see the "Getting Help from Uncle Sam" section, later in this chapter, to expedite your registration).

### Making it legal

A registration made within five years of the publication of your work becomes *prima facie* (legally sufficient) proof that your copyright is valid. After you introduce the registration in evidence, the burden of proof shifts to the infringing defendant, who must then establish the invalidity of your copyright or use another persuasive defense like "The devil made me do it."

### Giving public notice

Registration puts potential infringers on notice that your work is copyrighted, preventing copycats from pleading ignorance. Imagine that some deceitful character named Zook convinces The Bamboozle Company that he's the author of your song or the owner of the copyright. For a fee, Zook feloniously grants Bamboozle a license to record your ballad. In an action brought against Zook and Bamboozle, the latter can't plead ignorance and innocent infringement. The law presumes that the company checked the ownership of the copyright in the records of the Copyright Office.

### Making the most of your day in court

We hope you never have to bring a legal action to stop an infringement of your copyright, but if you do, it's good to go into court as soon as you can, armed with all the evidence you need to win your case.

- ✔ **Collecting more at court:** If you registered before the infringement, you can ask for statutory rather than actual damages. *Statutory damages,* contrary to actual damages, don't require proof and accounting of your losses. Instead, the judge looks at the conduct of the defendant to determine how much to give you, much like with punitive damages in a personal injury action. If you haven't yet exploited your work, you may be unable to show actual loss that you can attribute to the defendant's conduct. That's when statutory damages are a better deal. Even better, the law specifies minimum statutory damage amounts — which may top the amount of losses you could document and prove in court.

  Having your registration on file before your copyright is infringed also allows you to receive an award of attorney's fees when you win the infringement action. Considering what lawyers charge these days, that award may far exceed any actual or statutory damages.

- ✔ **Getting a second chance:** Your registration may be refused for a number of reasons, such as lack of substantiality, lack of original creativity, or mere functionality of the work (see Chapter 12). Of course, the refusal is the opinion of an application examiner and is never final. Talk to your copyright attorney. If, in his opinion, your application for registration has some merit, he'll suggest an appeal to a federal district court. An appeal takes time. (That's why it's always advisable to file your application for registration as early as possible and get the matter settled before you need to sue someone.)

  If you don't have time to pursue an appeal and want to go after an infringer right away, file a lawsuit despite the refused application, and name the Register of Copyright as additional defendant. The judge will first decide whether the denial of your registration was justified. If you win this first round, you're back in the game. If you lose it, you can either appeal to a federal circuit court of appeals or give up.

### Other benefits

Although getting to sue infringers is a primary benefit to registering your copyright, there are others:

- ✔ **Cashing in on your copyright:** Your registration is a public notice of your copyright claim. People interested in licensing your work or creating a derivative version can check the records of the Copyright Office, find your address, and offer you the deal of your life.

- ✔ **Stopping imported knockoffs:** If you file your certificate of registration with the U.S. Customs Service, its agents can stop the importation of counterfeit works without you having to go to court or know the identity of the infringer. The suspected goods will be impounded and destroyed after a period of time, unless their owners challenge the seizure in court within a specified period. We get into this in detail in Chapter 21.

## Timing is everything: When to register

To get the maximum protection, you should register your copyright within three months from first sale, distribution, or other disposition of your work. Any of these acts constitutes a *publication* of your work. That way you're covered for any infringement that took place right after the publication and before registration. But you don't have to wait that long. You may gain the following advantages by doing a pre-publication registration:

- ✔ Your pre-publication application allows you to confront and resolve any eventual registration problems very early in the game.

- ✔ The pre-publication registration acts as an early notice of your claim. It allows you to ask for statutory damages and attorney's fees from an early copycat or other infringer.

- ✔ The requirements for a pre-publication registration are less stringent than for a post-publication registration — you need to submit only one informal copy of your work, such as a manuscript.

- ✔ You don't have to file a post-publication registration unless you have added copyrightable material to your work.

- ✔ In a pre-publication application, you may group a number of related works, such as a series of posters or postcards in a single application. After publication, you can only bundle works that were published together, forcing you to file multiple applications.

- ✔ If you are creating a computer program or database that will be sold on CD-ROM, you can delete or block out trade secrets and other sensitive information from the copy of the program you submit with your pre-publication application. However, if you don't register until after publication, you can't omit anything from the required CD-ROM deposit copy. (See the sidebar "Preserving trade secrets in computer programs.")

# Finding and Filling Out Forms

Unless you opt to file your registration online as we discuss later in this chapter, you must apply for registration by using one or more of the forms supplied by the Copyright Office, whether you're applying for a pre-publication or post-publication registration. The choice of forms is dictated by the nature of the work in accordance with the categories listed in Chapter 12 or some special circumstances as we explain below. On these forms the applicant is referred to as the *copyright claimant* rather than the copyright owner, because until your application is approved, you can't be certain that you own a valid copyright.

- **Form TX:** All writings except plays, including computer programs.

- **Form VA:** Pictorial, graphic, sculptural, and architectural works, and any other unlisted visual art you may have created.

- **Form PA:** Musical, dramatic, pantomimes, and choreographic works. Motion pictures and other audio-visual works.

- **Form SR:** Sound recording works.

- **Form SE:** Serial works published in successive, numbered, and dated issues such as newspapers, magazines, newsletters, and other periodicals.

- **Form G/DN:** Complete month's issue of a newspaper.

- **Form GR/CP:** Group of individual contributions to a periodical, used always in addition to an application on form TX, VA, or PA.

- **Form RE:** Renewing a pre-1978 copyright registration.

- **Form CA:** Correcting or amplifying a prior registration, but not for changes in the content of a work (that requires a brand-new application). Also for correcting errors in the copyright notice (see "Marking Your Copyrighted Work," later in this chapter) appearing on the deposited copies or to reflect changes in ownership that occurred on or after the registration date.

You can use short versions of Forms TX, VA, and PA if you and your work satisfy these four requirements:

- You're the sole author and owner of the copyright (see Chapter 13 for info on ownership issues), and you're still alive (check your pulse).

- The work doesn't incorporate any pre-existing material (see Chapter 12).

- The work isn't a *work made for hire* (WMFH; see Chapter 13).

Get application forms by writing to the U.S. Copyright Office at 101 Independence Ave. S.E., Washington, DC 20559-6000 or by calling 202-707-9100. You can also access forms online at www.copyright.gov/forms.

## Handling multi-category works

Your work may include materials that fall into different categories. For example, a book about impressionist paintings probably contains a literary work and a number of pictorial works. A video production may include pictorial, dramatic, and choreographic works. You don't have to file a separate form for each work — just use the form for the work that's most prevalent in your creation. One registration will cover multiple copyrights in a single work, as long as you list all the categories on the application.

As with other legal matters, there are exceptions. Courts have been inconsistent when deciding whether a registration for a computer program on Form TX also covers the graphics generated by the program and displayed on a computer screen. Most judges have ruled in the affirmative, but it's a good idea to also file Form VA to cover the screen displays.

## Avoiding common mistakes

Although copyright registration forms come with guidelines on how to fill them out, many applications are rejected or delayed because of errors.Most errors are because the applicants (and even their attorneys) misunderstand the terminology used on the forms or the basic concepts behind copyright law.

The U.S. Copyright Office will ask for a correction if your application is defective, but if the examiner can't detect errors because facts are missing from your application, you may end up with a defective or completely invalid registration. Unfortunately, you could be in the middle of an infringement action before you discover a mistake that's fatal to your case.

In the following sections, we address the most common mistakes people make when filling out these forms and give you some additional guidelines — sometimes those on the forms aren't perfectly clear. This section applies also to online applications for registration.

### Lack of a title

Just like every file in your computer needs a name, the Copyright Office needs a handle to process your application. So make sure you enter a title, any title, for the work in Section 1 of the application form. "My Creation: Volume 1" will do if you can't think of something more specific (but being a creative person, we're sure you'll do better than that). The same title must also appear on the first page of the copy of your work that you submit with the application.

### Classification errors

Verify the category (or categories) to which your work belongs by reviewing the definitions in Chapter 12. Then pick the appropriate form from the list earlier in this section. "That's so simple," Simple Simon says. Yet misclassifying your work is one of the most common mistakes found in copyright registration applications. The consequences can be costly.

The names in the following sorry case have been changed to protect the guilty parties. Ruth wrote a catchy tune entitled "Pop Went the Zit" and licensed it to Hype, Inc., an advertising agency that used it in a TV commercial. Her attorney, Ira C. Blunder, Esq., filed a copyright registration by using a videocassette of a performance of the song as a deposit copy. Ira used Form PA, identifying the work as an audio-visual production rather than a musical work. A short time later Ruth filed a copyright infringement against Hype, Inc., for using her song beyond the term of the license. Here comes the judge — who dismissed the case because Ruth didn't have a copyright registration for her song.

Her registration was invalid because it claimed an audio-visual work created by Hype, Inc., and not by Ruth. Her legal eagle then compounded his mistake by filing a correction of the registration, using Form CA. Ruth gingerly ran back to court, sure that she now had a valid registration for her song. The judge quickly ruled that she still hadn't obtained a valid registration because you can't use Form CA to correct the nature of a work.

The moral of this story: Do your homework. Read the instructions on the forms, brush up your expertise by rereading this chapter, and carefully review all the forms before you send in your registration application. If you use an attorney, make sure he's expert in the field.

### Authorship errors

Many registration applications are rejected or found defective or invalid because the authors and the nature of their creations are improperly stated on the application form.

In a non-WMFH situation (see Chapter 13), each author's complete name and the nature of her contribution must be carefully entered in Section 2 of the application form, as shown in Figure 14-1. The nature of the contribution relates to the author's action — editing text or directing an audio-visual work.

You may list an author by either his or her full real name, with a pseudonym, or skip it altogether and check the Anonymous box. But watch for the effect of your selection on the duration of the copyright as explained in Chapter 12. You can skip the birth date. But if the author passed away, the date of death must be entered.

Figure 14-1:
Application
for copyright
registration,
page 1.

When registering a work or a portion of one created as a WMFH, you need list only the name of the employer or commissioning party, as Section 2c in Figure 14-1 illustrates. In this case, the editorial revisions were made by employees of Rising Tide Studios, Inc.

So many people are confused about the WMFH issue that the application examiner sometimes asks whether you really intended to designate a contribution as a WMFH. By the time you respond, the registration certificate is delayed by another month. So we suggest that you attach an explanatory note like the one in Figure 14-2 to your application and then mark the appropriate box. Doing so tells the examiner that you understand the nature of a WMFH and speeds up your application.

**Figure 14-2:**
Explanation of a contribution as a WMFH.

> *The contribution of author* _____ *is a work made for hire because it was created:*
> ☐ by an employee of author.
> ☐ under a work made for hire contract.

### False dates

You must give the completion date of the entire work in Section 3a of the application form. That's easy enough. If the work was published, indicate the date and country of first publication in Section 3b. Giving a false date, especially one that's later than the actual date, can invalidate your registration. If you don't remember the exact day or month, enter the earliest date you earnestly believe your work may have been published.

Publication occurs when you dispose of *copies* of your work, which means that you temporarily or permanently give up possession and control of at least one copy of the work by sale, rental, lease, or free distribution. For example, temporarily lending your novel to a publisher for consideration isn't publication. But giving copies of your manuscript (even an early draft) to your friends is.

Publication concerns physical copies that can be passed around. Disposing of the original isn't a publication. Neither is performing or displaying it publicly or transmitting it over the airwaves.

### Incorrect ownership

Enter the name and address of the current copyright owner as the claimant in Section 4 of the form. A copyright owner isn't necessarily the person in possession of the original work, but the entity holding the copyright. If the owner is different from the author named in Section 2, you must indicate how the copyright passed to the claimant — by contract, assignment, will, or other form of conveyance (see Chapter 13).

An assignment or transfer of exclusive rights must be in writing and signed by the transferor. A handshake agreement won't do.

## *Improper or missing source designation*

Failing to correctly identify pre-existing material incorporated in the work can be fatal to your registration because you're claiming authorship of something you didn't create. Pre-existing material can be anything you borrowed or copied from a previous work. We show you how to avoid misstating the source of the work on your application for copyright registration (see Figure 14-3).

| EXAMINED BY | | FORM PA |
|---|---|---|
| CHECKED BY | | |
| ☐ CORRESPONDENCE<br>Yes | | FOR<br>COPYRIGHT<br>OFFICE<br>USE<br>ONLY |

**DO NOT WRITE ABOVE THIS LINE. IF YOU NEED MORE SPACE, USE A SEPARATE CONTINUATION SHEET.**

**5** **PREVIOUS REGISTRATION** Has registration for this work, or for an earlier version of this work, already been made in the Copyright Office?
☒ Yes ☐ No If your answer is "Yes," why is another registration being sought? (Check appropriate box.) ▼ If your answer is No, do **not** check box A, B, or C.
a. ☐ This is the first published edition of a work previously registered in unpublished form.
b. ☐ This is the first application submitted by this author as copyright claimant.
c. ☒ This is a changed version of the work, as shown by space 6 on this application.
If your answer is "Yes," give: **Previous Registration Number ▼** PA XXXX  **Year of Registration ▼** 2002

**6** **DERIVATIVE WORK OR COMPILATION** Complete both space 6a and 6b for a derivative work; complete only 6b for a compilation.
a **Preexisting Material** Identify any preexisting work or works that this work is based on or incorporates. ▼

ENTIRE WORK EXCEPT UNDERWATER SCENES

See instructions before completing this space.

b **Material Added to This Work** Give a brief, general statement of the material that has been added to this work and in which copyright is claimed. ▼

UNDERWATER SCENES INCLUDING MUSIC, MONOLOGUES AND EDITING

**7** a **DEPOSIT ACCOUNT** If the registration fee is to be charged to a Deposit Account established in the Copyright Office, give name and number of Account.
**Name ▼**  **Account Number ▼**

b **CORRESPONDENCE** Give name and address to which correspondence about this application should be sent. Name/Address/Apt/City/State/ZIP ▼

JON J. JONES
RISING TIDE STUDIOS, INC.
P.O. BOX 9999
HOLLYWOOD HILLS, CA 90998

Area code and daytime telephone number ( 800 ) 000-1111   Fax number ( 999 ) 000-1112
Email J.J.@RTS.com

**8** **CERTIFICATION\*** I, the undersigned, hereby certify that I am the
Check only one ▸ {
☐ author
☐ other copyright claimant
☐ owner of exclusive right(s)
☒ authorized agent of RISING TIDE STUDIOS, INC.
Name of author or other copyright claimant, or owner of exclusive right(s) ▲
}
of the work identified in this application and that the statements made by me in this application are correct to the best of my knowledge.

Typed or printed name and date ▼ If this application gives a date of publication in space 3, do not sign and submit it before that date.

JON J. JONES  Date APRIL 1, 2003

Handwritten signature (X) ▼
x _____

**9** Certificate will be mailed in window envelope to this address:

Name ▼ RISING TIDE STUDIOS, INC.
Number/Street/Apt ▼ P.O. BOX 9999
City/State/ZIP ▼ HOLLYWOOD HILLS, CA 90998

**YOU MUST:**
• Complete all necessary spaces
• Sign your application in space 8
**SEND ALL 3 ELEMENTS IN THE SAME PACKAGE:**
1. Application form
2. Nonrefundable filing fee in check or money order payable to *Register of Copyrights*
3. Deposit material
**MAIL TO:**
Library of Congress
Copyright Office
101 Independence Avenue, S.E.
Washington, D.C. 20559-6000

Fees are subject to change. For current fees, check the Copyright Office website at www.copyright.gov, write the Copyright Office, or call (202) 707-3000.

\*17 U.S.C. § 506(e): Any person who knowingly makes a false representation of a material fact in the application for copyright registration provided for by section 409, or in any written statement filed in connection with the application, shall be fined not more than $2,500.

**Figure 14-3:** Application for copyright registration, page 2.

Section 5 of the form is self-explanatory and doesn't present any serious challenge, so long as you understand the differences between published and unpublished works, and between author and copyright claimant.

### Identifying borrowed material

You must fill out Section 6 whenever the work incorporates any pre-existing material, whether or not there was a previous registration. In Section 6a, briefly identify the pre-existing material. If the pre-existing material is the bulk of the work, you can just write "The entire work except . . ." and identify the new material, as shown in Figure 14-3.

If your work is a compilation, such as a cookbook that incorporates a number of previously published or uncopyrightable recipes, you must list in section 6b your own contributions, such as collecting, selecting, and arranging the recipes and any illustrations, ratings, or commentaries.

### Administrative matters

Section 7a is for attorneys and firms that have frequent dealings with the Copyright Office and have a deposit account from which fees can be paid.

Before you mail in the form, be sure to sign the application and enclose your check for the filing fee. We cover required identifying material for deposit in the next section.

# Depositing Copies of the Work

In a separate section of the Copyright Act, and in addition to registration, the law requires that you deposit in the Copyright Office two copies of the best edition of your creation for use by the Library of Congress. The rule applies to any substantial OWA. The word *substantial* is key — the Library of Congress isn't interested in miscellany, such as commercial labels, promotional pamphlets, and Aunt Helen's speech to the Garden Club luncheon.

However, as with every legal matter, there are exceptions, exemptions, and loopholes. In this section, we explain how to take advantage of them, and in particular, how to send material with your application for registration that in most cases will exempt you from the deposit requirement.

The deposit rules are lengthy, complex, and often changed. As much as we try to streamline them and translate the legalese, you may get lost. When in doubt, don't hesitate to run for help to a copyright attorney.

## *Meeting the deposit requirement with your application for registration*

With your application for registration, you must submit one copy of the work if it is unpublished, has only been published abroad, or consists of a contribution to a collective work. For a work published in the United States, you must submit two copies of the best edition of the work within three months of the publication date. (If the work is a sound recording, you must also provide the printed material that normally accompanies the recording, such as a jacket or insert.)

### *Selecting the copies*

Send in the most recent version of your work. So long as the same author created any previous, unregistered version, the registration will cover both versions. For example, the application for registration illustrated in Figures 14-1 and 14-3 would cover the original work. Note that in the sample, there was a previous registration mentioned in Section 5 of the form.

If you're not sure which version to send, choose the one that will be exposed to the public and is most likely to be copied.

Marcel sketched a line drawing, obtained a pre-publication registration for it, and applied a version of his design on T-shirts, which became hot sellers. Soon Keith, Marcel's competitor, copied the design, so Marcel sued Keith for infringement of the copyright in his T-shirt — that's for the entire design on his T-shirt including an adaptation of his drawing.

"Marcel and his T-shirt are all wet," Keith told the judge. "They're not covered by a registration." "You're so right," answered the magistrate, "I can see straight through it as if it were a wet T-shirt." He threw the case out of court. The drawing and the T-shirt are two distinct and different OWAs. Marcel should've sued for infringement of his drawing, or he should've filed an application for registration of his T-shirt design before going after Keith.

### *Sending photographs of three-dimensional works*

Three-dimensional objects and flat objects exceeding 96 inches in any dimension should be deposited as photographs, photoprints, or some other two-dimensional representation, except in the following situations where you must provide the real McCoy:

- ✔ Post-publication registration of a globe, relief model, or relief map
- ✔ Post-publication registration of a game consisting of multiple parts that are packaged in a container with flat sides and dimensions no greater than 12x24x6 inches, such as a Monopoly brand of board game

- ✔ Works reproduced on three-dimensional containers that can be readily opened out, slit at the corners, or otherwise made flat for storage and don't exceed 96 inches in any dimension, such as a cardboard model of a building

- ✔ Jewelry made of base metal (not gold, silver, or platinum) not exceeding 4 inches in any dimension

- ✔ Works or articles that are part of the registration of a published educational kit where the kit also includes a literary or audio-visual work

The photographs or photoprints must disclose the entire work shown from every side. If the work is already published, the copyright notice must appear in one of the photographs. You may add a close-up of the notice if it's not clearly visible on one of photographs. Mark all photographs or photoprints with the title of the work.

You must provide at least one dimension of the work by placing a ruler next to it when taking a picture or marking its dimensions on the back of a photograph or photoprint.

### Exceptions: Submitting a single copy of a published work

In some cases, you only need to send one copy or set of identifying materials with a post-publication registration:

- ✔ Three-dimensional cartographic representations, such as globes and relief models.

- ✔ Diagrams that illustrate scientific or technical information in linear or other two-dimensional form, such as architectural or engineering blueprints or mechanical drawings.

- ✔ Greeting cards, picture postcards, and stationery.

- ✔ Lectures, sermons, speeches (including Aunt Helen's), and addresses that are published individually and not as a collection of works.

- ✔ Musical compositions published in printed copies only, or both printed copies and electronic sound recordings, if the only publication took place by rental, lease, or lending.

- ✔ Published multimedia kits or any part thereof.

- ✔ Literary, dramatic, and musical works embodied in sound recordings. This exemption doesn't apply to the registration of a sound recording itself (see Chapter 12 for a definition of a sound recording).

- ✔ Choreographic works, pantomimes, and literary, dramatic, and musical works published only as part of motion pictures.

- Two-dimensional games, decals, fabric patches or emblems, calendars, instructions for needlework, and craft kits.

- Works appearing on three-dimensional containers such as boxes, cases, and cartons.

- Motion pictures. However, see the section on special deposit requirements later in this chapter.

- Computer programs with deleted portions as explained in the "Preserving trade secrets in computer programs" sidebar.

## Preserving trade secrets in computer programs

Computer programs often include proprietary processes you don't want to disclose to your competitors. Although material deposited in the Copyright Office for the Library of Congress may be accessible to the public, you can prevent unscrupulous copying by taking the following steps.

CD-ROMs are subject to more stringent post-publication requirements than other forms of recordings. If you plan to distribute your computer program on CD-ROM, make sure you file your application for registration before publication. If your computer program will be embodied in another type of machine-readable medium such as magnetic tapes or disks, punch tapes or cards, or firmware, you may wait until after the distribution of copies to file your registration.

However, you don't have to submit entire copies of your source code, but only *identifying material* (material that's sufficient to recognize your computer program without revealing the whole contents), consisting of partial source and object code, in one of these five formats:

- The first and last 25 pages of the source code, including the page bearing the copyright notice in the case of a post-publication deposit. You can block out pages containing sensitive information, if the blocked-out portion is smaller than the remaining portion.

- The first and last 10 pages of the source code listing with no blocked-out portion.

- The first and last 25 pages of the object code, together with 10 or more consecutive pages of the source code with no blocked-out portion.

- For computer programs consisting of 50 pages or less, the entire source code listing with up to 49 percent blocked out.

- If you're claiming the copyright in a revised portion of the program not contained in the first and last 25 pages, you must add 20 pages of source code representative of the revised material with no blocked-out portion. Alternately, provide any 50 pages of the source code representative of the revised material, with up to 49 percent of these 50 pages blocked out.

### Watching for special deposit requirements

The copyright registration of some types of works requires the submission of additional material:

- **Motion pictures:** The published or unpublished copy must be accompanied by a separate description of its contents, such as a synopsis or press book. (This goes for the video of your toddler's first steps, too.)

- **Works published on CD-ROM (including computer programs and databases):** The submission must consist of the entire CD-ROM package, including the instruction manual, and a printed version of the work embodied in the CD-ROM. In the case of a computer program, you must also submit a printout of the first and last 25 pages of the source code.

- **Holograms:** The submitted copy must include precise instructions for displaying the holographic images and photographs or other identifying material that clearly shows the displayed images.

- **Works published in both machine-readable and visually perceptible material:** The submission must consist of both types of materials. If the machine-readable material is on CD-ROM, however, you only need to include the identifying portion of the CD-ROM material: the title of the work, the copyright notice, and a portion of the work representative of the copyrightable contents.

### Asking for special relief

If the required material would cause you hardship, you may ask the Register of Copyrights for special relief, such as an alternate form of submission or the return of a valuable deposit copy. For example, supplying a copy of an expensive limited edition of a print may be prohibitive, or supplying an entire copy would be easier than providing any required identifying material.

## Formal deposit of the best edition

If you followed our instructions about the submission of material with your application for registration, you've probably fulfilled the requirement to deposit copies of the best edition of your work. However, if you only filed for a pre-publication registration, the Copyright Office may decide that the material you submitted isn't fit for conservation in the Library of Congress and request two published copies. If you don't comply, you face more than $2,500 in fines plus an invoice to cover the cost of purchasing the two copies on the open market.

If you didn't register your copyright (you'd be foolish not to), you must deposit two copies within three months of publication.

## Filing your application online

We hardly can believe it. The Copyright Office is entering the digital era — though very slowly. The Office is in the process of implementing an online registration procedure. The greatly simplified application process will use a single CO form for all types of OWAs. In July 2007, the Office initiated a beta-testing phase open to public participation. That test is still running, meaning you may take advantage of it and of the reduced ($35) filing fee. For more up-to-date information, see the Copyright Office Web site or go directly to `www.copyright.gov/fedreg/2007/72fr30641.html`.

# Marking Your Copyrighted Work

Placing a copyright notice on every published copy of your work, in one of the forms outlined below, fulfills some important functions. It

- ✔ Warns people that the work is covered by copyright and deters infringement.
- ✔ Prevents a person charged with infringement from claiming innocence.
- ✔ Increases damage awards for willful infringement.
- ✔ Improves your chance of foiling infringers with procedures such as restraining orders, preliminary injunctions, and seizure of counterfeit goods. A restraining order or a preliminary injunction stops the infringer until a trial on the issue or an amicable settlement of the case.
- ✔ Identifies the copyright owner.
- ✔ Informs the public of the date of publication.

## Formatting the copyright notice

A copyright notice consists of three elements:

- ✔ The word *Copyright,* the abbreviation *Copr,* or the symbol ©. Use the *circled P* in the case of a sound recording.
- ✔ The year the work was first published (distributed).
- ✔ The identification of the copyright owner (name, abbreviation, or symbol by which the name can be recognized).

Always use the © symbol. It's the only one recognized by certain countries under the Universal Copyright Convention.

If your creation incorporates material generated by the government, such as statistical tables, maps, or census data, exclude that material in your notice:

*©2003 Jane Deer excluding census data tables.*

*©2003 Jane Deer text excluding tables and maps.*

## Placing the notice

Depending on the nature of the work, you need to place the notice in a conspicuous place:

- **Book:** On the first page, the title page, or the back of the title page.

- **Magazine or other periodical:** Same as for a book or near the title, volume number, and date. One notice covers all articles in the periodical, except for advertising by someone other than the magazine owner.

- **Collective work:** On each separate contribution under or near the title or at the end of the contribution.

- **Work on machine-readable media:** Disks, tapes, or CD-ROMs must display the notice at sign-on, near the title, at the end of the screen-displayed image, on printouts, or on the medium or its container.

- **Movie or other audio-visual work:** Embodied into the work's medium, so that the notice appears near the title, at the beginning or end of the work, or with the cast of characters or credits. If the work lasts 60 seconds or less, the notice can be on the film or tape leader. The notice must also appear on the permanent housing (cassette body) or container (cardboard pocket).

- **Pictorial, graphic, or sculptural work:** On any visible part of the work. If the work is too small or doesn't have a front or back surface that can bear the notice, use a label or tag attached to the work.

- **Phonorecord:** On the label or any visible portion of the phonorecord.

You don't have to place a copyright notice on the original work, only on copies. If the work is not yet published, you don't need to have a notice, but displaying it on copies anyway is a good idea — just in case they fall into some unscrupulous person's hands. Just write it as *©2003 Jane Deer (unpublished).*

# Getting Help from Uncle Sam

During the last few years, the Copyright Office has greatly expanded the assistance services it provides to the public. Take advantage of the following resources (hey, they're free):

- ✔ A well-designed Web site at www.copyright.gov.

- ✔ An instant information service, available by calling 202-707-3000. The TTY line is 202-707-6737.

- ✔ User-friendly forms and very informative brochures that you can download from the Web site or order by phone at the previous numbers. Call 202-707-2600 to have explanatory circulars on most copyright topics (but not forms) faxed to you.

  Use the 24-hour Publication Hotline (202-707-9100) if you know which circular or form you need.

Direct mail enquiries to Library of Congress, Copyright Office, 101 Independence Avenue, S.E., Washington, DC 20559-6000.

Under the following very limited, extenuating circumstances, you may request to have your application expedited (which means your certificate of registration will be sent to you within two or three weeks instead of months):

- ✔ Copyright litigation.

- ✔ Import of counterfeit copies into the United States. File your registration with U.S. Customs so that its agents can seize the infringing goods.

- ✔ Contract or publishing deadline that depends your copyright registration.

You must request special handling in a letter accompanying your application for registration, explaining how you meet one or more of these special circumstances. You must pay an additional fee of about $700, along with the regular registration fee. Send your request and application to the Special Handling Department of the Copyright Office. For the P.O. Box number and specific fee amount, check Circular 10 on the Copyright Office Web site, www.copyright.gov, or call 202-707-3000.

## *Recording Copyright Documents*

Documents such as assignments, license agreements, court orders, and any legal papers affecting the rights of a copyright owner may be recorded in the Copyright Office where they're accessible to the general public and act as *constructive notice* to anyone. For example, you may want to record an assignment to you of Bill's copyright in his song, in order to warn people that they should deal with you and not Bill if they want a license to use the song.

You can send a copy in place of an original document providing it's accompanied by a sworn or official certification that it's a true copy of the original. Consult an attorney about what may constitute a valid certification. It varies depending upon the type of document and its source.

You should include a document cover sheet, available from the Copyright Office, and your check for the applicable recording fee.

# Part IV
# Protecting Your Commercial Identity

The 5th Wave                    By Rich Tennant

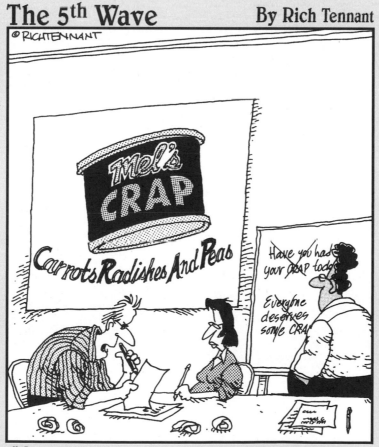

"How about this—'It's not just CRAP, it's Mel's CRAP'? Shoot! I hate coming up with a sales pitch for this client!"

# In this part . . .

Sure, you're probably familiar with that little ™ trademark symbol. But did you know that several other types of commercial identifiers, including trade names, service marks, and package configurations, are just sitting there waiting for you to put them into the game as well? All these commercial identifiers have a common purpose — to put an exclusive (and hopefully favorable) brand on your goods and services and give you an edge over your competition. We devote this part to breaking down the Xs and Os so that you can use the right commercial identifier for the job at hand.

We also demonstrate (with plenty of examples) what makes an effective mark and what types of identifiers you should avoid. After you decide to draft one or more of these players, you still need to make sure that they're the best pick. We lay out a game plan that walks you through the search for look-alikes (and sound-alikes) and outline how to register and use your trademark or servicemark.

# Chapter 15

# Flashing Your Badge

● ● ● ● ● ● ● ● ● ● ● ● ● ● ● ● ● ● ● ● ● ● ● ● ● ● ● ● ● ● ● ● ● ● ● ● ● ● ● ● ● ● ● ● ● ● ● ● ●

*In This Chapter*

▶ Understanding the roles and functions of commercial identifiers

▶ Making the most of your trade name or trademark

▶ Appraising the weight of a commercial identifier

▶ Striving for exclusive rights by using a distinctive moniker

● ● ● ● ● ● ● ● ● ● ● ● ● ● ● ● ● ● ● ● ● ● ● ● ● ● ● ● ● ● ● ● ● ● ● ● ● ● ● ● ● ● ● ● ● ● ● ● ●

*A* commercial identifier, such as your company name, the brand on your product, or the street name of your service facilities, is a goodwill ambassador, a herald, a promise — it's the first thing a customer sees or hears about your firm or your product. This first contact often determines the customer's attitude toward the business or product that the name identifies. Your commercial identifiers are your prime marketing tools. They also help the customer choose among a range of similar products or services.

When you start a new business or introduce a new product or service, you get a chance to create value out of nothing. By selecting strong, protectable, and effective commercial identifiers, you get inexpensive protection for your enterprise and the chance to catapult your products or services into a dominant market position. Yet the majority of businesspeople don't give this process much thought.

In this chapter, we define some terms and lead you through the maze of business names, trademarks, servicemarks, and other commercial handles and signposts. We also lay out how these commercial identifiers play a key role in any business, and perhaps most important, give you some ideas on what constitutes a distinctive and legally protectable trade name or trademark.

## A Commercial Identifier Inventory

We confess that we misused the term *trademark* in the title of this book. A trademark is actually just one type of commercial mark — the one that you apply to a product rather than a service establishment — even though it's commonly used to generically designate all kinds of commercial identifiers. But commercial identifiers are actually divided into three groups:

- **Product identifiers:** Commonly known as brands and formally called trademarks

- **Service identifiers:** Include servicemarks, certification marks, and membership marks (or association marks)

- **Company identifiers:** Also called *trade names* — typically these are business names and logos

In the sections that follow, we look at each of these identifiers in depth.

## *Marking a product*

The product identifiers most folks are familiar with are trademarks. A *trademark* is any name, word, phrase, slogan, symbol, design, shape, or characteristic that, when associated with a product, distinguishes it from other similar products. For example, the word Kodak is a trademark.

But any non-functional characteristic of a product or package can act as a product identifier. Without reading the words on the package, you know that a yellow package identifies a Kodak film, whereas a green box means Fuji.

Distinctive shapes, colors, and ornamentations of products, packaging, or places of business can act as product identifiers and are referred to as either *trade dress, configuration marks,* or *design marks;* whether they refer to the shape or color of the product or its packaging.

Here are some well-known examples of product identifiers:

- Dr Pepper, a mark identifying a soft drink

- "When it rains it pours," found on salt containers

- The circled three-pointed star symbol on the hood of a German car

- The log cabin shape of a maple syrup container

- The pink color of an insulating glass-wool material

- The fragrance of a laundry detergent

- The characteristic exhaust sound of an American-made motorcycle

The list is endless. Anything that customers can associate with a product that influences buying decisions qualifies as a product identifier (see Figure 15-1).

**Figure 15-1:**
Config-
uration
mark or
trade dress.

# Identifying a service

A *service identifier* is any name, word, phrase, slogan, symbol, tune, design, or characteristic that distinguishes a service from similar services offered by others. These include servicemarks, certification marks, and membership marks. For example, the mission church facade and tiled roof of a food service establishment identifies Taco Bell fast-food services. A squat building with a red-lined, square-topped roof designates a Pizza Hut restaurant. Here are some other well-known servicemarks:

- ✔ Mr. Goodwrench for an automotive repair service
- ✔ Prudential for financial services
- ✔ A red cross for the services of an international charitable organization
- ✔ The blue color of an airplane that tells you it's part of Jet Blue Airlines services
- ✔ The clownish character of the Jack in the Box chain of fast-food restaurants (see Figure 15-2)

As with product identifiers, there's no limit to what you may use to singularize your business and catch the attention of the customer.

A *certification mark,* shown in Figure 15-3, is a service identifier used to approve or certify the quality, accuracy, safety, performance, or authenticity of another's product or service. Some well known certification marks are

- ✔ The Good Housekeeping seal
- ✔ The Underwriters Laboratories seal

**Figure 15-2:**
Jack-in-
the-Box
restaurant
character
service-
mark.

**Figure 15-3:**
Certification
marks.

A certification mark differs from any other type of mark because its owner can't use it to qualify its own goods or services, but only the products or services of others.

A *membership* or *association mark* is another category of service identifier that indicates affiliation with an association. Membership marks are placed on badges, cloth patches, membership cards, pennants, and letterheads. They include political parties' emblems and distinctive religious symbols. See Figure 15-4 for an example. Some well-known membership marks are

✔ The Toastmasters International logo.

✔ The Girl Scouts of America trefoil design.

**Figure 15-4:**
Membership
mark.

In general, servicemarks fall under the same laws and regulations as trademarks. Certification marks and membership marks, however, are subject to special formalities and requirements that we address in Chapter 18.

## Naming a company

A company identifier, or *trade name,* identifies a firm and takes a few different forms:

- ✔ **Legal name:** This identifier appears on tax returns, judicial and administrative documents, and other official papers. Two well-known trade names are General Motors Corporation and Allstate Property and Casualty Company.

- ✔ **Shortened version of an official name:** Examples include General Motors, GMC, or Allstate. This abbreviation is sometimes called a *d.b.a.* (doing business as).

- ✔ **Adorned names:** These identifiers are also called *logotypes,* such as the word Allstate under the drawing of two superimposed open hands.

## Occupying multiple domains

A word or phrase can be used as a trade name, trademark, or servicemark. For instance, the letters GMC on a building could act as a trade name indicating administrative offices of the General Motors Corporation, a servicemark advertising automotive services, or a trademark promoting automotive vehicles or parts. Does it really matter? Yes, because the law treats each type of commercial identifier differently, giving more legal clout and protection to a trademark than to a trade name, as we explain in Chapter 18.

*Domain names,* which identify Web sites on the Internet, also fulfill both roles. A domain name is primarily a trade name when it resides on the World Wide Web. But it can also act as a trademark or servicemark when it's part of an advertisement, such as Ditech.com on TV.

# Putting Commercial Identifiers to Work

An effective commercial identifier, be it your trade name, trademark, or servicemark, plays three roles in your business scheme. It

- Promotes your products or services.
- Protects you against copycat imitations and other unfair appropriation of your reputation and goodwill.
- Generates profit when you exploit or trade it.

If a name is distinctive and appealing, it advantageously positions your products or services on the market, giving you a greater degree of promotion, protection, and profit. Customers easily remember and recognize the name and, therefore, are motivated to patronize your store or buy your product.

The distinctiveness of the identifier translates into legal clout, which in turn helps to protect your market position. (See the "Testing the Legal Strength of Commercial Identifiers" section, later in this chapter.) As the identifier gathers strength and reputation, it becomes a valuable commodity that you can lucratively exploit.

## Promoting your product or service

A good commercial identifier motivates the person who sees or hears it to buy the product or service it identifies, or it steers the potential customer toward the company that uses it as a trade name. Here are a couple examples:

- The trademark Mountain Dew, with its refreshing imagery of Alpine meadows under glittering dewdrops, suggests refreshment to the thirsty individual and motivates him to buy the soft drink it represents.

✔ A traveling businesswoman arrives in town after a long overnight flight. She has an important interview and needs to have her hair professionally done. In the phone book, she spots listings for Romance Stylists and Ernie's Salon. The lady has no idea about the reputation of these two establishments. But, chances are, she'll select the classy, glamorous-sounding listing and give poor Ernie the cold shoulder. The owner of the Romance Stylists shop has gained another customer, thanks to her motivating servicemark.

After a customer experiences and appreciates the quality of a product sold under a particular mark, he'll naturally return to it whenever he's faced with a choice between the known brand and several similar products. He'll also tend to recommend the product to a friend, who identifies it by its label.

Products that are identified with an inspiring and motivating trademark may promote themselves with little or no publicity. But if your identifier isn't very stimulating, your products must rely on their own merits or on a well-orchestrated and costly advertising campaign.

When you launch a new product under a unique and inspiring handle, the product acquires an advantageous market position that may be impregnable if subsequent competitors can't use that identifier or a similar one. For example, there's no patent or other legal impediment keeping you from manufacturing and marketing hook-and-loop fabric fastener strips. But how can you make any inroad into the market without using or referring to the Velcro mark, which confers a dominant market position to the pre-existing product, and contributes to the product's promotion and protection.

On the other hand, a mark like Treadmill on a line of treadmill exercisers is too generic to give you much marketing clout. Because you're not the only one making treadmills, your mark would also benefit your competition. And, if you later manufacture other exercise equipment, that mark won't fit.

## Protecting your product or service

When one talks about protecting a product, the first thing that comes to mind is a patent. However, the percentage of products on the market that are protected by patents is relatively low compared to products that derive their exclusive or advantageous market position from a strong identifier.

### Brand loyalty

An effective identifier favorably positions a product on the market against the competition. And anybody who introduces a new product or service can give it a protected name or mark that nobody else can use or even come close to. If the mark is fitting and memorable, the public will forever associate the mark with that product.

## Choosing marks over patents

Entrepreneurs and companies attempting to introduce a new product on the market shouldn't underestimate the broad and easily enforceable protection they can get by using a strong commercial identifier either in place of or in addition to the more costly patent protection. The legal community hasn't fully appreciated the protective role of distinctive trade names. It's no wonder that business and marketing people are, in general, unaware of the extent of protection that they can get from an effective moniker or a distinctive product configuration.

A fledgling company on a tight budget and needing effective protection for its new product should seriously consider adopting a good identifier. An identifier may be more appropriate and, in the long run, more effective at competitively positioning the product than a patent, which takes several years and large expenditures before it is granted and is difficult and expensive to enforce. A patent involves a public disclosure of the product's composition or manufacturing process and has a limited life. By contrast, a commercial identifier can be readily created, is valid as long as it is used, and can be expeditiously enforced, as we show you in Chapter 21.

Depending on your product, a commercial identifier is no substitute for a strong patent, but a good one may offer just the right degree of protection necessary to propel a product or service to a secure market position.

We'll bet a bottle of our favorite tequila that you can't name a competing brand to Velcro. What name comes to mind when you're in dreaming of feminine lingerie? Probably Victoria's Secret. These exemplary identifiers say nothing about the products, yet how effective they are!

After a customer is used to referring to a particular product or service by an effective *proprietary name* (legal jargon for a name that can only be used by its owner), that customer tends to ignore similar products or services offered by other companies with less familiar or less inspiring designations.

### The long arm of the law

After a product or service is favorably positioned on the market, a strong identifier protects it against unfair competition. The misappropriation of a trade name, trademark, or servicemark, or using a confusingly similar one, is prohibited by law. Such acts can be stopped by judicial orders, which are sometimes accompanied by seizure and destruction of the counterfeit goods or the closure of the offending establishment. See the "Testing the Legal Strength of Commercial Identifiers" section, later in this chapter, for all the ins, outs, and upside-downs on commercial identifiers and the law.

## Creating a new source of income

In ancient Egypt, names were believed to have an existence of their own, separate from the persons or things they designated. Commercial identifiers have turned this belief into a reality. Not only do commercial identifiers have an existence of their own, but they're also assets worth a lot of money. When you sell the business, that value can be converted into cold, hard cash. However, you can even "sell" the name and still own it, if you exploit the identifier in one of these ways:

- ✔ **Licensing:** This arrangement allows someone else to manufacture your product under your mark. For example, a shirt sold under the Hang Ten trademark may have been manufactured by a licensee of Hang Ten International.

- ✔ **Merchandising:** Under this method, you lease the use of your mark to others on a multitude of unrelated goods. Have you ever played with Star Wars toys? If so, you can see how the force is with LucasFilms.

- ✔ **Franchising:** A *franchise* is a contractual arrangement authorizing another firm to render services under your commercial identifier, such as McDonald's or Best Western. Franchising often includes some transfer of know-how and technical assistance by the franchisor to ensure the success, quality, and reputation of the products or services.

In a licensing, merchandising, and franchising venture, the company that owns the underlying commercial identifier is responsible for the wholesomeness and safety of the products or services. That company must, by law, exercise effective quality control over the products or services. We discuss all these options in greater detail in Chapter 20.

Although commercial identifiers aren't expressly bought and sold, they're indirectly the most traded commodity. Let's count the ways:

- ✔ When you buy a burger and fries from McDonald's, you're paying a few cents for the use of the famous name by the restaurant's owner, along with the dollars you're handing over for the meat and potatoes.

- ✔ If you're selling a business, you're not only selling your inventory and equipment, but also your *goodwill,* the company's reputation and recognition in the marketplace, that's represented by the company's trade name and trademarks.

- ✔ When stocks are bought and sold, investors are influenced by the value and performance of the company, represented by its trade name or trademark. For example, Consolidated Foods changed its name to Sara Lee in order to increase the value of that company's stock. The strategy worked and was the prime factor in doubling the value of the company's shares within the following 12 months.

# Testing the Legal Strength of Commercial Identifiers

Every IP right is based on a number of subtle legal concepts, and commercial identifiers are no different. Your right to the *exclusive* use of a commercial identifier and your ability to prevent imitations depend on two factors — its *distinctiveness* and the *unlikelihood of confusion* with other pre-existing identifiers. The more unique the trade name or trademark and the more dissimilar it is from commercial identifiers already in use, the easier it is to get court orders against a competitor trying to confuse the public with names that look, sound, or even feel like yours.

## Working toward distinctiveness

In "Putting Commercial Identifiers to Work," earlier in this chapter, we detail how distinct identifiers can help you promote products and services and turn a profit. But in this section, we concentrate on how distinctiveness affects your ability to legally protect your name or mark in the courts.

Trade names and trademarks have different degrees of distinctiveness. You can't protect a name or mark that exhibits no distinctiveness at all — and who would want to? If the mark isn't distinctive, it's completely useless and can even jeopardize your legal rights, as described in Chapter 18.

But as the level of distinctiveness increases, so does the legal strength of the moniker. By the term *legal strength,* we mean its clout — the ability to prevent others from using the same (or a confusingly similar) trade name or trademark. Position your company or product on an impregnable pinnacle by selecting very distinctive identifiers. The distinctiveness of a commercial identifier (or lack of it) can be laid out on a four-part legal strength scale:

- Generic: Think Apple when used to sell apples

- Descriptive: Think Apple when used to sell pies

- Suggestive: Think Apple when used to sell computers

- Arbitrary: Think ELPPA when used to sell anything (Unless this is an acronym for the Elephant Liposuction Prevention Program Authority that we're not aware of)

Only suggestive and arbitrary identifiers are inherently distinctive. Descriptive names or marks can sometimes become distinctive over time. A generic term is a dud incapable of identifying or protecting anything.

In case you're tempted, the law doesn't extend much protection to family names, and their registration as trademarks or servicemarks is subject to severe restriction. Check out Chapters 16 and 18 for information on the pitfalls of using your name.

### Starting with the generic

*Generic* trade names and trademarks (also *commonly descriptive* ones) have no legal strength at all because they're mere dictionary definitions that apply to all products or services of a kind no matter their sources, and the courts allow no one to monopolize the common language.

How about a simple example? Previously, we pointed out that using the trademark Treadmill for treadmill exercisers isn't very creative or effective from a marketing standpoint. It also brings other baggage:

✔ Somebody else probably is already using the same word as part of a trade name or trademark for a similar product, which is likely to drag you into damaging conflicts, consumer confusion, and costly litigation.

✔ Legally, it would be impossible to register, and therefore difficult to enforce, such a generic label against future imitations.

Selecting that mark would be a pretty dumb move. Yet hundreds of entrepreneurs make this mistake every day when they name their companies or products.

One such company is a bedroom and bathroom-product retailer who chooses Bed & Bath as a servicemark. They then get upset when a competitor comes up with Bed Bath & Beyond, because the newcomer is likely to steal much of the goodwill already accumulated under the mark Bed & Bath. However, the original retailer couldn't do anything about it because the only two terms appearing in both servicemarks are common English words that name the type of products sold by these businesses.

Similar reasoning shows you that a muffler shop that operates under Discount Mufflers can't prevent another muffler shop from placing a "Discount Mufflers" sign over its door. Likewise, Imported Auto Parts, Discount Towing, and Auto Repair Specialists are also ineffective marks.

Don't succumb to the temptation of picking a generic term for your company or product because it confers no distinctiveness to your trade name or trademark. If you go generic, you're buying a heap of trouble.

### Moving on to descriptive

One notch above a generic term is a descriptive trade name or trademark. It's not quite the dictionary definition of your product or service, as a generic name often is, but a *descriptive* trade name or trademark still only describes a common characteristic or function of the product or service without distinguishing it from similar names.

Vision Center is a descriptive trade name for optometric services. It's not a common definition, but it tells you a lot about the services provided.

Although a descriptive name is a vast improvement over a generic one, it's not the best choice unless you can put up with a degree of risk.

The law recognizes that a descriptive trade name or trademark may eventually acquire some legal strength, and be considered distinctive, through continuous and exclusive use, extensive advertising, and the development of a reputation. Eventually, the name takes on a *secondary meaning* that identifies a specific company, product, or service.

After five years of steady and exclusive use, you can file an application for registration to legally protect your name or mark as we explain in Chapter 18, but you still have to tolerate close imitations by competitors.

The following names have acquired secondary meanings:

- ✔ The mark Marineland for a theme park featuring live sea animals is highly descriptive of any attraction featuring marine life. However, after many years of use, it's now associated with a chain of marine parks in Florida and California.

- ✔ About 100 years ago, Ford was just a family name. Now, it has become a very distinctive brand (trademark) of automotive products.

### *Reaching distinctiveness*

A distinctive name is so unique that it may have no relation to the product it identifies, or it may merely hint at some characteristics of the product. A distinctive name gives you the biggest marketing advantage and the greatest legal protection. Distinctive commercial identifiers fall into two categories:

- ✔ **Suggestive:** A suggestive identifier implies, rather than describes, a characteristic of the designated product or service:

  - • Rejuvia for skin care products doesn't describe anything specific, but does suggest rejuvenation, a fountain of youth.

  - • Old Hearth for bakery goods immediately reminds you of old-style bread making in wood-fired ovens.

  - • Visa for credit card services tells you that, armed with that company's card, you can go anywhere to buy anything.

- ✔ **Arbitrary:** An arbitrary or fanciful identifier is either a known word or phrase that has been given a new meaning or one that's totally made up. Both types are unique, original, and unlikely to be accidentally used by another business:

  - • Jellibeans for a skating rink

  - • Google for an Internet search engine

- Exxon for automotive fuels
- Lego for sets of building blocks

Arbitrary identifiers have the most legal strength. They're protected against imitation from the outset. They can muster a very broad scope of protection that goes beyond strongly similar terms, and extends over identifiers that merely suggest a relationship with existing designations.

### Courting success (and failure): Distinctiveness on trial

The protection and legal clout a trade name or mark provides is proportional to its distinctiveness. Although the strength or weakness of the identifiers wasn't the only factor weighed by the courts, the verdicts pretty much followed the rule that a good, distinctive identifier deserves a wide scope of protection, but a weak, descriptive one must endure close competition.

- ✔ The owner of the distinctive Lego trademark stopped a competitor from using the mark Mego.

- ✔ The mark Lessbucks Coffee was refused registration in view of the prior registration of Starbucks.

- ✔ The operator of a skating rink under the Jellibeans servicemark prevented a competing rink from using the servicemark Lollipops.

- ✔ Stouffer Corporation, owner of the Lean Cuisine mark, couldn't prevent a competitor from using the mark Michelina's Lean 'N Tasty.

- ✔ First National Bank of Sioux Falls, with a foolishly common and weak trade name, couldn't prevent another bank from using the equally insipid name First National Bank of South Dakota.

Look at the wide difference between Jellibeans and Lollipops! By contrast, although First National Bank of South Dakota closely resembles First National Bank of Sioux Falls, the court didn't find any confusion problem. The proof is in the originality (distinctiveness) of the name.

# Avoiding the likelihood of confusion

The second factor that affects the protection afforded to any commercial identifier is the unlikelihood of confusing it with pre-existing identifiers. State and federal laws forbid the commercial use of any trade name or trademark that is *"likely to cause confusion, or to cause mistake, or to deceive."*

When you buy a yellow package of film, you expect to find a high-quality product manufactured by the Eastman Kodak Company without reading the name on the package. You rely on the yellow color. You'd be very upset, with good reason, if you later discover that the product was made by some fly-by-night outfit. Fortunately for you — and Kodak — that can't happen in the United States because the law gives the Eastman Kodak Company several very powerful means to weed out unscrupulous entrepreneurs who try to ride on a well-known mark's trade dress (the yellow color of the package) to deceive and bamboozle unsuspecting consumers.

How far can a company go to prevent competitors from using monikers or configuration marks that are copies or imitations of its own trade names and trademarks? Or, looking at it from the opposite perspective, how close can you get to an existing commercial identifier when you select a name or trade dress (without getting your hand slapped)? The short answer is very simple: It depends. The full answer is more complex. You need to consider several critical factors to assess the likelihood of confusion between commercial identifiers. The most important is the distinctiveness of the pre-existing trade name or trademark. Other factors to consider are the similarity of the names or marks, the similarity of the goods or services, the respective channels of commerce through which the goods are marketed, the costs of the goods, and the sophistication of the typical buyer. We address this in Chapter 17.

For now, just remember that the *likelihood of confusion* test in combination with the concept of *distinctiveness* determines how much protection your commercial identifier will enjoy.

# Chapter 16

# Coining the Next Household Name

• • • • • • • • • • • • • • • • • • • • • • • • • • • • • • • • • • • • • • •

• • • • • • • • • • • • • • • • • • • • • • • • • • • • • • • • • • • • • • •

*U*nfortunately, good commercial identifiers almost never come to mind in a flash of inspiration, and they're rarely found by accident. They can't be collected with much confidence from public naming contests. Instead, they must be built painstakingly from the ground up, piece by piece, keeping the legal and marketing ramifications in mind. You can't use haphazard or subjective, and consequently unreliable, approaches to find an effective name — you need to apply a structured methodology.

We're not here to magically turn you into a professional namesmith. But we do spell out the basic steps of a methodology so that you can recognize a good commercial identifier when you see one — and come up with your own. Even more important, we give you the savvy to avoid the worst naming mistakes.

Laying out all the name-coining rules would take a dozen or so chapters. So, we simply give you the basic principles behind coining effective names the same way lawyers master the law — by studying a few prior cases. After defining the basics, we analyze a number of commercial identifiers, some more desirable than others, before suggesting practical naming techniques.

Commercial identifiers should be evaluated under two distinct criteria: marketing power and legal clout.

# Marketing Power: Components of Good Commercial Identifiers

*Marketing power* is the ability to attract customers and favorably position the business, product, or service against the competition. *Legal clout* is the capability to prevent competitors' use of the same, similar, or even vaguely related identifiers.

In Chapter 15, we touch upon the legal aspect of identifiers. Legally speaking, a good commercial identifier must be

- Distinctive
- Unlikely to be confused with another identifier

Good news: An identifier that meets these two legal factors also provides marketing power. This situation is one of those rare cosmic events where the law is pretty much in synch with the real world. And the reverse is also true: An identifier that packs a good marketing punch is also usually granted broad protection by the law.

Commercial identifiers aren't limited to names. The category also includes graphics, logos, and three-dimensional configuration marks. The same rules apply for all types of identifiers. If you use a drawing of a bicycle to identify your bicycle shop, you're using a generic designation that anybody is free to copy — and customers are free to ignore. Instead, call your bike shop, for example, Tour de France and use the Eiffel Tower as an icon to make your shop memorable and distinctive.

You must be wondering, "How can I give marketing power to my business name or other commercial identifier?" In this section, we start you down the Marketing Superhighway by outlining the three tasks a successful identifier must accomplish and by providing some case studies. Later, in the "Trying the Tricks of the Trade" section, we clue you in on tools you can use to build a savvy commercial identifier.

If you can foot the bill, we recommend working with a specialized marketing firm or a naming consultant to develop your commercial identifier. With the info in this chapter, you can be an informed client, take an active role in the process, and ensure that the identifier reflects your vision.

## A blueprint for building a commercial identifier

Commercial identifiers are your goodwill ambassadors and your best advertisements. Think about a radio or TV commercial. Its purpose is to turn the customer on to a company, service, or product. A good and effective commercial identifier does the same thing by

**A.** Attracting the attention of the targeted customer.

**B.** Establishing a bond, relationship, or common interest with the potential customer.

**C.** Offering a concrete or abstract benefit to the customer.

In a TV commercial, these three tasks are often done in 30 seconds of words and images. Your challenge in creating a commercial identifier is to perform all these tasks with a single word, a short phrase, a graphic image, or a unique package.

## Dissecting success stories

The following examples show you how a number of successful commercial identifiers have mastered their ABCs.

### Hang Ten

Hang Ten is a trademark for beachwear.

**A.** This mark gets attention with its hard-hitting sound and its intriguing word association for those who aren't familiar with its meaning.

**B.** The phrase is borrowed from Southern Californian and Hawaiian surfer jargon and refers to a maneuver where your ten toes hang over the nose of the surfboard. That meaning is reinforced by the accompanying logo of two footprints, as shown in Figure 16-1. Because the mark speaks their language, surfers, surfer wannabes, and other "beach bums" immediately recognize it and develop a feeling of kinship toward the product it identifies.

**C.** The mark screams: "Buy and wear my clothes, and you'll become one of those legendary curl-riders — or at least look like one."

**Figure 16-1:**
Hang Ten
trademark
name and
logo combi-
nation.

### Apple Computer

Apple is, of course, the trade name of a computer manufacturer, whose original logotype is shown in Figure 16-2.

**A.** Two wizards from Silicon Valley broke through the clutter of minicomputer manufacturer names like Control Data, Digital Equipment, and other quasi-generic, nerdy, techno-geek monikers by selecting a fresh, somewhat incongruous, and pleasantly evocative name that immediately caught the attention of the newbies and spurred a cultlike loyalty among many of them.

**B.** The company initially targeted the educational market — of which Apple still keeps a considerable share. What more endearing (and enduring) symbol of education than the legendary apple Johnny takes to his teacher?

**C.** That bonding symbol is reinforced by a sharp logo of an apple with a bite taken out of it. This is a powerful invitation to take a bite of the good life the company's products will bring to you.

**Figure 16-2:**
Apple Computer original trade name and logo combination.

### Amazon.com

Amazon.com is the domain name of a major retailer on the Internet.

**A.** The name is arbitrary and consequently very distinctive. It's at the beginning of the alphabet, quickly noticed, and very easy to remember.

**B.** Amazon is a very simple, easily spelled word that triggers three friendly and fascinating impressions among potential customers. First, the reference to the Amazon River conjures adventure. Second, it subliminally suggests amazement. Third, the image of Amazonian warriors suggests strength. The term is fluid, yet strong, and reinforces the imagery of strength and adventurous discoveries. It is the epitome of a customer-friendly name.

**C.** The imagery of the longest river on earth with all its tributaries spread over an immense basin symbolizes the many and vast resources of the company. It tells you that you can find anything you want on its site.

You can really see the strength and marketing power of Amazon.com when you note that the company very handily survived while other dot-coms were dropping like flies.

### NyQuil

NyQuil is a trademark for a cough medicine.

  A. Here's a distinct coined name with a fanciful sound that's concise, yet stretched out by its fluttering ending. Pure poetry, we'd say.

  B. To the person afflicted with an annoying cough, the term is soothing and endearing.

  C. The name is composed of two word fragments reminding us of "night" and "quietness" or "tranquility," and so promises a peaceful night.

# Trying the Tricks of the Trade

Namesmiths have a broad palette of elements and concepts they can draw on to paint powerful commercial identifiers. In this section, we briefly go over some of the basic and most effective technical and artistic name-coining approaches.

One of the biggest mistakes you can make is to focus too much on your company, product, or service and forget your target audience. Take some time to analyze your potential customers, and you have a better chance of choosing a name that packs a powerful punch. You can look at a number of factors to define the audience:

  ✔ **Geography:** New England and the Southwest are very different parts of the country. The servicemark Del Taco may not ring a bell for many New Englanders. By the same token, many Latinos and other Southwest residents may have no idea what Scarborough Fair "should" conjure up in their minds.

  ✔ **Age group:** Know whom you want to attract. The mark Twinkies is perfect for children; Healthy Choice probably couldn't help you there, but it does speak to an adult population concerned with their health.

  ✔ **Educational level:** You don't have to be a rocket scientist to understand and respond to marks such as Mr. Clean, Cover Girl, and Rainbird. By contrast, Arpeggio and Rejuvia are addressed to a more sophisticated audience. Microkeratome (for an eye-surgery tool) speaks only to the highly educated ophthalmologist.

You can play with other factors, such as income level, ethnicity, and even political leanings to further focus your identifier toward a specific group of customers.

## Defining the message

You have to decide what message you want your commercial identifier to convey to your targeted audience. Here again, think market rather than product or service. Don't tell the homemaker that your vacuum cleaner has a high-tech motor-and-blower assembly with sound baffles. Tell her that it's quiet enough to use next to her sleeping infant. Forget features. Think results. In the NyQuil name, the message isn't about the therapeutic ingredients of the cough medicine — it's the promise of a good night's sleep.

## Using your imagination

We're always amazed at how clever and entertaining entrepreneurs are when naming their dogs or pleasure boats, but how trite and dull they can be when selecting their commercial identifiers. They're too close to their creations and can't take their noses off the grindstone long enough to look at the market. Digital Equipment and Control Data are trade names developed by blind techies; Apple Computer is a name devised by people with vision.

## Devising a commercial

Because your commercial identifier operates as an advertisement, why not begin the naming process by writing a script for the best commercial you can dream up for your company, product, or service?

Be serious about it. Carefully analyze whether your commercial conveys a basic concept or term around which you can coin a new name. This is exactly what professional namesmiths do. Have your associates or marketing gurus do the same. The process helps you get a consensus about what you can offer to the customer. After you agree on the message that the identifier must convey, it's all downhill to the selection of that perfect name.

## Playing the scale of name-coining options

Your commercial identifier can't simply define your company, product, or service, or the name won't have any legal clout or protection (see Chapter 15). Don't make it too descriptive either. The more descriptive a commercial identifier, the less protection it carries. But, what you can't say explicitly can be implied or suggested by a mere word or phrase.

### Coining a new term

Instead of using words from the English language or another language, coin a brand-new word:

- ✔ **Join two or more words.** KitchenAid on kitchen appliances or Sunkist on citrus fruit.

- ✔ **Fuse two words by sharing some letters.** Travelodge (travel and lodge) for roadside inns; Ameriprise (American and enterprise) for financial services and Telytics (telecom and analytics) for telecommunication consulting services.

- ✔ **Tack a prefix or suffix onto a word.** Microsoft for computer software and Woolite on a fabric detergent.

- ✔ **Clip the beginning or end of a word.** Fanta (from fantastic) for soda.

- ✔ **Abbreviate and then merge words.** Jazzercise (from jazz and exercise) for aerobic studios.

- ✔ **Imitate a common word.** Numberjack (which imitates lumberjack) for accounting services.

### Making allusions

What you can't say directly, you can convey in a roundabout way:

- ✔ **Use a symbol.** Greyhound suggests the speed of a bus service and Rosetta Stone for language-teaching software symbolizes a key to knowledge.

- ✔ **Evoke an image or sensation with a reference.** Mountain Dew on a soda, or Sandals for a tropical vacation resort.

- ✔ **Select a positive term.** Bounty, Power, and Vigor for example.

- ✔ **Turn a common, descriptive term into an attention-catching phrase.** Two-Bit Tow is equivalent to Discount Towing, but a lot more elegant and distinctive.

- ✔ **Provide a role model.** Craftsman on tools and Cover Girl on cosmetics.

### Personalizing your mark

Using a fanciful character as a mark — like the Jolly Green Giant on canned vegetables, Mr. Clean on household cleaning preparations, or Dutch Boy on cans of paint — offers a good opportunity to devise very clever commercials because people tend to bond with a friendly cartoon character. The character mark turns into an effective and inexpensive advertising agent.

# Coca-Cola: The real story

Coca-Cola is probably the best-known mark in the entire world. For better or worse, this product is an icon of American culture, and Coca-Cola is often cited as a model mark. Well . . . not so fast.

In 1886, the drink was originally touted as a medicinal elixir by its inventor, Dr. John Styth Pemberton, for it contained a stimulating extract from coca leaves and a caffeine-loaded extract derived from kola nuts. Back then, people believed that those two extracts had therapeutic qualities (and there were no drug tests). With the product rather than the public in mind, the drink was named Coca-Cola. If you've read this chapter this far, you know that the mark merely described the ingredients of the drink and therefore was initially unprotectable.

After the use of the coca leaf extract was banned, the first half of the mark was no longer descriptive and became merely suggestive. In the meantime, *cola* had become a generic name for a type of soda. Those guys at Coca-Cola Co. ended up with a mixed bag, but through extensive advertising, they boosted that mark to the pinnacle where it stands today.

However, the mark has its problems: Every time Coca-Cola is advertised, other brands such as Pepsi Cola and RC Cola derive at least half the promotion benefits. When Coca-Cola Co. opens a new market in an underdeveloped country, the other cola manufacturers take a free ride on its coattails because the Coca-Cola Co. has already familiarized the new consumers with the term *cola*. That wouldn't happen if the mark didn't contain a generic term.

We're the last one to denigrate the many aesthetic qualities of that mark. It's well balanced, sonorous, and rhythmic because of its double alliteration and syncopated syllables. However, we personally prefer another type of bubbly — Dom Perignon, named after the monk who put the fizz into Champagne wine.

## Jazzing up the name

The aesthetic qualities of a commercial identifier have a great deal of impact on its powers of attraction and retention. *Aural impact,* the harshness or softness of a term, can help convey the right image. NyQuil has a soothing sound. Jazz up a name with an *onomatopoeia* (a word whose sound imitates nature), such as jingle, splat, peck, and pop. For example, Cougar expresses the roar of a wildcat, and Cascade imitates the sound of falling water.

## Joking around (tastefully, of course)

Humor is a great attention getter. Don't overdo it, but the right amount can impress your commercial identifier indelibly into the psyche of your potential customer. Banana Republic as a servicemark for activewear stores and Social Security on a cologne have just that right touch of witticism that we like in a name. Jogstrap on clutches used to hold weights while running and No Deer Not Tonight on a wildlife repellant spray might be pushing the boundaries of good taste, but they're certainly memorable.

### Say it pretty

Don't be afraid to take a bit of poetic license and give your commercial identifier flamboyance, but not pretension. Jellibeans and NyQuil are both smooth, melodious words. Fruit Of The Loom is another pleasant moniker. Try the following literary techniques:

- ✔ **Use alliteration.** Alliteration is the repetition of sounds in syllables, as in Cascade and Two-Bit Tow.

- ✔ **Think rhythm.** Put some rhythm in your name, as in Coca-Cola or Dom Perignon.

- ✔ **Match sight and sound.** Use the coincidence of sound and image to emphasize your message. A great example is the mark Jaguar, where the harshness of the word combines with the image of the ferocious wildcat to convey the power and machismo of the sports car.

## Avoiding the Seven Deadly Sins

Knowing how to avoid commercial identifiers that could to lead you into a marketing fiasco or embarrassing situation is essential. The cardinal sins of commercial identifier development are platitudes, pride, puffery, and plagiarism. Also, make sure that no scarecrow, skeleton, or scatology lurks behind the name you create. . . . Let us explain.

## Platitudes

A generic phrase like The Builder's Mart for a construction-material outlet, Discount Muffler for a muffler shop, or Lite (or Light) on a low-calorie brew identifies nothing because the phrase can't distinguish you from anyone else. Miller Brewing Company made the mistake of introducing the first low-calorie beer in the industry under the commonly descriptive mark Lite and spent a lot of dough promoting it. Within a few months, several of its competitors were marketing their own light beers, some of them under the mark Lite.

A platitude is born from the strong temptation to use a commercial identifier that tells people about your business or product. If you insist on doing so, do it with style and imagination by using some of the tricks we suggest earlier. Rose-Colored Glasses for optometric services is merely suggestive and therefore quite distinctive. You may also add a generic term to a distinctive and fanciful one, as in Apple Computer.

If you need to be more specific, add an explanatory term or phrase to your distinctive identifier (see Figure 16-3).

Many companies are burdened with the surnames of long departed founders or a descriptive technical name that no longer fits its product line. In these situations, the management may resort to crunching the cumbersome corporate identifier down to an acronym or a few initials. For example, National Cash Register turned into NCR, and Minnesota Mining and Manufacturing morphed into the 3M Company. However, because you have only 26 letters to play with, there's a high probability of conflicts with similar names. Furthermore, initials carry no message and therefore are not distinctive, motivating, or memorable.

**Figure 16-3:**
Here's a dstinctive servicemark with an explanatory phrase.

## Pride

To be effective in the marketplace, a name should be distinctive and, if possible, unique. In most cases, there's nothing distinctive in a surname. The yellow pages directories are replete with Smith Brothers, Inc., Smith Communication, Smith & Sons, and so on. Also, family names are not readily registrable. See Chapter 18. They seldom can be sold to a successor owner. The new owner may not be interested in your name. You'll lose the money you would get for the goodwill attached to your name and some tax advantages.

Except in those instances where a personal name has already acquired notoriety, like George Foreman or Yves Saint Laurent, identifying a company product or service with a personal name is never advisable.

Using a name that describes an outstanding characteristic of your product is also a mistaken show of personal pride. The developer of the Chem-Dry mark for carpet cleaning services may be very proud of the process she developed, but the homeowner doesn't give a hoot how the carpet is cleaned, as long as it's cleaned. The term Chem-Dry is pretty descriptive and uninspiring. A competitor could closely imitate the name with impunity.

## Puffery

Highly laudatory phrases, such as The Best Beer in America, are considered merely descriptive and are neither registrable nor protectable.

## Plagiarism

You may be tempted to copy or imitate a successful commercial identifier in order to take a little ride on your competitor's coattails. After the impressive commercial success of a chain of toy stores operating under the servicemark Toys "R" Us, a plethora of 'Something "R" Us' names appeared on the market. These copycat businesses soon had to change their names, at a great loss in goodwill and reputation — not to mention damages and attorney's fees. In Chapter 21, we show you how easy it is to shoot down the imitator of a distinctive name. So don't fall into temptation and let the evil of plagiarism spoil your business venture.

The three main reasons for staying clear of names similar or too close to an established one are

- ✔ To protect yourself against accusations of infringement.
- ✔ To avoid restraining orders, injunctions, or seizure of your goods.
- ✔ To avoid being forced to change your commercial name after developing some goodwill and reputation under the ill-chosen moniker.

## Scarecrows, skeletons, and scatology

When selecting a commercial identifier, stay away from words that may have negative connotations. Terms that suggest death, suffering, and other painful implications may sometimes creep into a commercial identifier. For example, the word *pane* may be misunderstood as *pain*.

Also, make sure that the name you choose doesn't have another meaning or connotation in a different language. If your product is destined for foreign distribution or a predominantly Hispanic or Asian market in this country, verify that your identifier doesn't evoke something morbid, ridiculous, or obscene in the foreign idiom:

- ✔ In Japanese, the word *shi,* which means four, has the same sound as the word for death. The Korean word *sa* has a similar problem. Avoid both sounds when branding a product to be exported to Asia.
- ✔ The mark Nova on a car, with a shift of emphasis to the last syllable, means "It won't go" in Spanish.

- In Germany, the term *mist,* as in the curling iron mark Mist Stick, stands for *manure*.

- The French word *camelote* means shoddy merchandise.

- The Pschitt brand of Perrier soda means *fizz* in French. We don't have to tell you how that term is perceived in an English-speaking market.

- When the slogan used to promote Parker pens — "It won't leak in your pocket and embarrass you" — was translated into Spanish, it read, "It won't leak into your pocket and make you pregnant."

Globalization requires that all new commercial identifiers be acceptable in any market where they may be introduced. We recommend you consult an international dictionary of obscenities.

# Chapter 17

# Searching for Name Availability

· · · · · · · · · · · · · · · · · · · · · · · · · · · · · · · · · · · · · · ·

· · · · · · · · · · · · · · · · · · · · · · · · · · · · · · · · · · · · · · ·

**Y**ou're very excited — you've just come up with the perfect name for your new business. But is it up for grabs? Probably not. Finding an available trade name or trademark on your first try is like winning the lottery! Count on researching at least three options before you stumble on an available moniker. In this chapter, we fill you in on what an availability search is (and what it isn't) and the purpose of a search. We then describe what an appropriate availability search involves, outline a search strategy that you can use, and explain how to analyze your findings.

We restrict our comments to word identifiers. Common graphical elements like "triangles" and "arrows" are too common to narrow search results. Unless your mark uses a fairly uncommon graphical element with a well-known definition (for example, a Gaelic cross), there's no practical way to research prior use of graphic and configuration marks except by thumbing through thousands of pages of trademark registers and electronically searching for keywords in the description of these marks found in some of these registers.

## Practicing Prudence

An *availability search* is a careful look at a range of commercial identifiers that can be found on the Web and various business and legal databases (including state and federal trademark registers) to find out, as a first step, whether anyone is already using your choice of trade name or trademark.

After you uncover one or more prior uses, two questions must be answered:

- ✔ Can you use your moniker without infringing the rights of prior users?
- ✔ Can you obtain the benefits of a federal registration (see Chapter 18)?

An availability search is essentially a legal process. Deciding what and where to search and analyzing the results of the search requires a good understanding of the legal strength and likelihood-of-confusion concepts we explain in Chapter 15. Although you can do some of the basic legwork, you may have to consult your IP professional to decide whether your trade name or trademark is available and registrable.

## What an availability search is not

We can't overemphasize the need to conduct an appropriate availability search before you place a commercial identifier in business. (See Chapter 15 to review the types of commercial identifiers.)

Many people (business attorneys included) believe that the secretary of state's office, whose role is to regulate corporations and limited liability companies, "clears" a name before accepting it as a company identifier. Thus, these folks don't bother searching any farther than the secretary of state's office.

But the secretary of state only checks the name for direct conflict with other names on the state corporate register — he or she couldn't care less if other laws prevent you from using that name. They would be happy to allow you to use Betty Crocker Taxidermy, Inc., as long as you pay your corporate dues. By this time we hope you already know how General Mills, Inc., would feel about your new name. Reserving a business name in your secretary of state's office or having it accepted as a corporate identity doesn't mean that you can use the name commercially whether locally or nationwide.

If you're operating in one of the more enlightened venues, such as California, you're particularly at risk because the courts there give precedence to the first user anywhere in the United States. Some other states allow you to use a mark that's used in another state as long as you're the first local user.

## Reasons for doing an availability search

Just in case you're not quite convinced of the necessity of conducting an availability search, here are a few legal and financial difficulties a search can help you avoid:

✔ **You can get sued:** Adopting a commercial identifier that copies or imitates an existing one may be an actionable act of infringement.

✔ **Judges get angry:** If you're convicted of infringing on the rights of a prior user and you carelessly neglected to conduct a search before using the identifier, the court won't treat that as a show of bad faith, but could penalize you for negligence by increasing the damages awarded to the plaintiff. However, if evidence exists that you had a prior warning or strong suspicion that the mark was already taken, the judge may consider your failure to search as willful and intentional infringement and order you to pay the offended party's attorney and other court costs.

✔ **Your application for registration can be denied:** The disappointment and financial losses associated with the United States Patent and Trademark Office (USPTO) denying your application for federal registration because your mark conflicts with an existing one are substantial. (We discuss federal registration in Chapter 18.)

✔ **You may face a costly change of identifier:** If you launch your company or product under an infringing name, you'll soon have to change it. Think about the loss of goodwill that you'll incur and the cost of promoting a new name.

✔ **You might go to jail:** Under the Trademark Counterfeiting Act, you can be jailed for as much as ten years, pay up to $2,000,000 in fines, or both.

✔ **You may find yourself in bad company:** We assume you're a straight shooter — you took the time to buy this book — so you probably want to do an availability search because you believe in your company, service, or product and want it to stand on its own in the market. You don't need to piggyback on the goodwill developed by a similar trade name or trademark, and you don't want the public to confuse your commercial identity with one with a bad reputation.

# Defining the Scope of Your Search

The extent of your search depends on the identifier that you want to use and register. So before you get ready to search, make sure that you understand your own identifier. You can then set the search boundaries.

## Assessing your choice of identifier

The scope of your search and the interpretation of your search results (see "Analyzing the Results," later in this chapter) depend upon two factors:

✔ The legal strength of the identifier

✔ The intended field and territory of use

The *legal strength* of a commercial identifier is its ability to prevent other businesses from using the same or confusingly similar identifiers. So your first order of business in the great name search is to assess where your prospective commercial identifier falls on the *legal strength scale* — generic, descriptive, suggestive, or arbitrary — which we outline in Chapter 15.

After you've taken your legal-strength reading, you need to delineate the anticipated *field and territory of use.* In other words, define the nature and utilization, collectively called the *definition,* of your goods or services and the geographical areas where they'll be marketed. It's a three-step process:

1. **Write a concise definition of the nature, role, or function of the business, product, or service for which you want to use the prospective identifier.**

   Here are some examples:

   - A business manufacturing automotive engine parts
   - An engineering inspection and certification service for dwellings
   - A single retail shop for high-end female fashion apparel
   - A series of medical tomography scanners
   - A nationwide fast-food restaurant chain
   - An adult table game

2. **Compare your product or service definition with those found in the *International Classification of Goods and Services* in order to determine which *international class* (IC) or classes you should search.**

   The International Classification is a multinational system of grouping goods and services into different categories. You can read the definition of each IC in Chapter 1400 of the *Trademark Manual of Examining Procedure* (TMEP), accessible on the USPTO Web site.

3. **Write down the jurisdictions where the commercial identifier will be used.** This refers to one or more counties, a state, or a number of states.

   The identifier of any commercial activity that affects foreign or interstate commerce is considered as used in the entire country. This includes businesses serving tourists and travelers, such as hotels and restaurants.

## Setting boundaries

Good news! Unlike the patent search that forces you to consider everything published anywhere in the world (see Chapter 7), U.S. commercial-identifier-protection laws, although subject to a few limited situations that we explain in Chapter 19, make you search for trade names and marks only used within the United States and, in some cases, only in their actual territory of use.

So, you've narrowed your search down to the good ol' USA and to one or more ICs. But that's still a pretty big sea to swim in — you need to narrow it even farther. Enter your old friend — the legal-strength scale:

- ✔ **Distinctive:** If your commercial identifier is distinctive because it's either suggestive or arbitrary, you must extend your search to practically all areas of commercial activities. The trademark Kodak, for example, could refer to anything, so you'd need to look wider than the photographic industry and into every IC.

  Folks before you already have a ton of legal protection for their distinctive marks. But after you clear your distinctive mark, you're afforded the same protection.

- ✔ **Descriptive:** If your commercial identifier is merely descriptive, you can limit your search to fields related to your industry. If you're searching for the trade name Boston Brewers, limit it to the wine, beer, and liquor classes. The downside is that even if you find no one else using your mark, a descriptive mark offers very little protection against infringers.

- ✔ **Generic:** If your commercial identifier is generic, don't bother searching because anyone is free to use it.

---

## Commercial identifiers: The world tour

Currently, the laws regulating the protection of commercial identifiers stop at our national borders. This is incompatible with the globalization of trade, especially because the names of foreign establishments, products, or services are now familiar to many Americans.

Even when foreign companies or products have no commercial presence in the United States, their names are easily recognized. Most people know that La Scala identifies an opera house in Milan, and that Le Louvre is the name of a museum in Paris. An American customer seeing an art print bearing the name Le Louvre would probably think that the production and distribution of that print are sponsored by the French museum. In France, the term *Champagne* doesn't designate just any old bubbly, but the highly praised product of a small territory east of Paris. In the past, the generic use of the word *champagne* in the United States caused a lot of friction between our commercial representatives and their indignant French counterparts, who like to wash down their frog legs and escargots with *le vrai Champagne, sacré bleu!* The controversy has now been settled in favor of France through an international trade agreement. It remains to be seen whether the term "sparkling wine" ever acquires the same panache.

Slowly, legislation is catching up with the new global economy. Most industrial countries are moving toward standardization of their trademark laws, and the United States is joining more international treaties and conventions. Someday, we can expect to have a worldwide system regulating the use of trade names and marks.

If your name is a combination of words, try to identify the word or words that are least descriptive of your goods or services. For example, for the name Lonely Loon Escort Services, focus your assessment on Lonely Loon.

Check out Table 17-1 for an idea on where to draw your search boundaries.

| Table 17-1 | Search Parameters for Beauty Parlor Names | |
|---|---|---|
| *Position on Legal-Strength Scale* | *Mark* | *Search Boundaries* |
| Generic | HAIR & NAILS | No search necessary |
| Descriptive | PERMANENT WAVES<br><br>CALIFORNIA CARE | County cosmetic-products and personal-care businesses found on the Web and state and county commercial registers |
| Suggestive | A CUT ABOVE<br><br>SHEAR DELIGHT<br><br>BEAUTY AND THE BEST | State cosmetics-and-toiletries-goods and personal-care businesses found on the Web and state and county commercial registers |
| Arbitrary (existing word unrelated to goods or services) | PASSION FLOWER<br><br>ARABIAN NIGHT<br><br>DOMANI | U.S. cosmetic-and-toiletries-goods and personal-care businesses found on the Web and state and federal trademark registers |
| Totally arbitrary (newly coined word) | XOKKOX<br><br>CAPIX<br><br>JUVERA | All categories of goods and services nationwide found on the Web and all state and federal trademark registers |

# Carrying Out Your Search

Unlike many countries, the United States has no authoritative, centralized national register that you can check to make sure that no one has already acquired your prospective identifier. In the U.S., your exclusive right to use a commercial identifier is based on your using it first — and continuously — in commerce (or filing an Intent-to-Use application for registration on the Federal Register, as we explain in Chapter 18).

The states and the Feds maintain nonmandatory registers of product and service identifiers commonly called *trademark registers.* As to company identifiers, various registration systems exist at the state level, but not at the federal level. Most county administrations maintain registers of fictitious commercial identifiers, including sole proprietorships and partnerships operating under an assumed name as part and parcel of their administrative and regulatory activities. For the same reason, state governments keep records of corporations, limited liability companies, and partnerships.

Millions of commercial identifiers are used in the U.S., but only about a quarter of them are registered in the USPTO. But even the hundreds of thousands of commercial identifiers that aren't recorded in any readily searchable register are protected against even unintentional imitation. Therefore, an availability search can never provide you with 100 percent assurance that your prospective identifier isn't already taken — just your luck, right? — but it *can* improve your odds, so here you go.

In order of importance, there are four excellent places to search. If you find the name you had in mind already taken on your first go-around, at least you've saved some time that you can devote to coming up with another name.

# On the Internet

The Internet, that cornucopia of information, is a bonanza for name searches. You need only type in a word, and the search engine fetches hundreds — sometimes thousands — of references. Sometimes the volume retrieved is so overwhelming that you need to narrow it down by adding words to the search criteria. You can request an advanced search, where you can search on a number of keywords or an exact combination of words. For example, if you search for *tornado* as a mark for a drain cleaner, you get over three million references with one search engine. But If you enter the combination *tornado* and *drain,* you get only around 27,000 results. At least it's a start, right?

If your name uses a "borrowed term," — an already existing word, such as *tornado* — your search will turn up hits where the word is descriptive rather than part of a commercial identifier. To reduce these hits, try subtracting words related to the descriptive use. For example, try "tornado -weather" (Many search engines interpret a minus sign immediately in front of a word as *not*). However, keep in mind that this may eliminate some useful hits as well.

If you don't find your moniker on the Internet, you have a pretty good chance that nobody is already using it. But unless you have coined a very unique term like Kodak or Xokkox, you're more likely to hit so many references that you have to sift through and then interpret them, as we explain next.

Some marks that haven't been used in commerce may have been reserved by Intent-to-Use applications for registration with the USPTO. Because they aren't being used yet, the marks may not appear on the Internet. So don't think that you're safe using your chosen identifier just because you didn't spot it on the Internet. You must go to the next step and search the USPTO database.

## In the USPTO database

The USPTO maintains a comprehensive database of all marks that have been applied for, including those that were refused. The database also lists all marks with current or expired registrations. You can access it through the Trademark Electronic Search System (TESS) at www.uspto.gov.

Federal registration is open only to marks used in interstate or foreign commerce. Therefore, only those marks are included in the USPTO database.

Choose the Search option under Trademarks to get started. First, click the New User Form Search (Basic), where you can enter a single word, a combination of words, or an exact phrase. Note that you can also search by serial number or owner.

If you get too many hits, go back to the Search Form page and click the Structured Form Search (Boolean). This lets you specify different criteria on which to search, such as the actual mark; the classification; the publication, filing, or registration date; or the description. For example, if you're searching *Alibi* for a bar, enter **Alibi** as a search term and select Non-Punctuated Word Mark from the corresponding drop-down field list. Then enter **43** (lodging, food, and drink establishments) as the second search term, and select International Class from the second drop-down box. For a washcloth, search for Rubadubdub as a Non-Punctuated Word Mark with 24 (textile goods) as the International Class.

If your search results in "No TESS records were found . . ." — no hits — don't start celebrating just yet. Double-check to make sure that you haven't misspelled your name or used some overly restrictive criteria. The USPTO search syntax is a little different from the typical Internet search engine's. When in doubt, try using the same syntax to search for a well-known trademark that must be in the database.

You can also focus your search by specifying the exact product or service, such as *Alibi and bar* or *Rubadubdub and washcloth,* using the Goods & Services category from the drop-down field box. Make sure you try different definitions of your goods or services. For example, after *bar,* try synonyms such as *tavern, barroom, saloon,* or *lounge.* After plugging in *washcloth,* also try *towel, sponge, wash rag, bathrobe, bathtub,* or *washbasin.*

## At state trademark registers

Many states and counties have their public records on the Internet, so you can easily check the records of corporate and other limited liability company identifiers and fictitious business names and marks that have been registered in the states that are part of the territory of use. To find these sites enter your state name followed by "secretary of state"; or your county name followed by "county recorder" in your search engine. Choose the hit that seems like a government-run site, usually not a .com. Some private databases also provide access to state registers, as well as some business name records. See the "Setting boundaries" section, earlier in the chapter.

A state register only records marks used within that state.

## Through private database services

A few private companies provide trademark search services or direct access to some name databases. The best-known are Thomson and LexisNexis. You can conduct an in-depth search for a mark, including USPTO records and state trademark registers, on Thomson's www.ialog.com. If you want someone to do the search for you, Dialog.com can refer you to a professional researcher in your field by clicking on Search Services on the site. Lexisnexis.com gives you access to a huge warehouse of information, but it isn't organized for a practical and thorough commercial identifier search. You can search it to find some names and information about their use.

Access to these databases is restricted to paid subscribers; however, most private database services allow you to pay as you go by credit card.

## Using foreign searches

If you're planning to export your products or services, you may want to verify that your mark doesn't conflict with any mark used in other countries.

Many foreign trademark registers are accessible online. Each country has its own way of doing things, so be prepared to master a new search syntax for each country of interest. Find these sources by typing in the name of the country of interest followed by "trademark office" into your favorite Internet search engine. Again, use the site that looks most like a government site instead of a commercial site trying to get your business. Stay away from the .com and .co extensions. If you want more confidence in your search result, use a native trademark agent to conduct this type of search. Most domestic intellectual property (IP) attorneys have correspondents in major industrial countries whom they call upon for international inquiries.

The World Intellectual Property Organization (WIPO) in Geneva, Switzerland, maintains databases of international trademark applications and registrations filed under the Madrid system. This system allows you to get a single international trademark registration which gets submitted to the individual country trademark offices you designate (for more, see Chapter 19). For trademark info, look on the organization's Web site, www.wipo.org, and work your way from the intellectual property section to the trademarks area. The organization's Madrid Express Database (http://ipdl.wipo.int) provides a concise listing of international trademark applications and registrations filed under the Madrid system. The ROMARIN database offers more detailed information and broader search options for all trademarks filed under the Madrid system.

The laws pertaining to commercial identifiers vary from country to country. In most parts of the world, you can only acquire exclusive rights by registration. We recommend that you consult an IP attorney before you spend time and resources checking foreign trade names and marks.

# Analyzing the Results

Remember, finding no reference to your prospective name in all the available sources of commercial identifiers is no guarantee that it's available. Because so many commercial monikers are unregistered and unsearchable, the possibility of inadvertently infringing on some obscure yet protected trade name or trademark is always there. On the other hand, finding out that your baby is already in use doesn't necessarily prevent you from using it as well.

If you do find that your commercial identifier (or something resembling it) is already in use, you have to consider the legal issue of whether using this identifier is likely to cause confusion in the marketplace.

Only an IP specialist can give you a fairly reliable answer on this complex question, but even that would only be a guesstimate. Because the standards for determining likelihood of confusion are so imprecise and dependent upon the circumstances of the case, many attorneys and law firms plainly refuse to issue a definitive opinion on the subject. Foolish would be the attorney who cleared a name of all risks of infringement.

Yet you have to make that judgment, unless you decide to drop any candidate name that is identical or vaguely similar to one already in use. Because of the sheer number of names and marks already used in commerce, you may have to change your selected name dozens of times before you stumble on that unblemished pearl nobody has seen before. The best we can do for you is to lay out the most common criteria that the courts use to decide the issue of infringement of commercial identifiers and give you a few examples.

## *Determining likelihood of confusion*

Common sense is your best guide in analyzing likelihood of confusion between your commercial identifier and those you find during your search.

Likelihood of confusion is hard to define. Courts are still trying, without great success or consistency, to quantify likelihood of confusion. It really boils down to a logical, honest, fair evaluation of all the circumstances.

First, ask yourself earnestly, "Am I trying to launch my product or business on the coattails of a well-known one?" We've noticed that many people do just that without admitting it to themselves. We mention elsewhere that the servicemark Toys "R" Us triggered a flurry of imitations. Then there was the Depot craze: Home Depot, Office Depot, Auto Depot, and so on; and the Club vogue: Sam's Club, Price Club, Auto Parts Club, and a few others. Avoid this type of piggybacking if you want to steer clear of legal problems.

Although the various courts use slightly different standards to determine the likelihood of confusion between two commercial identifiers, we describe the most used factors in the following sections.

### *Legal strength or weakness of the pre-existing identifier*

The protection afforded to a commercial identifier is proportional to its distinctiveness (see Chapter 15 for more on this). You can't apply an arbitrary term to any kind of product or service, no matter how your predecessor used it. The Eastman Kodak Company was able to prevent the use of its unique mark on watches and other products totally unrelated to photographic goods.

If the name you want is suggestive of your product or service, you may be able to use it — even if it's already used for a different type of product or service — because a suggestive term doesn't immediately make the customer think of a specific product or service. For instance, in order to make the connection between the servicemark Tour de France and a bike shop, you have to know what the famous competition is about, and then speculate that bicycles or bicycle-related goods or services may be involved. Finding that the mark has already been used in connection with casual wear wouldn't, under normal circumstances, prevent you from using it for your bike shop.

If you settle for a descriptive term like The Hair Palace for your beauty shop, salons in other states or counties with the same name are no problem. The controlling issue is whether a customer may frequent both establishments.

Watch out for a local service that sells related goods online under the same brand name. If The Hair Palace in Asbury Park, New Jersey, sells hair relaxer under the same name on its Web site, you may have a problem using the name for your salon in California, regardless of whether you sell relaxer.

### Quality of the prior goods

A mark used on high-quality goods is entitled to more protection than one used on average or low-quality merchandise. For example, if you plan to sell expensive, high-fashion dresses for "full-figured" ladies under the mark Strong & Striking through up-scale fashion shops, you might not be in conflict with the owner of the same mark who sells ready-made women's wear through Wal-Mart and Target stores because there's little chance that your customer would patronize this type of department store.

### Similarity of the two identifiers

The similarity in appearance, sound, and meaning of the two identifiers is taken into account. Obviously, the more your commercial identifier resembles the pre-existing one, the more likely the confusion among the customers.

The courts tend to give more importance to the sound of a mark than its look, so you can't get away with misspelling an established name. Cauddac won't differentiate your goods from Kodak, and Pleidow won't distinguish your product from Play-Doh. That said, adding a logo may be enough to negate any likelihood of confusion, especially when the marks are descriptively weak.

### Similarity of the goods or services

You need to give considerable weight to the similarity of your goods or services to those of your predecessor. Again, a small difference between the marks or the goods may get you off the hook if you're dealing with a descriptively weak mark, but you won't get away with imitating a suggestive or famous mark even if your goods or services aren't similar. For example, a toiletry manufacturer was allowed to use the mark Sport Stick in connection with its deodorants, despite the fact that another party was already using the mark Sport-Stick on a lip balm. However, you can't sell or do anything under the mark Playboy because it's such a famous, and, therefore, strong name.

### Likelihood of bridging the gap

You must also anticipate that the person already using your selected identifier for different goods or services may one day bridge the gap by offering the same goods or services as yours. Say you plan to offer a college transcript registering service under the name Curriculum Now knowing that Curriculum.Com already operates a résumé-writing sevice. What's the likelihood that Curriculum.Com may offer a college transcript processing service in the future? You may be exposing yourself to future infringement problems. Use your best judgment. Don't guess. Err on the side of caution.

### Marketing channels

Are your goods likely to appear next to those with the similar mark? Could your loan brokerage services and other services with the same mark be offered by the same bank or financial establishment? If so, that would cause customer confusion, so you must abandon the name. If the identifier is descriptive, a slight difference in marketing channels may be sufficient to preclude likelihood of confusion.

### Cost of the goods & sophistication of the buyer

The likelihood of confusion is increased when goods sold under similar marks are inexpensive and subject to impulse buying. Candies and magazines fall into this category. More expensive and complex products, such as automobiles and computers, are less subject to name confusion because they require more customer consideration of their functions and capabilities. Very expensive or customized equipment for discriminating buyers is almost immune to confusion. Better-educated people are less likely to be confused. All things equal, marks used to sell goods to 10-year-olds face a tougher time overcoming a likelihood of confusion than marks used to sell goods to PhDs.

# Putting it all together

In the end, the only way to analyze your search results (especially if you found an identical or similar identifier) is to look at *all* the criteria listed previously to determine whether your prospective mark is a good choice. Say you're about to market a new type of CAT scan machine to be sold for a quarter-million dollars to medical groups, hospitals, and health centers. Your marketing group has coined the mark NovaRad, but an availability search uncovers NovaRay, used for X-ray equipment and also marketed to the healthcare and medical research fields. Take a look at each of the factors outlined in the previous sections and see where you come out:

 ✔ NovaRay is suggestive and deserves a broad scope of protection.

 ✔ The NovaRay X-ray equipment has been sold for many years and maintains a good reputation in the field.

✔ *Ray* and *Rad* (short for radiation) are quasi-synonymous words, making the marks NovaRay and NovaRad very similar.

✔ The two brands of equipment are used in the same field, by the same people, for the purpose of looking into someone's anatomy.

✔ The manufacturer of the NovaRay device may someday expand its product line to CAT scan equipment, as has already been done by companies like General Electric and Siemens.

✔ The two machines are sold through the same channels of distribution.

Here you've gone through six of the criteria and have come up with six good reasons to coin another moniker. However, the "sophistication of the buyers" test will save the day and trump all. Is there any chance that the MDs and PhDs who purchase your equipment will be confused about the source and purpose of such an expensive piece of equipment? No way. Therefore, the first six negatives present no obstacle to using the NovaRad mark.

There's no foolproof way to analyze the likelihood of confusion between two commercial identifiers. Although some factors, such as the strong legal clout of the senior mark, carry more weight than others, a certain factor may override all the others, as in the NovaRad example. Common sense must be your guide, and you'll have a good chance of avoiding any legal difficulties.

# Chapter 18

# Establishing and Registering Your Commercial Identifier

*I*n the United States, you acquire your exclusive rights to a distinctive commercial identifier by simply making commercial use of it. However, in this chapter we show you the many advantages of registering your mark. Here we deal mainly with registering a mark with the USPTO — a rather complex and lengthy process. Registration of a mark on a state trademark register varies from state to state but is relatively uncomplicated. We cover the ins and outs of the registration process and then provide some info on the follow-up work you need to do after registration.

In these few pages we can't cover all the complex aspects of applying to register a mark. Filling out, filing, and processing your application for registration in the U.S. Patent and Trademark Office (USPTO) usually raises intricate legal issues and requires some tough choices on your part. Moreover, your application will be handled by a USPTO trademark attorney, so unless you're using the services of a competent lawyer, you'll be at a great disadvantage. Even though the standard application forms are adequate in most cases, any unusual circumstance requires some legal massaging beyond what these forms allow. The bottom line? Don't dispense with the advice and services of a good intellectual property (IP) professional.

You'll find in documents E2 on the CD the collection of papers related to an actual trademark application registration with all its intricacies from A to Z.

# Gaining Exclusive Rights to a Commercial Identifier

In order to secure exclusive rights to a commercial identifier you must do two things. First, you have to select a distinctive identifier (described in Chapter 15). Second, you have to use that identifier in connection with commercial activities. In the following list, we describe activities that qualify as commercial use for each type of identifier:

- ✔ **Trade name, corporate identity, and fictitious business name:** Entered on state or county records; applied to a sign, advertisement, or distributed promotional material; or used on business cards, letterhead, checks, offers, estimates, shipping papers, invoices, or other documents

- ✔ **Trademark:** Put on labels, tags, containers, point-of-sale displays, documents accompanying the product, or on the product itself

- ✔ **Servicemark:** Used on signs, business cards, letterhead, clothing patches, promotional materials, offers, job estimates, or other documents

- ✔ **Membership mark:** Used like a trademark or servicemark or on cards, emblems, or other items carried or used by members

- ✔ **Certification mark:** Used on a document or article to show compliance with certain certification requirements

# Registering Your Commercial Identifier

The most effective way to shore up the exclusive rights you have acquired through use of a commercial identifier is to register it as a mark with the USPTO — and in some cases, on one or more state trademark registers. Foreign trademark registration is covered in Chapter 19.

Registration isn't readily available for company identifiers, but only for product, service, membership and certification identifiers — in other words, for marks. But you can often dress up a company identifier as a registrable mark. Here are a few examples:

- ✔ You've named your manufacturing company Ionic Scientific Manufacturing Company, Inc. Strip that name down to Ionic Scientific and establish that moniker as a trademark by applying it to your products. Then register the mark to protect and bolster both your mark and company identifier.

- ✔ You've named your business Bean Brain Accounting Services Associates. Highlight Bean Brain on your business cards and put "Accounting Services" under it as an explanatory legend. Then register Bean Brain as a servicemark.

State registration may give you certain state legal remedies that attach only to locally registered marks. Many states process registrations within a few months — much more quickly than the USPTO. State registration may be your only resort if you can't qualify for federal registration. Let your IP professional decide whether state registration is a good idea for you.

The USPTO registers your mark on the Federal Principal Register (or the Supplemental Register, which we discuss in the "Going to jail: Switching to the Supplemental Register" section, later in this chapter). But before you get a registration certificate, your application must survive a USPTO trademark attorney's thorough examination and any eventual opposition by some other dude displeased by your mark (covered in the "Getting published and dealing with opposition" section, later in the chapter).

In general, registering your mark doesn't give you any ownership rights that you didn't already have, but it does give you a procedural advantage to stop an infringer in a wider geographic area. It does the following:

- **It arms your attorney.** It's a really big stick to beat away someone trying to copy or imitate your mark in the U.S. and its territories.

- **It acts like the deed to your house.** It tells the world that the USPTO has investigated your mark, confirmed your ownership, verified its commercial use, and concluded that the mark is valid and enforceable.

- **Anyone doing an availability search will find your registration.** Anyone as smart and honest as you are will keep clear of your mark.

- **The burden of proof shifts to the infringing defendant.** In a legal action, introducing your registration certificate shifts the burden of proof away from you. Without a registration, you'd have to prove that you own the mark by introducing evidence that you used the mark first.

- **You can get temporary restrictions placed on the infringer.** Registration makes it easier to get a restraining order, preliminary injunction, or seizure of counterfeit goods while awaiting trial. These temporary, but very effective and often decisive, remedies usually stop an infringer dead in his tracks.

- **You get federal protection.** When you register your mark, you're protected by federal laws. Federal courts have broader jurisdiction and powers than state courts. And without a federal registration, you can't go before a federal judge without proving that the accused infringer is headquartered in a different state.

- **You can stop the entry of infringing foreign goods.** U.S. Customs can seize imported goods bearing your marks and eventually destroy them if the importer doesn't challenge the seizure.

- **You can obtain cancellation of domain names that conflict with your mark.** See Chapter 21.

- **International registration is easier.** Federal registration makes it easier to register your mark abroad under many international treaties and conventions (in some foreign jurisdictions, it's a requirement).

## About those symbols

Allow us to clear up some common misconceptions about the ™, SM, and ® characters you see next to some commercial identifiers. ™ (for *trademark*) and SM (for *servicemark*) have absolutely no legal significance. They simply indicate that someone is claiming the identifier as a mark. If the mark is distinctive and properly used, as we explain at the end of this chapter, the status of the identifier should be obvious without the symbol. If the mark is descriptive and weak, using such a symbol doesn't do much to improve its status.

The ® symbol is another matter. It's an international symbol indicating that the mark is registered at the national level (in the U.S., that's on a federal register). Using the ® symbol before registration is a misrepresentation that can torpedo your application. Failure to use it after registration precludes you from collecting monetary damages from a convicted infringer.

## *Establishing eligibility*

To qualify your mark for federal registration, you must use it *in commerce.* For the purposes of registration, that means you've used your mark in connection with the sale of goods or the advertising or rendering of services in interstate commerce, in foreign trade, or in any other activity regulated by Congress. A use of the mark in *intra*state commerce doesn't qualify for federal registration because it is not activity regulated by Congress. Lodging and food service establishments, shops, and other commercial enterprises catering to tourists and travelers are considered to be in interstate commerce.

Any mark that meets these criteria, including configuration marks (see Chapter 15), can be registered — except for a mark that

- ✔ Contains immoral, deceptive, or scandalous material — so much for registering "&*%$@."

- ✔ Incorporates the flag, coat of arms, or other insignia of either the United States or any individual state, municipality, or foreign nation.

- ✔ Is a deceptive geographical indication of the origin of a wine or spirit.

- ✔ Disparages or falsely suggests a connection with any person, institution, belief, or national symbol.

- ✔ Uses a name, portrait, or signature that identifies a living individual without his or her written permission.

- ✔ Includes the name, signature, or portrait of a deceased U.S. president during the life of his widow, without her written permission.

✔ Is generic, commonly descriptive, functional, or misleading.

✔ Is likely to be confused with a commercial identifier in use by another.

✔ Is primarily a surname.

Restrictions are subject to interpretations developed by court precedents. For example, the two first prohibitions didn't prevent the registration of a representation of a condom decorated with the stars and stripes.

As we're sure you know, laws are often complicated and confusing — why should trademark laws be any different? But although the U.S. trademark laws have so many exceptions that even lawyers can get tangled up in them, keep in mind that you can register some otherwise ineligible marks after they acquire secondary meaning (see Chapter 15). This exception covers marks that comprise a surname or one that's merely descriptive or functional. You can go ahead and enter your ineligible mark on the Federal Supplemental Register, however, until it acquires a secondary meaning (see the "Going to jail: Switching to the Supplemental Register" section, later in this chapter).

## Putting your intentions to good use

You can have the world's most original, distinctive, marketable, ironclad mark or name, but unless you legitimately use it in interstate commerce, you don't have a leg to stand on when you submit a regular application to register it with the USPTO. However, in the interim, you can get some protection by stating your intentions (no false pretenses). You have two filing options:

✔ **In-Use application:** You must wait to file your application for registration until the mark is used in commerce. This is called a *Prior-Use* application by the USPTO and others. We like *In-Use* better because it clearly shows you are *still* using the mark — required for registration.

✔ **Intent-to-Use (ITU) application:** This application reserves your right against any other subsequent applicant to obtain a registration for a great mark you've created but haven't yet used in commerce. But, you can't get a certificate of registration based on an ITU until you can prove you have used the mark in interstate commerce. See "Completing the ITU process," later in this chapter. There's no good reason to delay filing an application for registration after you settle on a distinctive mark.

A trademark or servicemark must be genuinely used in the general course of business and not as a token mark for the purpose of registration only. Besides being tacky, selling some of your product to visiting family members at Thanksgiving won't cut it. Unless you're already in business and able to sell your goods or provide the services, don't even try to file an In-Use application because a false application may result in an invalid registration.

You're not a bird, and you don't want a worm, but in the world of ITU applications, being early gets you the following advantages:

✔ The filing date of your ITU application retroactively becomes the date you acquire your mark after the registration is granted. This is how the ITU protects your mark — after you file, you can even stop someone who uses the mark in commerce before you, but after your application.

✔ Your ITU application is posted on the USPTO and other databases where it can be discovered during an availability search.

✔ A USPTO trademark attorney examining another application for the same or a similar mark can cite your ITU application to provisionally refuse registration to that applicant.

✔ Your ITU application allows you to file an application in another country. If you file the foreign application within six months of your ITU application, the U.S. filing date is recognized as the priority date abroad.

# Preparing Your In-Use or ITU Application

The process of registering your mark begins with preparing and filing your application. (We detail the rest of the process in the section "Pushing Your Application Through the USPTO," later in this chapter.) Although it's still possible to prepare the application on paper and file it by hand or mail, you're asking for trouble going that route. The USPTO trademark division has jumped into the deep end of electronic filing without a life preserver and expects you to join them. When you try and access the old printable forms, they redirect you to their electronic entry screens. Using the new forms helps you avoid omitting important information. At the end of the entry process, you can either click Submit and be done, or you can print the forms, mail them in along with a larger fee, and wait a longer time while the USPTO reenters the same information by hand, with typos, into the same system. In the trademark filing area on the USPTO Web site, you can prepare your entire application on-screen, and then either choose to file electronically or become the biggest stick-in-the-mud and print the application in order to file by mail.

Whichever option you select, click on the link to apply for a new mark and then on Trademark/Servicemark Application, Principal Register. You can also prepare applications for registering collective membership marks, collective trademarks/servicemarks, and certification marks. A *collective trademark/ servicemark,* such as Sam Stop for RV parks, is a mark adopted by an association for use only by its members in connection with their goods or services to distinguish them from those of nonmembers. By contrast, a *collective membership mark,* such as Hell's Angels, simply indicates membership in an organization, but is not used in connection with any goods or services.

Filing an online application is advantageous for several reasons:

✔ Electronic applications get to the USPTO instantly and are given priority over mailed-in applications.

✔ The USPTO requires an extra filing fee for paper applications.

✔ As soon as you file your application with the USPTO, you can trace it, amend it, and generally keep better control of it via the Internet.

The USPTO's online forms are improving every week and cover most of the special circumstance filings we've recently encountered. However, your lawyer may have her own forms that accommodate exceptions or special circumstances.

You're now ready to fill out your application. In the next few sections, we guide you through the form, pointing out the critical legal issues and how to handle them along the way.

## Warming up with the TEAS wizard

If you prepare your application online, the USPTO provides you with a set of preliminary questions — a wizard — to tailor the application to your needs through its Trademark Electronic Application System. Of course, because it seems that any U.S. Government body derives its level of funding based on the number of acronyms it employs, the USPTO simply calls this system TEAS. This was very easy to remember during the early days of the system, as it *teased* you into thinking it adequately covered every possible filing scenario. Nowadays the system is very robust.

The USPTO provides a further incentive to making life easy for the USPTO by charging only $275 per class (instead of the usual $325 per class) if you use the TEAS Plus Form rather than the standard TEAS Form. The TEAS Plus Form is less flexible, requiring you to use only the goods/services definitions approved by the USPTO (you can find these in the Acceptable Identification of Goods and Services Manual), and to pay all class fees upfront. It also requires properly sized image files for your mark and specimens (if you are filing an In-Use application).

Carefully read the instructions provided regarding which form to use. Unless you are pretty comfortable manipulating computer image files, have a good idea that your mark is available, and have found all your goods/services descriptions in the Acceptable Identification of Goods and Services Manual, you should stick with the standard TEAS Form.

If you're not to sure exactly what you will eventually sell under the mark but want to protect many different types of goods, from T-shirts to back scratchers, you may want to file under the standard TEAS form and pay only one filing fee at the time of filing.

The first screen of the TEAS wizard asks you whether you are an attorney. If you've listened to our advice, your hotshot attorney will answer yes. However, if you are new to the TEAS system, just say no. At this point you probably do not have any "previously saved data" either, so just leave that optional field blank.

## Providing applicant info: Defining the owner

You may file the application on behalf of

- ✔ Yourself as an individual.

- ✔ A corporation.

- ✔ A general partnership.

- ✔ Another type of business entity, such as two or more individuals jointly, a marital community, a trust, a limited partnership, or limited liability company.

This owner definition isn't a matter of choice but a statement of fact. The mark and its registration must be owned by whoever stands behind the product or service, because the mark carries an implication of warranty of quality and commercial fitness of the goods or services it identifies. If the product fails or is adulterated, the owner of the mark can be sued for any resulting loss or injury to the customer.

The owner must sign the declaration at the end of the form either when the application is filed or later as requested by the examiner. Here's the skinny on who must sign a non-individual application:

- ✔ In a joint application, all applicants must sign the papers. To avoid this inconvenience, you can call the joint venture a general partnership.

- ✔ For a partnership, at least one general partner must sign the application.

- ✔ An officer, such as the president, CEO, COO, or CFO (and *not* a director or manager), handles the honors for a corporation.

- ✔ For a limited liability company, the manager signs on the dotted line.

- ✔ The trustee of a trust puts pen to paper.

About your mailing address: Remember that this information becomes part of the public record. If for whatever reason you do not want your home address listed, make sure you've already arranged a P.O. box address to supply here.

Although most of us are very familiar with the convenience, cost savings, and organizational benefits of e-mail, some people change their e-mail address more often than their bed linen. If you fall into this category, think twice before authorizing communication between the USPTO and you via e-mail only. We recommend using e-mail, but only if you make yourself check the status of your application at the USPTO Web site every couple months just in case you accidentally missed some important communication from the USPTO.

## Defining the mark

Marks that incorporate graphics, shapes, colors, or other nonverbal characteristics require special attention. In the sections that follow, we provide some insight into graphic marks and trade dress and then provide form-specific instructions.

Your mark may consist solely of one or more colors applied to a particular object, such as a product, a packaging, a store sign, or a building. A color mark, just like a product shape, isn't considered inherently distinctive until it has acquired secondary meaning. Therefore you can't register it on the Principal Register until that time. (For information on the Supplementary Register, see the section "Going to jail: Switching to the Supplemental Register," later in this chapter.)

### Graphic mark

If your mark comprises verbal and design elements (including fanciful lettering), such as the one shown in Figure 18-1, you can file for:

- **The literal part (made of one or more typed standard characters):** The character, word, or phrase only
- **The design part:** The graphics only, if they can stand alone and aren't part of the lettering
- **The whole enchilada:** Both the characters and graphics

Note: A mark that consists only of standard characters is commonly called a *word mark,* even if it consists of a single punctuation character.

**Figure 18-1:**
Combining
word and
design into
one mark.

To obtain the maximum coverage and get the most bang for your buck, register only the part that exhibits the greatest legal strength.

 ✔ If you have a strong word mark, you can get broad coverage by filing for the literal part only. A person needs only to copy or imitate that part to create a likelihood of confusion among the public. In the TEAS wizard, make sure that the Standard Characters button is selected.

 ✔ If you have a nondescriptive and motivating design, you may want to obtain registration for that design only.

The odds that someone would copy both parts of the mark are relatively low. You can catch more flies with a limited form of the mark.

If you have a weak word mark, combining it with a graphic, even a fanciful one, won't save the mark from rejection. You cannot register the name Bike Shop even if you jazz it up with fancy graphics of a bike and the Eiffel Tower.

### Configuration mark

Distinctive shapes, colors, and ornamentations of products, packaging, or places of business can act as marks and are referred to as *trade dress* or *configuration marks* (see Chapter 15).

You can only register the trade dress or packaging of a product or the style of a business establishment if that unique approach isn't practical or functional. When defining such a mark, describe only its non-functional aspects.

For instance, if the product is a screwdriver with a series of diamond-shaped engravings on the center of the handle, the mark should only define a series of diamond-shaped engravings around the midsection of a screwdriver handle, not the screwdriver or the screwdriver handle. The drawing must depict the engraving in full line and the rest of the screwdriver, or just the handle in dotted lines. See the section "Entering the mark and preparing the drawing," later in this chapter.

The shape of a product normally isn't considered to be inherently distinctive until it has acquired a secondary meaning, but a package design can be. Don't bother filing for registration of a mark that's not inherently distinctive before it's been in commerce for a few years and you can submit some evidence of secondary meaning in the form of testimonials or a public survey. Until then, you can file for registration on the Supplemental Register (see the section "Going to jail: Switching to the Supplemental Register," later in this chapter).

### Entering the mark and preparing the drawing

If your mark consists of a word or phrase with nothing other than standard English punctuation or sanctioned typographical elements, check Standard Characters on the application and enter the mark in the box in all upper-case. For a design or configuration mark, check Special Form (Stylized and/or Design) and submit an image-file drawing as instructed. Unless you want to claim color, the drawing must be in black and white lines only, including shading. The lines must be sharp, solid, and uncrowded. Gray tones or tints aren't permitted. Although a true black-and-white, 1-bit-per-pixel format is preferred, the USPTO will allow an 8-bit grayscale image containing some transitional gray pixels.

If you're applying for a mark consisting of mixed uppercase and lowercase letters, you can still make a standard character claim. Be sure to click on the Preview USPTO-Generated Image button to ensure that your standard character mark appears the way you want it. If your mark uses foreign punctuation that does not appear in the Standard Character Set, check the Stylized or Design Format box, but simply submit an image with the word mark typed in the middle of it.

A graphic mark should be easily reproducible in any media. Tell your designer to avoid complex graphics, halftones, and blended colors. Ideally, your mark should be suitable for rendition on a rubber stamp. Such a mark greatly simplifies the preparation of your application.

Lastly, the TEAS wizard asks you to check a box if you want to enter an additional statement. For Pete's sake, do not check this box. Don't go blabbing about how you specifically designed your ATOMS brand building block toys to mimic the function of real atoms. In other words, in the application stage, the less said the better. But your lawyer may use this space for entering an appropriate legal statement about the history or composition of the mark that'll enhance the application and expedite its examination.

## Classifying and identifying your goods or services

How you classify and identify your goods or services not only influences the protection your mark will get, but also determines the types of prior marks that can be cited against your application.

If you haven't already done so, define the areas of commerce where your mark is used and then compare that definition to the identifications (IDs) found in the International Classification listings. (See Chapter 1400 of the *Trademark Manual of Examining Procedure* (TMEP) on the USPTO Web site: www.uspto.gov.)

Click the Searching ID Manual button to use the online Acceptable Identification of Goods and Services Manual. You can then search out the proper IDs by using keywords.

Start broad by using only one word. It's better to page through the possible IDs and note the ones that apply instead of trying to type the exact wording. Also, think up some common synonyms for your goods and other closely related goods. For example, if you plan to sell hand lotion, don't forget to try searching for "cream" or "gel" as well. One of your hits might also display synonyms or similar goods you may want to consider.

You can use the same mark on goods or services that fall into several classes. For example, if you're manufacturing leather articles, you may have to select all the following classes:

- ✔ Class 18 (Leather goods) for handbags, briefcases, luggage, wallets, purses, and belts
- ✔ Class 14 (Jewelry) for watch straps
- ✔ Class 16 (Paper goods) for desk pads and checkbook holders
- ✔ Class 20 (Furniture) for jewelry cases
- ✔ Class 25 (Clothing) for jackets, pants, shoes, and boots
- ✔ Class 26 (Fancy goods) for leather belt buckles
- ✔ Class 34 (Smokers' articles) for cigar and cigarette holders

If you want to try your hand at creating your own description, click the Entering Free-Form Text button. In the box labeled Listing of Goods and/or Services on the form, enter a definition for each type of good or service associated with your mark. Don't use a class code, but find a description that's as close as possible to one found in the International Classification. Be prepared for the trademark examiner to object to your wording, and provide you with suggestions as to proper wording. But don't let the examiner bamboozle you into using words that are narrower than you deserve and certainly not ones that do not describe your goods.

### Filing for In-Use versus Intent-to-Use classes

The type of application you're filing affects the classes that you list:

- ✔ **In-Use:** On a regular application, list only goods and services already offered in commerce.
- ✔ **Intent-to-Use:** No limit on the types of goods or services you can list in each class. You can always drop items later when you need to prove you've used the mark in commerce (see the section "Providing evidence of commercial use," later in this chapter).

If you have a combination of goods and services, some already in commerce and some not yet in commerce, you may file a cost-saving single application. Simply make sure that the In-Use goods are listed as a separate entry from the Intent-to-Use ones. Then select a different filing basis for each entry. However, you should watch for the pitfall discussed later in this chapter in the section "Completing the ITU process."

If you're trying to keep costs down, keep in mind that your filing fee is based on the number of classes you specify in your application. At the time of this writing, the filing fee is $325 per class, using the standard online TEAS form. That means the filing fee for the leather products example earlier in this chapter would be $2,275. Ouch! You may choose to file your application, paying the fee for only one class, but this will prompt an office action request that you pay for the remaining classes. If you're lucky, the examiner won't find any conflicting other marks so you'll know by the time you are required to pay the additional fee whether the mark is available in those classes.

### Specifying the dates of first use

If you're filing an In-Use application, you must enter two dates for each class or goods or services:

- ✔ First use of the mark anywhere, including limited use within one state
- ✔ First use of the mark in commerce, as defined earlier in this chapter

The two dates are the same if the goods or services were placed in commerce at the outset.

### Providing evidence of commercial use

In an In-Use application, you must submit one specimen of use for each class of goods or services. You may use an image file showing the trademark on a label, tag, container, or the product itself. You can also show a servicemark on a sign, advertisement, business card, letterhead, brochure, proposal, invoice, or other document that describes the goods or services. Either way, the document must be scanned or photographed and saved as an image file on your computer for later attachment to your application.

### Correspondence information

The TEAS wizard prepopulates the correspondence address fields with the same information as the applicant's address entered earlier. If you want correspondence sent elsewhere, you may enter a different address in the fields provided. Check the box if you have appointed a Domestic Representative. If you live outside the United States, you must appoint a U.S. resident or company to receive and accept papers on your behalf.

## Signing and filing the application

To electronically sign the declaration at the end of the application, you may use any name, word, letters, codes, or symbols you choose between slashes, such as */jd signature/*. Then file the application by clicking Validate and following the fee payment instructions. Alternately, you may print and sign the paper application, scan it back into your computer, and attach it at this screen — or you can mail it in. Your electronic or mailed application will be accepted without a signature (not recommended), but you'll be asked to mail a signed declaration later.

If all goes well, and your credit card still has some life left in it, you'll receive a "Success" screen listing your application serial number. Make sure that you print this page or write down the serial number. You will use it to access the status of your application at the USPTO Web site.

## Pushing Your Application Through the USPTO

After you get that "Success" screen, you may think you're home free. Think again. The journey of an application through the USPTO is longer than Dorothy's journey down the yellow brick road.

About six months from your filing date, your application lands on the desk of a trademark attorney. That's when the fun begins. An In-Use application that's not challenged takes about 18 months to mature into a registration. Each interim action by the examiner adds another 6 months — and an opposition (see "Getting published and dealing with opposition," later in the chapter) adds 16 to 24 months. For an Intent-to-Use, you must add about 6 months to these figures, plus whatever time (up to 36 months) you take to place your goods or services in commerce after you receive a *notice of allowance* (see "Completing the ITU process," later in the chapter.)

Contrary to a patent application, which can be expedited for a number of reasons (see Chapter 9), the Commissioner of Trademarks very rarely gives any application priority.

The examination of an application for registration of a mark parallels the examination of a patent application (see Chapter 10). One difference, though, is that your mark application isn't confidential. The bad news? Anyone can see what you're up to. The good news? You can check the current status of any pending application or registration — including your own — on the USPTO Web site at www.uspto.gov.

The rules outlined in the Trademark Manual of Examining Procedure (TMEP) guide the examination process. The TMEP is periodically updated and available by subscription from the U.S. Government Printing Office (http://bookstore.gpo.gov) or you can download it free from www.uspto.gov/go/tmep.

In the sections that follow, we tell you how your application for registration is processed. This information applies to In-Use and ITU applications, but the ITU process has a few additional steps, which we outline in the section "Completing the ITU process," later in the chapter.

## Passing (or failing) the examination

When your application hits the USPTO, an examining trademark attorney is assigned to your case. Your first contact with this person may be receipt of a request for corrections to some technical defects in your application, such as insufficient fees or missing information. Then after the examiner completes a thorough availability search on your mark, you receive a first report on the status of your application, some six to ten months after your filing date.

The examiner's report may include a combination of objections and refusals to register. The report always specifies how much time (in most cases six months) you have to answer. Objections and refusals are never welcome, of course, but they don't *necessarily* put an end to your pursuit either.

---

# Finding the right lawyer

Any attorney who practices in one of the 50 states or the District of Columbia may represent you before the USPTO during the examination and prosecution of your trademark application. He or she doesn't need any special certification or examination, unlike a patent attorney.

Although many lawyers who aren't IP specialists will take a mark-registration case, you can't expect these occasional trademark practitioners to give you the same quality of service as an IP professional who keeps up with the frequent changes in the laws pertaining to commercial identifiers. Carefully investigate the qualifications of any professional before you hire.

---

The report is in formal language, written by and for an attorney, and cites controlling authorities, such as sections of statutes, regulations, and court decisions. To repeat: Don't go it alone; consult your IP attorney.

You have to answer the report by filing an amendment with supporting arguments. An *amendment* is a legal document that answers every objection or ground for refusal and either accepts or contests each of the examiner's findings and decisions. The name comes from the fact that it often includes a modification of the application. There's no fee required unless you have to split the goods or services into one or more additional classes, in which case you must pay the standard filing fee for each added class.

After a couple of exchanges with the examining attorney, you'll either get a preliminary approval or face a final refusal to register the mark. After the preliminary approval comes the publication step, which we explain below. A final refusal leaves you with two options — appeal the decision or let the application lapse and pick another mark.

Promptly answer any communication from the examining trademark attorney. Failing to do so may cause your application to be declared *abandoned*.

If your application is declared abandoned because you failed to timely answer the examining attorney, or pay a fee, you can apply to revive it. File a petition to the Commissioner of Trademarks, within two months of the notification of abandonment, in which you allege that the abandonment was unintentional.

## Dealing with examiner objections

The most common objections are improper identifications (examiners often prefer the word *recitations*) of goods or services or a wrong classification.

In most cases, the examining attorney suggests a new recitation of goods or services and their appropriate classifications.

Don't blindly accept suggestions from the examiner without considering their impact on the scope of your mark and the cost of the registration. You know your product or service better than the examining attorney. Her suggestion may miss the mark (ha ha!) and not give you the coverage you need. Also, each added classification raises the filing fee and other subsequent fees.

The examining attorney may also ask you to disclaim a descriptive part of your mark and even suggest a wording for the disclaimer. In other words, you're asked to agree that you don't have any exclusive right to that portion of your mark. If you don't agree that that portion is merely descriptive, present a convincing argument against the need for a disclaimer.

### Facing rejection

If the examiner's report contains a refusal to register, all is not lost. You can also contest that decision. The following list outlines the most common grounds for refusals and the ways that you can rebut them. You must answer a refusal to register the mark with an amendment.

- ✔ **Likelihood of confusion with a registered mark or company identifier:** If the refusal is based on likelihood of confusion, you must try to distinguish your mark from the trade names or marks cited by the examining attorney by applying the tests outlined in Chapter 17. Your argument should rely on pertinent court decisions and other authorities that can overcome those cited by the examining attorney.

- ✔ **The mark isn't distinctive, but merely descriptive or is primarily a surname:** If registration is refused on the ground that the mark isn't distinctive, you can show evidence of the contrary in the form of intensive advertising campaigns, commentaries culled from newspapers and other publications, or written testimonials by competent individuals.

  If you've used the mark in commerce for at least five years, you may establish secondary meaning by filing a statement, ending with a declaration (similar to the one at the end of the application filing form, preferably with supporting evidence) asserting that the mark has become distinctive through substantial, exclusive, and continuous use for five years.

- ✔ **The mark is disqualified under the eligibility requirement:** If your mark is declared ineligible for registration, there's a good chance you made a fatal mistake in your selection. However, a good attorney can sometimes get you past this most formidable obstacle. With laws, nothing is set in concrete. It's mostly a question of time and money. (See the section "Establishing eligibility," earlier in this chapter.)

### *Going to jail: Switching to the Supplemental Register*

If your mark was rejected on the grounds that it isn't distinctive, the examining attorney will routinely suggest that you switch your application to the Supplemental Register until you can show that it has acquired secondary meaning. One big advantage of doing this is that after your mark is on the Supplemental Register, examining attorneys can cite your mark against other applications for an identical or similar mark.

You can apply for registration on the Supplemental Register at the outset if your mark isn't inherently distinctive — such as a new color mark. However, think twice before doing this because registering on the Supplemental Register amounts to putting your mark in jail for those few years. You're publicly admitting that it's merely descriptive and very difficult to enforce against an imitator. Moreover, such a registration does not carry all the advantages attached to a Principal Register entry, even though it allows you to file an infringement action in a federal district court.

Choosing the Supplemental Register depends upon your situation. If you've already used the mark for a few years, and there's little chance you'll have to sue someone in the near future, a Supplemental Registration could work for you. However, if you just started and have five years ahead of you to establish secondary meaning, and if you may have to go to court before then, you're better off without the stigma of a descriptive mark imposed upon you by a registration on the Supplemental Register.

## Getting published and dealing with opposition

Upon preliminary approval, the examining attorney sends you a *notice of publication.* This notice gives you the date upon which your mark will be published in the *Trademark Gazette* for oppositions. This weekly publication of the USPTO contains, among other items, a list of applications that have recently been granted preliminary approval for registration. (You can access the *Trademark Gazette* on the USPTO Web site.)

Anyone who objects to your registration can file an *opposition* with the USPTO within 30 days of the publication date. People with objections can also file requests for an extension of that 30-day period. You receive copies of these requests. If someone files an opposition, your application is sent for a spin before the Trademark Trial and Appeal Board (TTAB).

The TTAB conducts a trial under the Federal Rules of Civil Procedure (FRCP) to determine whether your mark and that of the opposing party are in conflict and, if so, who has priority of use. Needless to say, this is a complex and costly battle that must be fought between lawyers.

Opposition is usually based on a perceived conflict between a mark to be registered and a commercial identifier used by the opposition. But opposition can come from other quarters as well. Anyone who can demonstrate that he could be adversely affected by your registration can file and fight an opposition. If I think your mark disparages my person or ethnic group, or even offends my moral or religious beliefs, I have a basis for opposition.

## Receiving the USPTO's seal of approval

If you encounter no opposition, or if the opposition is settled in your favor, the next step depends upon the type of application. If you filed an In-Use application, your registration will be issued without further ado, about three months from the end of the opposition period (or any extensions).

After you receive your certificate of registration, you must place a notice of registered status next to the mark. The notice can consist of the legend *Registered in the United States Patent and Trademark Office,* the abbreviation *Reg. U.S. Pat. & Tm. Off.,* or the international symbol ® placed next to the upper right-hand corner of the mark when possible. Failure to use the notice may prevent you from collecting damages and legal expenses from an infringer, although you may still stop the copycat.

## Completing the ITU process

If you filed an ITU application, your travails are far from over. About three months after the expiration of the opposition period (or your successful fight against the opposition), the examining attorney sends you a Notice of Allowance. That means your mark is registrable pending use in commerce. You now have six months from the date of the Notice of Allowance to use your marks and submit a Statement of Use with the required fee ($100 per class at the time of this writing). A registration is usually issued about three months after the filing of the Statement of Use.

You can't get a registration in the U.S. until you use the mark in commerce.

You can file your Statement of Use electronically at the USPTO Web site. Simply visit the trademarks area and select the option for responding to a Notice of Allowance.

You can extend the period before you have to file your Statement of Use in 6-month increments, up to five times, for a total of 36 months from the date of the Notice of Allowance, by filing a Request for Extension of Time for Filing a Statement of Use. Each time, you have to pay the required extension fee, which is currently $150 per class. Your first request is automatically granted, but with each subsequent request, you must provide some credible reason why you haven't yet used the mark in commerce.

If you miss a deadline, the entire application is declared abandoned.

A few circumstances call for special procedures. Here are the most common:

- **Amendment to Allege Use:** If you've used the mark in commerce between the date of your ITU application and before the approval for publication, you may file an Amendment to Allege Use during that interim period. When the USPTO receives the amendment, your ITU application turns into an In-Use application. Simply use the same form (and pay the same fee) as for a Statement of Use.

- **Splitting the application:** If you've only used the mark in commerce on some of the goods or services listed in your application, you can revise your application after receiving the Notice of Allowance by either

  - Deleting the unused goods or services and filing a Statement of Use covering the goods or services already in commerce.

  - Dividing your application into two — one for goods or services already in commerce, the other for the ones that aren't. Each application may cover a different category of goods or services. You may have to pay an additional filing fee to cover a divided class.

If you filed an application combining In-Use and ITU goods or services, when the entire application is approved, you'll get a Notice of Allowance for the In-Use part. However, no registration will be issued for either ITU or In-Use goods or services until you file a Statement of Use on the ITU items.

If you miss a deadline, the entire application will be declared abandoned. This is one reason that filing a combined application is not recommended.

## Appealing an adverse decision

You can appeal — all the way to the U.S. Supreme Court, if you want to — an adverse decision by the examining attorney. Figure 18-2 illustrates the appeal routes. Basically, you can appeal an adverse decision by the examining attorney on a purely regulatory matter, such as a final request to submit a drawing or amend a recitation of goods or services, by petition to the Commissioner of Trademarks. However, you must appeal an adverse decision on a substantive matter, such as a refusal to register the mark, to the TTAB.

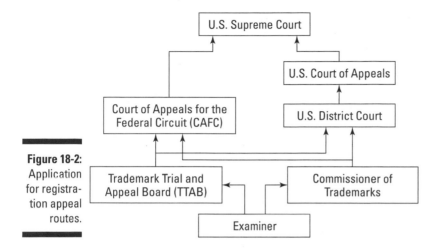

**Figure 18-2:**
Application
for registra-
tion appeal
routes.

If the Commissioner of Trademarks or the TTAB goes against you, you can appeal either to the Court of Appeals for the Federal Circuit (CAFC) or to a federal district court. If you appeal in the federal district court, you can introduce new evidence because a new trial or examination of the facts will be conducted in that forum.

Any adverse decision by the federal district court can be appealed to a U.S. Court of Appeals. A decision by either the CAFC or the U.S. Court of Appeals can be appealed to the U.S. Supreme Court. And if the U.S. Supreme Court says no, you're out of luck. We don't think God has a trademark office.

If the mark you want to register is already used, but not in your market area, you may apply for a *concurrent use proceeding* to obtain exclusive rights to use the mark in the territory not occupied by the senior user. You may apply by amendment after the examiner cites likelihood of confusion as grounds for refusing your registration. The matter goes to trial before the TTAB, where you become the plaintiff and the senior user is the defendant. The procedure is akin to an opposition.

## Facing cancellation

Your registration is never completely secure. Before it becomes incontestable, as we explain in the next section, a person who misses the deadline for opposition gets a second chance to petition for a *cancellation* of your registration on the same grounds. A cancellation is conducted before the TTAB just like an opposition. That means, as with other adversarial proceedings, your attorney and the petitioner's will slug it out with interrogatories, depositions, motions, and other costly maneuvers (see Chapter 21 for more).

Your registration will be cancelled if do not respond to a petition for cancellation or if you lose the contest. At its sixth anniversary, your registration is automatically canceled unless, during the preceding year, you file a Section 8 Affidavit of Continued Use stating that your mark is still used in commerce. (The name refers to a section of the federal trademark law called the Lanham Act.) Along with the affidavit, you have to provide evidence of commercial use by submitting a specimen of the type required with the original application for registration. The affidavit can be filed late with a surcharge as long as it's filed within six months after the six-year deadline.

## Making your mark and registration incontestable

If, after five years, no court has decided against your ownership of the mark, and no one is currently challenging it, you can sew up your registration for good by filing a Section 15 Affidavit of Incontestability before the mark's sixth anniversary. The affidavit must state that the mark has been in continuous use for the last five years, is still used in commerce, and is not the object of an adverse ruling or involved in current adverse proceedings.

After the Section 15 document is filed, a cancellation can only be brought on one of the first seven exceptions listed in the section entitled "Marks Eligible for Registration." Your mark registration can't be cancelled because of likelihood of confusion with another mark or a trade name or because the mark is merely descriptive or primarily a surname. The affidavit can be filed late with a surcharge within six months after the six-year deadline.

## Renewing your registration

Your registration will last as long as you use the mark in commerce, providing it's renewed every ten years. During the ninth year of each renewal period, you must file another Section 8 Affidavit, showing that your mark is still used in commerce. You must also request a renewal for another ten years. Again the renewal can be filed six months late with a surcharge. After that, you have to refile and start over from scratch regardless of the fact that you've never stopped using the mark.

You can combine Sections 8 Affidavit of Continued Use and 15 Affidavit of Incontestability in one document and do the required post-registration filings online. Go to the USPTO Web site, Trademarks section, choose Filing Online, find the File a Post-registration form, and choose the appropriate declaration.

# Losing Your Commercial Identifier

You can lose your exclusive rights to a company identifier or mark under the following circumstances:

- **Failure to use:** If you don't use your commercial identifier for two or three years and show no intent to use it in the future, someone else can assume that you abandoned it and begin using it. To keep your identifier, you must show credible evidence that you intend to use it and were prevented from doing so by circumstances beyond your control. Proving these circumstances is difficult, if not impossible. Use it or lose it.

- **Authorizing uncontrolled use:** The law protects exclusive use of an identifier to give the public a reliable indication of quality. For example, you buy Kodak film because you know it's a quality product. Authorizing someone else to use your mark without controlling the quality of the products or services is considered fraud that creates a defense to allegations of infringement, and a ground for cancellation even after your mark has become incontestable.

- **Using the mark as a substantive:** A mark must always *qualify* a product or service. Never use it as a noun ("Drink Sanka") or, worse yet, as a verb ("You can Xerox any documents"). Your advertisement should say (in effect), "Drink Sanka brand of coffee" or "You can duplicate any document on our Xerox copier." If you don't treat your company name or mark as a valuable qualifier, others won't either. Your mark can lose its distinguishing character and become unenforceable. Some other examples of companies that run the risk of their marks becoming generic are Google, Band-Aid, and Kleenex. Pay attention to advertising by these companies, and you'll often see them discouraging use as a noun or verb.

  Where possible, one should "play it safe" by typing a mark in bold, uppercase letters, or some other way that makes it stand out in text, followed by a generic term — for example, "Our comfortable **TIPPYTOE®** slippers will keep your feet warm." In this way you easily avoid uses which could diminish the strength of your own mark, or the mark of another, prompting a complaint.

  Only use the ® symbol after obtaining a federal registration.

- **Unfair use:** You can't take advantage of your strong commercial identifier to impose obligations that go beyond your exclusive rights. A common example of misconduct is when a fast-food franchisor insists that all franchisees buy their disposable tableware from the franchisor. This unduly extends the rights and advantages conferred by the mark and its reputation to unrelated products, and unfairly limits the choices available to the franchisee who might be able to purchase these supplies on better terms from other sources. Other abuses of a mark include forcing a trademark licensee to also accept a license under a copyright or patent. Depending on the degree of coercive conduct, the owner of the abused moniker can lose some or all of his exclusive rights.

✔ **Failure to go after infringers:** If you tolerate infringement, competitors may assume that you deserve a very narrow scope of protection. This clears the way for the copycats to use it. The longer you delay pursuing an infringer, the less likely you'll be able to stop him.

✔ **Genericness:** If you're lucky enough to have a successful and profitable product marketed under a strong mark, the public may eventually adopt your mark as the generic term for that kind of product. The court may then declare your mark generic and unenforceable. This has happened before: Aspirin, linoleum, and cellophane were all famous brand names.

✔ **Misuse of a certification mark:** Placing a certification mark on your own goods, using it for a purpose other than certifying another's goods or services, or losing control over its use subjects it to cancellation.

# Part V
# Making Your IP Rights Work for You

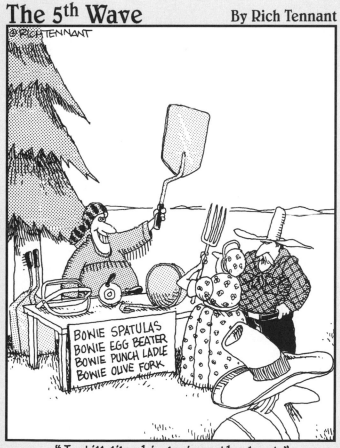

The 5th Wave                    By Rich Tennant

BOWIE SPATULAS
BOWIE EGG BEATER
BOWIE PUNCH LADLE
BOWIE OLIVE FORK

"I still like his knives the best."

# In this part . . .

*W*e talk about what you can do after you've acquired your U.S. patent, copyright, or commercial identifier. If you're planning to do business abroad, your work isn't quite done yet. You need to know how to protect your IP overseas, so grab your passport, stow your carry-on bags, and get ready for an IP overseas getaway.

And now that you've spent a bunch of time and money (or blood, sweat, and tears) to get that protection, find out how you can use your intellectual property to increase profits. Finally, we show you what to do if someone infringes on your IP rights (stockade not included).

# Chapter 19

# All Abroad: Protecting Your IP Rights in Other Countries

· · · · · · · · · · · · · · · · · · · · · · · · · · · · · · · · · · · · · · · · · · · · · · · ·

*In This Chapter*

▶ Deciding whether to file a patent overseas

▶ Discovering three basic rules of foreign patent filing

▶ Taking full advantage of multinational filing systems for patents

▶ Finding out about foreign design and plant protection

▶ Uncovering the details of overseas mark protection and copyrighting

· · · · · · · · · · · · · · · · · · · · · · · · · · · · · · · · · · · · · · · · · · · · · · · ·

"**T**ravel is fatal to prejudice," wrote Mark Twain in The Innocents Abroad, a book about the wanderings of a motley gang of American tourists through Europe and the Middle East. If you have a narrow-minded idea that foreigners are less industrious or entrepreneurial than Americans, filing patent applications overseas can quickly set you straight. Acquiring foreign patents or registering your mark abroad can be extremely costly, complex, and time consuming. So, carefully ponder the pros and cons of obtaining foreign IP protection before casting your money to wayward winds. Because the patent process is the most complex IP right, most of this chapter focuses on utility patents (see Chapter 4). But we talk about plant and design patents, commercial identifiers, and copyrights at the end of the chapter.

# Pros and Cons of International Patents

You're probably wondering whether you really want to go to all the trouble and expense of applying for international patents. A worthy question. And the answer is different for everyone. So, before you plunge ahead or slink away, take a look at the following reasons to file — and a reason to stay "local."

## Counting the ways: Why file abroad?

If you have a good, solid invention, not just a pipe dream, but one that has a reasonable potential of being used outside the United States, filing abroad can give you a real competitive edge by protecting you from infringers, increasing your licensing payoffs, and getting licensees in the first place.

With few exceptions, a patent offers no protection beyond the borders of the country that granted it. Although your U.S. patent lets you take anyone to court who makes, markets, or sells your patented gizmo anywhere from sea to shining sea, it has no sway in a foreign tribunal. Getting a foreign patent lets you police the world, or at least the most-developed nations.

Considering the universal high cost and uncertainties of legal proceedings, you probably can't afford to sue abroad. But few can afford to be sued. So you gamble that your foreign patents will deter potential infringers.

Getting a foreign patent helps you leverage your licensing clout and collect royalties on the overseas activities. Here's an example. The good news is that you've been granted a solid U.S. patent and successfully negotiated a lucrative, exclusive license with Titanic Tools, Ltd. (TTL), a Fortune 500 company that agrees to pay you $1 for each of your two-handled flyswatters it makes or sells. The bad news — you didn't file for a patent abroad and now all application deadlines have elapsed. Don't be surprised if Titanic then has the swatters manufactured in China for sale all over the world. You're only entitled to royalties on units sold in the United States — nowhere else. The law forbids the use of your U.S. patent to extract royalties for your licensee's activities anywhere you don't have patent coverage. However, if you had patent protection in China, TTL would have to pay you royalties on its entire production, and you could've asked for a higher royalty rate. The greater the territorial coverage, the higher the royalty.

Having overseas patent coverage makes you more attractive to potential licensees. Most large companies shy away from an invention if they can't secure a monopoly in most industrial countries. Ever-expanding globalization of commerce discourages heavy investments in tooling, marketing, and other start-up costs for a product that competitors can freely copy outside the U.S.

## Adding it up: Is it worth the money?

The substantial cost of obtaining and maintaining foreign patents is really the only factor that should prevent you from implementing an overseas patent program. Of course, cost is a pretty major factor, especially because most inventors seldom seek only one patent. As the technology is improved, they file additional applications, often for multiple patents in each country.

How much is substantial? As a rough estimate, plan to spend between $5,000 and $7,000 per patent per country just to get the application filed, and probably another $1,000 per patent per country per year to keep it going — what with maintenance fees (unlike the U.S., many foreign countries charge these every year during the pendency of your application) and other agent charges. Throw in an office action and an amendment or two and you can add another $3,000 per patent per country during the four years it takes to obtain the first generation of patents. Let's see: 12 countries, $60,000 here, $12,000 there, another $36,000 over there, and soon you're talking real money. In some English-speaking countries like Canada, India, or Australia, the costs may be less, but they're higher in Japan, France, and Germany.

After you get your patent, the maintenance fees continue per patent per country per year, for the life of the patent (typically 20 years from priority). These fees can range from a few hundred dollars a pop but can grow to over a thousand as the patent nears expiration. These figures are valid no matter which filing strategy you choose. (We discuss different strategies later in this chapter.) For example, if you file in the 12 major member nations of the European Union, plus Canada, Australia, Japan, China, South Korea, and Mexico (a relatively modest program), you need a potbellied piggy bank holding between $90,000 and $125,000, the bulk of which you need upfront. We don't have ESP, but we can probably answer your next question: No, you can't handle your foreign application yourself. Even your U.S. patent attorney must hire a correspondent patent agent in every targeted country. We include all these guys' fees and other charges in our estimates.

Don't even think about starting an overseas application program unless you're certain you can finance it to completion. In our experience, many folks and small businesses abandon their applications halfway through the process for lack of funds. The large sums they've already spent (and can't recover) would've been better spent on research and design (R&D) or marketing.

Try to be creative and let someone else pay the piper. If you can license your invention early, be a tough negotiator and insist that the big guy, your licensee, pay for the acquisition and maintenance of foreign patents.

Under international treaty, your lowly U.S. application (which now sounds like a bargain, eh?) automatically provides you with nearly worldwide protection — for a time (one year automatically, and up to two and one-half years if you file the PCT application discussed later). During that time you should find a licensee who can eventually pay for the foreign patents. During the one to two and one-half year window after U.S. filing, you have a great bargaining chip: the right to patents worldwide. But after the window closes, the bargaining chip goes away, and your invention becomes public domain everywhere you didn't file.

## Making the decision

Your decisions boil down to the same basic consideration: Are benefits you and your business will receive by filing abroad worth the cost? It's a business decision only you can make. Your patent lawyer can only answer peripheral questions about the topics we just discussed.

We can tell you that the simpler the technology, the more foreign protection you need, because it's more likely to be copied.

In each country, look at the revenue potentials of each patent and the adverse consequences of not being covered. Do the math, carefully add up your resources, and then make your best educated guess. We'd be leading you astray by giving you more definite guidelines. Every business decision is a gamble. This could be your biggest one.

We cannot stress enough the cost advantage provided by the international patent treaties — even if you're Bill Gates and your invention is a known winner. So, listen up Bill, unless you need to sue somebody in Morocco right away, you should probably file your U.S. patent application first and hold off filing in most foreign countries until the treaty deadlines approach. Otherwise, you're throwing away a year's worth of interest. But don't forget about those countries that didn't sign on to the treaty. So Bill, if you need to sue in Peru, make sure you file there, too — woo-hoo.

# Basic Rules of Filing for Foreign Patents

Before we get going on how to actually file a patent application abroad, we want to outline three basic rules you need to keep in mind from the start.

- ✔ **Keep your invention secret:** U.S. patent law gives you one full year to file a patent application after public disclosure, but most other countries don't allow you to have a patent if your invention was disclosed, without a confidentiality agreement, before you filed your U.S. patent application. Casually showing your homegrown prototype to Gus, your friendly neighbor, may constitute such a disclosure. You don't need a confidentiality agreement with your attorney. She's already under a legal obligation of strict confidentiality.

- ✔ **Get a foreign filing license:** As a U.S. citizen or legal resident, you can't file for a patent application or generally disclose your invention abroad before you obtain a *license* (a permit to do so) from the U.S. Government. Such a license is routinely returned to you with your U.S. patent application receipt (see Chapter 9). You risk severe punishment, even prison, and the inability to obtain a U.S. patent if you file an unauthorized application abroad.

If your invention relates to nuclear energy or national defense, the license may be delayed or denied. In critical cases, the Department of Defense may request a secrecy order, and you could be denied the right to a patent that would disclose sensitive information. However, the government does owe you reasonable compensation (see Chapter 9).

✔ **File foreign patent applications within one year from the filing date of your U.S. application:** This is critical if you want to claim priority based on your U.S. filing date under the Paris Convention, as we explain later. If you don't take advantage of this, you may lose your chance at foreign patents if your invention becomes known, either through publication of your U.S. application or the issue of your patent.

The publication of an application or the grant of a patent constitutes a public disclosure of the invention. If this rule weren't enforced, any unscrupulous individual who reads the published document could claim to be the inventor and file her own application. Foreign patent authorities don't investigate priority of invention contests, as is done by the USPTO, as we explain in Chapter 9.

As long as you keep your invention confidential, you can file applications abroad more than one year after filing your U.S. application. But you don't get the advantage of an early priority date and may lose the patent to someone filing overseas just ahead of you. The absolute deadline occurs when your U.S. application is published, about 18 months after its filing date or when your U.S. patent is granted, whichever comes first. To sum it all up: If you keep the invention secret, you have about 18 months to file abroad, but if you go public, you have only one year from your U.S. filing date. Mark your calendar about ten months from your U.S. filing date to remind you that you only have two months left to start your overseas filing process, and also about five months thereafter to warn you of the publication deadline.

We want to add a fourth rule of our own: Let your patent attorney handle all your filing overseas through her own stable of foreign correspondents. Don't wait until the last month before any deadline. She or the correspondents may need time to prepare translations and obtain certified copies of assignments.

# Where Should You File?

With the universal high cost of patents, few individuals or small businesses can afford a comprehensive foreign patent program. Even huge multinationals carefully select the countries in which they apply for patent protection. These decisions can be difficult in the early stages of your business venture as you teeter between the need to conserve financial resources and your desire to secure a broad marketing territory for your invention.

In general, give priority to countries that offer a good potential market over those that only have advanced manufacturing capabilities. When you control the most important markets, nobody else is interested in making the product. For example, if your product relates to surfing equipment, you should seek protection in the Western European nations, Australia, Brazil, and Japan. You can probably bypass Taiwan, South Korea, and China although these last countries are prime manufacturing candidates.

If the invention has worldwide applications, target the most prosperous countries rather than the most populous. The most popular choices, in order of preference, are: Western Europe, Japan, Canada, Australia, Mexico, Taiwan, New Zealand, Israel, South Africa, South Korea, and Brazil. The nature of your invention dictates where you apply. Obviously, you won't sell many snowmobiles in Australia. However, there are exceptions. For instance, if the manufacture of the product requires very sophisticated metallurgical techniques and precision machinery, get adequate patent protection in countries that specialize in that kind of manufacturing, like Germany and Japan, and perhaps forego filing in other big market countries.

Research the population, average personal income, and manufacturing capabilities of the countries you're considering. Don't rely on your attorney's recommendations, except in connection with expenses for each foreign application. The attorney has a duty to help you obtain the maximum protection in as many countries as possible, but he's not a marketing expert. Most attorneys are reluctant to discourage you from filing in any particular country because that country may one day offer a lucrative market or be of particular interest to a potential licensee.

Enforceability is another important concern. Even though markets are booming in the Middle East, it's still the wild Wild West when confronting infringers there. Your IP professional can help identify those countries you may want to research a little more before going ahead with a patent.

Don't forget to seek out the advice of your friendly foreign business contacts, including distributors or manufacturers. They may have a thing or two to tell you about the practical value of patents in their country.

## The typical approach to foreign patents

For many, the trick is to delay filing and hence delay shelling out your cash, for as long as possible. You can choose from two basic strategies to delay filing in individual countries and still get the patent coverage you need. You can file individual patent applications in each country you choose within the 1-year deadline provided under the *Paris Convention*, or you can further delay filing for another 18 months ($2^{1}/_{2}$ years from the date you filed your U.S. application) in most countries under the handy-dandy *Patent Cooperation Treaty (PCT)*. We outline both options here, with pros and cons.

## Filing under the Paris Convention

If you want to get a patent in only two or three countries or obtain a patent quickly, you should apply directly with those countries. You must also apply directly with any country that isn't a member of a multinational patent-filing system, such as a good number of South American nations.

Most countries are members of the Paris Convention for the Protection of Industrial Property (Paris Convention), which outlines basic rules and IP protections. The Paris Convention gives you up to one year after the filing date of your first patent application in your own country to file a corresponding application in a member country and get the earlier filing date as your *Convention priority date* (often shortened to *priority date*).

That priority date defines both your priority of invention and filing. The Convention priority date is the best thing since the Swiss Army knife. If someone else has filed an application for the same invention in that country after your priority date and before your foreign application is filed, your application trumps that other guy's. Also, if any document describing your invention is published during that interim period, it won't be cited against your foreign application. The priority date for trademarks and design patents under the same convention is limited to six months. The Convention priority date can be claimed in a single country application as well as in the multinational patent applications discussed later in this chapter.

 A few countries haven't ratified the convention. For a list of signatories, go to www.wipo.int/treaties/en/ShowResults.jsp?lang=en&treaty_id=2. Taiwan is an exception, but the U.S. and Taiwan have a separate bilateral treaty that provides the same filing convenience to American inventors.

In addition to providing a way to eliminate interim patent applications by another inventor, the Convention makes it easy to meet two of the three rules in the section "Basic Rules of Filing for Foreign Patents." If you take advantage of the Convention, you need only keep your invention confidential up to the date of your U.S. filing. You can start selling your super-duper squabulators the next morning and file foreign applications, initiating them either at home or abroad, up to 364 days later. Your foreign applications are considered to have been filed on the same date as the U.S. one. You must specifically claim the benefit of your U.S. filing date in each application.

Make sure that the foreign patent agent asks for this one-year convention-priority benefit when preparing your application, because it's not automatically granted. However, this benefit costs you — government authorities extract a few more bucks from your pocket. Your agent also wants his pound of flesh for checking the right box on the application cover letter. Then you're often asked to provide a certified copy of your original U.S. application that the USPTO gladly sends you for an extra fee.

## Multinational patent applications

Some small, mostly developing countries have established a common patent authority that can grant you a single multinational patent enforceable by the courts of all participant nations — a real bargain in terms of cost and time.

- **The Office Africain de la Propriete Industrielle (OAIP)** with headquarters in Yaoundé, Cameroon, groups the former French colonies of Benin, Burkina Faso, Cameroon, Central Africa Republic, Chad, Congo, Côte d'Ivoire, Equatorial Guinea, Gabon, Guinea, Guinea-Bissau, Mali, Mauritania, Niger, Senegal, and Togo. The OAIP accepts patent applications in English and French.

  Currently, the OAPI doesn't conduct any substantive examination. An OAPI patent that's enforceable in all the member nations is granted without warranty of validity. The patent validity issue remains to be resolved at the time of trial when you sue an infringer.

- **The African Regional Industrial Property Organization (ARIPO)** in Harare, Zimbabwe, covers the former British possessions of Gambia, Ghana, Lesotho, Malawi, Mozambique, Sierra Leona, South Africa, Sudan, Swaziland, Uganda, United Republic of Tanzania, Zambia, and Zimbabwe. The ARIPO language is English. The ARIPO conducts a formal examination of the application before granting a patent.

- **The Eurasian Patent Office (EAPO)** operating under the Eurasian Patent Convention (EAPC) in Moscow, gathers the former Soviet republics of Armenia, Azerbaijan, Belarus, Kazakhstan, Kyrgyzstan, Republic of Moldova, Russian Federation, Tajikistan, and Turkmenistan. Applications must be in Russian. The EAPO conducts a substantive examination only upon request when you file your application.

## Filing under the European system

The members of the European Union (EU) and a few candidate nations have instituted a well-rounded patent system, administered by the European

Patent Office (EPO) located in Munich, Germany and in The Hague, Netherlands.

The contracting states are Austria, Belgium, Bulgaria, Croatia, Cyprus, Czech Republic, Denmark, Estonia, Finland, France, Germany, Greece, Hungary, Iceland, Ireland, Italy, Latvia, Liechtenstein, Lithuania, Luxembourg, Malta, Monaco, the Netherlands, Norway, Poland, Portugal, Romania, Slovakia, Slovenia, Spain, Sweden, Switzerland, Turkey, and the United Kingdom. That list will grow as other nations join the EU. For a nominal fee, an EPO application can be extended to Albania, Bosnia, and Herzegovina, Macedonia, and Serbia in anticipation of their future admission.

The EPO accepts patent applications in English, French, or German, but after the application has been approved in one of the three official languages, the claims must be translated into the other two. The patent can then be filed in any one of the designated countries to be issued by the local patent authority. If the country doesn't accept one of the three official languages, the patent must be translated into the national idiom. You get the same patent granted by all countries, but each in a different national language. Lately there has been some effort to relax these outdated restrictions. Check out the latest info at www.epo.org.

Why didn't the EU originally adopt a simple system similar to OAIP, ARIPO, or EAPC, where one patent in a single language is valid in all member countries? First, national pride. Can you imagine the French giving full faith and credit to a patent document in English? Also, European patent agents outside Germany, where the first EPO opened, didn't want to be left out and insisted that the patent be provided in each nation and in each applicable national language. So, after your patent application has been approved by the EPO, thanks to the services of your German or Dutch patent agent, you must hire patent agents in member countries you selected on your application. They translate into Italian, Portuguese, Finnish, or whatever. At this point, you've paid your U.S. patent attorney, the German patent agent, and agents in some other designated nations. Also, you need to pay a plethora of government charges and translators — two more reasons to keep your application short and simple.

## Filing under the PCT

Under the *Patent Cooperation Treaty* (PCT), over 100 nations operate a common, uniform application process for utility patents. The PCT lets you submit a single patent application in your own domestic patent office to reserve the right to file that application in any contracting nation. Moreover, the PCT integrates the Paris Convention, and counts among its members the multinational patent authorities including the EPO.

By filing a PCT application in English with the USPTO in Washington, you can postpone entering your application abroad for two and one-half years from the priority date of your initial U.S. application. WIPO, headquartered in Geneva, Switzerland, administers the PCT. This system lets you to postpone the heavy cost of filing overseas, giving you time to test-market your invention. By the 30th month, you should know whether you're going to get a worthwhile patent. By then, you either have your U.S. patent, or you've undergone a fairly complete examination. (See Chapters 4–10 for the whole patent story.) If it looks like you're not getting a good patent, you can abandon your foreign filing and save a bundle. PCT membership changes constantly. Check the list at `www.wipo.int/pct/guide/en/gdvol1/annexes/annexa/ax_a.pdf`.

A PCT application goes through four stages: the filing stage, the international stage, the regional stage (for some countries), and finally, the national stage.

There is no such thing as an "international patent." An International Patent Application filed under the PCT is primarily a way of delaying filing in individual countries. If you need to sue someone for patent infringement in Morocco, you still need a Moroccan patent — and a few dirhams.

If you want to file your application in the USPTO, at least one inventor needs to be a U.S. citizen. Otherwise, you have to file at WIPO. PCT procedures, regulations, and fees are in a constant state of flux. What we write today may change by the time you read this. Check the USPTO Web site.

### Filling out the filing stage

You begin by filing your PCT application with the USPTO, which serves as the receiving office. Fortunately, you can file your PCT application in the same format as a regular U.S. utility patent application, but on A4 paper (8.26 11.69 inches). See Chapter 8 for more on utility patent applications.

1. **Find the forms you need to fill out. You need**

   - A Request form.

   - A Transmittal Letter form.

   - A Power of Attorney form (when applicable).

   The USPTO offers the forms and guidelines (`www.uspto.gov`). Click on Patents, and then Patent Cooperation Treaty. Click Chapter I for the forms.

2. **Fill out the Transmittal Letter and Power of Attorney forms.**

3. **Next fill out the Request form. It comes with ample instructions.**

   • Follow the instructions to the letter or you may be rejected.

   • Claim the filing date of your prior U.S. application — so long as it was filed no more than a year before the PCT application — in order to establish the earliest possible priority date.

   • Sit down before tackling the Fee Calculation Sheet, part of the Request form. The total may exceed $3,000 for filing.

4. **Send in your application.**

   You may fax or mail your application, but you get a discount when you file electronically, and save even more if you use the PCT-EASY software. Check out the *PCT Applicant's Guide* on the USPTO Web site.

   Your PCT application *must* be filed by the one-year anniversary of your U.S. application. No amount of whining will overcome this strict deadline. Also, if you're mailing your application, a postmark won't cut it. The USPTO provides special filing procedures, using Express Mail by the U.S. Postal Service where the filing date is your Express Mail "date in" date. If filing online, remember the filing date and time is the time in Washington, D.C. If you're in Honolulu, and you wait to file until after dinner on the deadline, Cinderella may have already left the ball. It's best not to wait. If you have a question, ask your IP pro.

5. **The USPTO, as a receiving office, verifies that your application conforms to applicable regulations and that you paid the fees.**

   You also get time for corrections or additions before the application is forwarded to the International Bureau at WIPO for the second stage.

---

# The French made them do it

The PCT administration is essentially European in style and mentality. The French, who think the autocratic way is the only way and favor forms over substance, have had a major influence on these procedures. Every form must be filled out exactly as prescribed. Your last name must be entered first and your first name last. Your country of residence can't be listed as *United States of America, U.S.A.,* or *U.S.* No sir. It must be *US* with no periods, period! And so it goes, with a multitude of meticulous rules that, just because they're so detailed, must be constantly updated. Fortunately, the good people in the USPTO bend over backwards to help you with all these PCT procedures. They often graciously correct your mistakes instead of returning the application.

### *Going through the international stage*

The International Bureau deals only with the multinational aspect of the application, which is the International Stage. Because the PCT was approved in two separate parts, the treaty is divided into two chapters. Member countries can observe the limited provisions of Chapter I, which includes an anticipation search but no examination of the merits of the invention, or adhere to the whole treaty, including Chapter II, which includes an examination of the claims based on the findings of the Chapter I search along with a written opinion on patentability by an examiner. Both chapters are processed during the International Stage. Currently, all PCT nations are bound by both chapters. Some future members may limit their participation to Chapter I. Check www.wipo.org for the current members' status.

In Chapter I, a few months after your application reaches the International Bureau, your claims will be subject to an anticipation search, better known as the *international search,* conducted by the *International Searching Authority* you designate — either the USPTO, the EPO, or the Korean Intellectual Property Office (KIPO). Even though there is no rigorous examination under Chapter I, the searcher (usually an examiner) will indicate which of the prior art references he found have bearing on each of your current claims.

United States IP practitioners don't seem to agree on the best searching venue, but we suggest letting money versus the scope of search be your guide. The EPO currently costs about $2,500, the USPTO about $1,800, and the KIPO about $250. Selecting the EPO may offer a better opportunity to flush out prior foreign patents but at a high cost. Selecting the USPTO will likely result in the same list of prior art references found in your earlier U.S. application. For low cost, you can't beat the KIPO, but don't rely too heavily on the results, and there can be additional translation costs. The EPO can't be selected for certain biotechnology or business method inventions. If you have questions, contact your IP pro.

After you review the *International Search Report,* you have the opportunity to amend your claims. Exactly 18 months from the priority date, the application, search report, and any amendments will be published for the entire world to read. Before the end of the 19th month from your priority date, you can initiate the Chapter II phase by filing a Demand for International Preliminary Examination of your application. (Get the form by clicking on Chapter II in the PCT section of the USPTO Web site.)

Rules always change among the members of the PCT. The list of countries that still observe the Demand and International Preliminary Examination requirement has shrunk to a point where many applicants don't bother filing the Demand. Now, nearly all countries accept filing of the application in their respective patent offices within 30 months from the priority date based on

Chapter I alone. Consult your IP specialist to decide. If you file a Demand, you should receive a report on the International Preliminary Examination a few months afterwards. Typically, you have another opportunity to amend your claims before entering the regional and national stages. On entering Chapter II with a Demand, you also have at least 30 months from your priority date to file applications in the countries that adhere to Chapter II.

You must file your application before the expiration of the 19th month from your priority date in those few countries that require adherence to Chapter II.

### Entering the regional stage

After the International Publication of your PCT application, you can move on to getting the actual patents by filing your PCT application with one of the three regional patent authorities mentioned earlier: OAIP, ARIPO, and EAPO. These must be filed within the same time period as if they were being filed into individual countries. You can also file your application in the EPO under the same time constraints. The EPO conducts an examination and then issues a patent that can be entered in any designated country in the European group. In most EPO countries, after the patent is issued, it only needs to be translated into the national idiom before it becomes locally enforceable.

During the regional phase, your attorney's local correspondent deals with the multinational organizations on your behalf. The office reports are sent to your attorney for your review and instructions on how to answer any objection or rejection. Don't be surprised if the process drags out over a year or two.

### Entering the national phase

Some countries, including the U.S., Australia, Canada, China, and Mexico, don't belong to a regional group. You must send your PCT application to each one separately through your attorney's local correspondent. Your PCT application may be subject to a complete new examination, just as any domestic (non-PCT) application. Some countries skip the new examination if you accept the results of the Preliminary International Examination (if you haven't amended your claims after that examination).

Before entering the national phase (and plunking down about $5,000 per country), check with the foreign agent to see whether that country's laws allow additional delay. For example, Canada provides an additional 1 year delay (up to 42 months from the priority date) for only a few hundred dollars.

You must have a local patent practitioner (usually a foreign correspondent of your U.S. attorney) at each level and pay local fees, making it all expensive.

### Selecting the proper filing protocol

Often, the most economical route to foreign patent protection involves first filing your U.S. application and then 12 months later filing a PCT, and then 18 months later filing in the national or regional offices. This is the "traditional" approach that typically results in your knowing whether or not you're going to get a worthwhile U.S. patent before incurring the high cost of foreign national phase filings. However, the PCT and regional patent authorities offer you two slightly different domestic and foreign patent filing scenarios (one of which may better saddle your foreign patent horse):

- ✔ Instead of first filing a formal U.S. application, you first file a provisional application in the U.S. (see Chapter 7). Within a year, file a formal application under the PCT and in non-PCT countries. Later, you can enter your PCT application in the USPTO as part of the national stage. This method is particularly effective if you're on a limited budget, or need to refine your invention before finalizing your applications. The downside is: Granting your patent in the U.S. is delayed (Figure 19-1).

- ✔ File a provisional application in the U.S., and within a year file a formal application in the U.S., the PCT, and non-PCT countries. This approach postpones the big expenses associated with regional and national filings for at least 30 months, but expedites the issue of your U.S. patent.

# What's a Utility Model?

Instead of getting an expensive utility *patent*, some countries offer a kind of stripped-down form of utility patent protection called a *Utility Model*. This is generally cheaper and easier to get, but is weaker and doesn't last as long. If your invention isn't all that innovative, and you're worried about spending a lot on a patent application just to see it denied, a utility model might be just the ticket. The requirements and scope of protection are often different for every country, so ask the agents in each country of interest what's required.

**Figure 19-1:** Typical delayed foreign filing under the PCT.

Because there is no Utility Model protection in the U.S., your IP professional may not have a good familiarity in this area. Be sure to ask her about obtaining updated information on Utility Models in your foreign countries of interest, especially if your invention has weak patentability.

# Filing for Design Protection Abroad

Only the United States offers design patents (see Chapter 5), but many countries offer similar protection for industrial designs. The scope of protection is about the same. The major difference: In many countries, the duration of protection is less than the 14 years under a U.S. design patent.

The European Union provides *Community Design* protection for a new appearance of a product that exhibits "individual character." This protection requires lower standards of novelty and non-obviousness than a U.S. design patent does. The Community Design protection has a term of 5 years from the deposit of a graphic representation of the design, and can be renewed four times for a total span of 25 years. Applications to register a Community Design are processed by the Office for Harmonization in the Internal Market (OHIM — often called the European trademark office) in Alicante, Spain. Information about the OHIM registration process is at http://oami.eu.int/. After the registration is granted, it's enforceable in all 27 member nations of the EU without having to obtain a separate registration in each country.

The Community Design protection is typical of what is available in most industrialized countries. You can register industrial designs in Africa with the OAIP and the ARIPO (see the section "Entering the regional stage," earlier in this chapter, for more info on these regional patent authorities). The conditions and procedures are similar to applying with the OHIM. These applications have to be handled by the local correspondents of your attorney.

You may also want to check out the *International Deposit of Industrial Designs Agreement* (The Hague Agreement). About 30 nations adhere to this agreement, which offers basically the same type of protection as the Community Design. Check the WIPO site or ask your attorney. Any type of application for design protection abroad can claim a priority date upon a design patent application filed in the USPTO no more than six months before filing abroad, instead of one year for a utility patent.

Have a local IP practitioner handle your filing or deposit. Most U.S. practitioners maintain a network of correspondents for that kind of filing. Requirements vary from country to country. A design doesn't usually disclose any kind of technological breakthrough and, consequently, isn't subject to the foreign filing license limitations imposed on utility applications.

# Protecting Your Plant Overseas

About 35 countries, including the United States, Japan, the United Kingdom, France, Germany, Canada, Australia, Italy, Spain, Argentina, and Mexico, are members of the *International Convention for the Protection of New Variety of Plants* (UPOV). Under this convention, a member country must give a plant breeder exclusive rights to the reproduction of a sexually reproductive or vegetatively propagated new plant for a minimum of 15 years. The new plant must be clearly distinguishable from commonly known varieties by at least one characteristic, and must be stable in its sexual reproduction or vegetative propagation. Under the U.S. implementation of the treaty, called the *Plant Variety Protection Act* (PVPA), administered by the *Plant Variety Protection Office* (PVPO) of the Department of Agriculture, the term of the protection is 25 years for trees and vines, and 20 years for other plants.

This protection is broader than that obtained under a U.S. plant patent (see Chapter 5). Note that in the United States, and theoretically in any other country with a plant patent system, a new plant can be protected in any particular country under either the UPOV registration or a plant patent, but not both. When applying for registration in a member country, you may claim a filing priority date based upon either your U.S. application for a plant patent or your registration under the PVPA filed within the last 12 months.

# Protecting Your Mark Abroad

On November 2, 2003, the United States joined the Madrid System for the international registration of marks by signing the *Protocol Relating to the Madrid Agreement Concerning the International Registration of Marks* (the Madrid Protocol). This treaty lets you to apply for registration of your mark in at least 70 countries with the click of a button and — by European standards — for a meager fee. The Madrid system is administered by the International Bureau of the World Intellectual Property Organization (WIPO) in Geneva, Switzerland. WIPO handles the prosecution of your international trademark application and, if approved, forwards the registration the designated individual foreign country trademark offices for approval.

Before the treaty, a U.S. resident had to apply for registration of a mark in each country, at the average cost of $1,000 per country just for the original application, except when using the European Community's Office for Harmonization in the Internal Market (OHIM) or the OAPI and the ARIPO in Africa to get a registration enforceable in all of their member states.

---

## The march toward global trademarks

The Madrid Protocol is a momentous event and a major step toward a global mark protection system. In the United States, unlike most other jurisdictions, we have a unique system of mark registration and protection that is predicated upon use of a mark rather than its entry in a government register. Many complex adjustments to the rules of the game had to be arduously negotiated by U.S. representatives to accommodate the peculiarities of our system. This is one of the reasons it took us 112 years to accede to this convention, first signed on April 14, 1891.

---

# OHIM, why bother?

Even though the European Community joined the Madrid Protocol in October 2004, filing a Community Trademark (CTM) application directly with the OHIM still has some advantages. For instance, a registration under the Madrid Protocol in the OHIM or any country is totally dependant upon your U.S. application and registration during the first five years from application. If your application is refused or successfully protested, or your registration is cancelled during this five year period, all your Madrid Protocol registrations can lapse. By contrast, non–Madrid Protocol applications in individual countries or the OHIM don't even require you to file in the United States first. The registration lives or dies on its own. For more about the European Community mark, go to the OHIM Web site at `http://oami.eu.int/`.

# Let's all go to Madrid virtually

Applications for registration under the Madrid Protocol are handled by WIPO in Geneva and must be based on a *domestic registration or application* (you must first apply in your own country) and filed through your domestic trademark office. The online filing procedure at the USPTO is simple:

1. **File your WIPO application online, using the same application program you used to file your U.S. application (see Chapter 17).**

2. **You don't have to repeat the info from your domestic application.**

   Just enter your serial number, and the software combines your online entries with the information from your previously filed U.S. application and whisks the package to WIPO in Switzerland at the click of a button.

Be careful about changing any of the prepopulated information supplied by the USPTO. Making changes will delay and could prevent certification of your application by the USPTO to WIPO.

## Copyrighting overseas

International conventions and treaties, subscribed to by almost every country, mandate that each nation gives nonresidents the same copyright protection it extends to its own citizens and legal residents, with no registration or other formality. So, in principle, there's no compelling reason to register your copyright abroad.

However, some countries, like the United States, grant special procedural rights to owners of registered copyrights. If you're concerned about infringement of your copyright in a particular country, have your IP specialist look at the copyright regulations in that jurisdiction to see if you could benefit from a local registration.

3. **The filing fee for all designated countries can also be paid online to the USPTO.**

   A U.S. applicant designating about 25 countries in a Madrid Protocol application saves about $20,000 over filing in each country separately.

4. **You should receive filing confirmation by e-mail right away.**

   This number (and your old U.S. serial No.) will allow you to access the status of your application online.

If you follow the directions and did not have to change any of the prepopulated information in the forms, your application could be certified by the USPTO and forwarded to the International Bureau (IB) of the WIPO within hours. The IB will check for irregularities and let you correct any before approving your international registration. But now your international registration needs to be approved by each country you've designated. Each conducts its own examination and may issue a rejection based on similarities with existing registrations on its own register. If that happens, you'll need to hire an agent in that country to help you address and overcome the rejection. Even if this happens, the process is still no more expensive than if you had filed in the individual countries at the outset.

# Chapter 20

# Making 'Em Pay: Licensing Your IP Rights

## In This Chapter

▶ Exploiting your IP rights

▶ Avoiding tax and antitrust problems

▶ Marketing your assets

▶ Maximizing the income from your musical works

*A*lways develop your IP assets with an eye towards letting these assets, and your IP rights to them, work like a lucrative investment. The royalties they generate, just like dividends and interest, can keep your wallet bulging — without your lifting a finger. That dream has become reality for many astute entrepreneurs who took advantage of licensing opportunities that rewarded their creativity. You can license your invention, know-how, original work of authorship, or commercial identifier as long as it is protected by a patent, trade secret, copyright, or trademark. In this chapter, we explore the different kinds of licenses and government requirements to comply with — and touch on developing a licensing plan and dealing with music business quirks.

## Types of Licenses

Your driver's license gives you the permission to do something that you previously couldn't do under the law — take your jalopy out for a spin on the public highway. This permission is given by the government, which owns the highway, to you as part of a deal. For that license to remain in effect, you have to uphold your end of the deal: drive responsibly, follow the rules, and pay your taxes — otherwise they will take your license away.

A *license* is a contract between two parties. The *licensor* is the owner of an IP asset and its corresponding IP rights. The *licensee* is an individual or company willing to use the IP assets in exchange for the payment of royalties or other valuable considerations. For example, if the IP asset is an invention and the IP right a patent, the licensee can practice the invention without being sued for infringement by the patent-owning licensor.

A license doesn't actually transfer an asset or right — it just gives the licensee permission to use the IP asset, backed by the licensor's promise not to cancel that authorization as long as the licensee keeps up her end of the bargain by making required payments. A license is like the lease of a house, where the landlord gives the tenant permission to live there as long as he pays the rent on time. A license is different from an *assignment,* which is an outright transfer of an IP asset or right, which is like selling a house.

There are six types of licenses, according to the underlying type of IP right:

- ✔ **Patent license:** This license permits use of one of these IP assets:

    - A technological breakthrough, such as a better mousetrap

    - An ornamental design, such as the shape of a perfume bottle

    - A variety of plant, such as a new species of cotton

    You can license your asset before you get your patent, because a license is a contract that stands independently from the patent. Courts recognize that when a manufacturer takes a license from an inventor, the former is buying insurance (with the royalties as the premium) against being sued for infringement if and when the patent is awarded. After the license agreement is signed, it doesn't matter whether the patent is granted. The manufacturer must pay royalties for the duration of the agreement.

- ✔ **Trade-secret license:** A trade-secret license is a contract to have the licensor disclose proprietary and confidential information to the licensee in exchange for a payment and a promise to keep the information under wraps. This is common in the chemical field where it's relatively easy to keep formulae and manufacturing processes secret, and is often more practical than getting a patent (see Chapter 4).

- ✔ **Copyright license:** A copyright license allows the licensee to enjoy one or more of the copyrights listed in Chapter 12. Copyright registration isn't a prerequisite to the granting of the license, but recommended for the reasons outlined in Chapter 14.

- ✔ **Trademark/Servicemark license:** This license authorizes someone else to operate under one or more of your commercial identifiers. The law requires that you keep some quality control over the activities of your licensee so that the customers who relied on the quality of your goods or services in the past will not be deceived.

Nowadays, many products aren't made by their original manufacturers but by firms that use the trademark under license from the original manufacturer and strict quality control conditions. A Hang Ten brand of shirt may have been manufactured by one of many domestic and foreign licensees of Hang Ten International.

In the U.S., registration of a mark isn't a prerequisite to the license, but it is recommended (see Chapter 18). But mark registration is required in other countries where the right to a mark isn't based upon a first use in commerce, but upon entry on a government register.

✔ **Merchandising license:** This is a copyright or trademark license, or a combination of both, where the range of goods upon which the mark or the copyrighted work is used goes beyond its original purpose. Certain commercial identifiers are so strong, recognized, and widely accepted that they can be rented out for use on a wide variety of goods. For instance, a movie studio may license the use of a cartoon character on a variety of children's products from toys to book bags.

Merchandising is pure IP exploitation that depends on the value of the copyrighted material or commercial identifier itself, and not the quality or reputation of the original products or services. For example, the Dior mark appears on a multitude of products, from garments and perfumes to sporting goods.

✔ **Combination license:** In a combination license, several IP assets and rights are bundled together, such as when a manufacturer is authorized to produce and sell a patented article under the licensor's mark and package it with copyrighted graphics. This type of license is subject to antitrust limitations. See "Avoiding illegal entanglements," later in the chapter.

A *franchise* is a trademark or servicemark license with rules about how the licensee (or *franchisee*) shall conduct the business according to a method imposed by the licensor, called the *franchisor*. This type of contractual relationship includes some transfer of know-how and technical assistance by the franchisor (coupled with a hefty down payment by the franchisee). Fast-food franchises are a familiar example, where a franchisee acquires a restaurant carrying the franchisor's servicemark and prepares and serves food under a set method and under strict quality control.

A servicemark license that involves some operating control (instead of just quality control) by the licensor is treated as a franchise — a critical distinction because, due to the large initial investment and high royalty rates, franchises are subject to special regulations by state and federal authorities.

# Inspecting Basic Elements of a License

Before you can negotiate any type of license agreement, you must understand the important parts of the agreement and the specific legal clauses that you need to include — so we throw in examples from a patent license to give you some legal lingo to chew on. These clauses can be adapted to cover licenses for other types of IP assets and rights.

This outline of the basic clauses in a license agreement isn't exhaustive. Like any contract, the license agreement must include a number of additional clauses relative to future improvements, technical assistance, warranties, legal action against infringers, termination, notices, arbitration, and attorney's fees, just to name a few. Our goal is to make you aware of the key issues you should address when exploiting your IP assets. You need the assistance of a competent IP specialist to negotiate and draft the license agreement.

## Defining IP assets and rights

You must first clearly define the IP asset and/or right you're licensing:

> *Licensor is the sole owner of an improvement in an auto-focusing mechanism for cameras (The "Improvement"), disclosed in a pending U.S. utility patent application entitled Auto-focusing Mechanism for Outdoor Surveillance Video Camera under Docket No. 200-1 at the offices of Sue-Ann Dannoy, Esq. in Alexandria, Virginia (the "Application") from which and from continuation applications thereof a number of domestic and foreign patents are expected to issue (the "Patents").*
>
> *Licensee wishes to obtain the right to manufacture and sell several types of cameras using the Improvement.*

*Note:* Until it is published, a patent application isn't identified by its serial number — always keep that information confidential.

## Granting permission to use your IP

This clause defines the scope of the permitted activities, and is the most important part of the license agreement.

### Exclusivity

The *exclusivity clause* states who gets to use the invention.

✔ **Exclusive:** The licensor waives any right to practice the invention or to authorize anybody else to do so.

✔ **Co-exclusive:** The licensor reserves the right to practice the invention himself or through his company, but agrees to license only the licensee.

✔ **Non-exclusive:** The licensor reserves the right to practice the invention and can also license third parties in competition with the licensee.

In general, an exclusive license carries higher royalties than the other two. Only an exclusive licensee can file legal actions against infringers.

### The grant clause

The clause must be very specific in order to avoid future disputes. For the sake of illustration, this license contains multiple exclusivity provisions. Most licenses have a single exclusivity clause.

> *Licensor grants Licensee:*
>
> *a) an exclusive license and permission to manufacture, offer for sale, sell, and use digital still cameras incorporating the Improvement with right to sublicense others to do the same,*
>
> *b) a co-exclusive license and permission to manufacture, offer for sale, sell, and use analog and digital video cameras incorporating the Improvement without right to sublicense others to do the same; and*
>
> *c) a non-exclusive license and permission to manufacture, offer for sale, sell, and use analog still cameras incorporating the Improvement without right to license others to do the same.*
>
> *Licensor reserves the right to manufacture, offer for sale, sell, and use said analog and digital video cameras, without right to license others, and to manufacture, offer for sale, sell, and use said analog still cameras and license others to do the same.*

Notice how a single word, such as *exclusive* or *co-exclusive*, buried amid other legal gobbledegook, can drastically change the meaning of the clause.

### Territory and field of use

An owner of any type of IP assets and rights can divide and parcel the geographical areas and commercial fields where the invention can be practiced or applied. In this illustration, each license has a distinct territory:

> *Said exclusive license shall be limited to the consumer market in the United States and Canada and shall not extend to cameras primarily intended for professional or industrial use.*

*Said co-exclusive license shall be limited to the United States and Canada in any field of use except geographical mapping and law enforcement surveillance cameras.*

*Said non-exclusive license shall apply worldwide without any restriction.*

### Duration

To avoid allegations of abusive conduct, the duration of the license must be no more than the life of the patent or any other applicable IP right. A patent license agreement should specify that if no patent is issued, the duration should be no more than 20 years (the maximum life of a utility patent).

*The term of the above licenses and the obligations imposed on the Licensee in this agreement shall not last beyond the expiration of the last of the Patents. In any territory where no patent has issued within ten years from the effective date of this agreement, said license and obligations shall expire on the twentieth anniversary of said date.*

## Getting paid: Remuneration

The law allows great flexibility in setting up the payment for the license. Payment may comprise

✔ One or more lump sums

✔ Royalties based on net proceeds, number of items made or sold, costs of goods, or any other readily verifiable parameter

✔ A combination of the above

Advances against royalties, delayed payments, stepped-up or stepped-down royalty rates based on sale proceeds or number of items sold, and guaranteed remittances can be used to fine-tune the agreement to the circumstances:

*Licensee shall pay Licensor each of the following:*

*A non-refundable lump sum of $5,000.00 on each anniversary of the effective date of this agreement.*

*During the first 10 years of the term of this agreement, royalties at the rate of $10.00 per camera manufactured under said exclusive and co-exclusive licenses, and at the rate of $3.00 per camera manufactured under said non-exclusive license; plus 1% of the net proceeds from the sales of all types of cameras. After the 10th anniversary of the effective date of this agreement, said royalty rates shall be reduced by one half.*

*A royalty advance of $25,000.00 upon execution of this agreement by all parties. Licensee shall not apply more than $5,000.00 per month out of said advance payment against royalties payable to licensor.*

The details of the remuneration clause are usually dictated by the business circumstances — the financial status and marketing clout of the licensor, the anticipated sales, the required investment in tooling and marketing, and so on.

A minimum performance clause should always be included in an exclusive license because you depend entirely upon the licensee's performance to exploit your IP asset. Such a clause may use a sliding scale to keep the licensed company on its best behavior. For example:

> *Licensor shall have the right to terminate this agreement by thirty day written notice to the Licensee in the event that the total amount of monetary remuneration received by Licensor does not exceed:*
>
> *$50,000.00 during the first full calendar year,*
>
> *$150,000.00 or one half of the total monetary remuneration received by licensor during the preceding calendar year in any subsequent calendar year, whichever is greater.*

## Reporting

Except when license fees are fully paid upfront or by a fixed payment schedule, the licensee should be required to periodically report its production and/or sales and pay the applicable royalties:

> *Within thirty days from the end of each calendar year, Licensee shall provide Licensor with a report of the number of cameras manufactured under each of said licenses and of net proceeds collected by Licensee during said calendar year and shall tender payment of royalties applicable to said number and proceeds.*

## Trademark licenses

If the license authorizes the licensee to use or operate under your mark, you must include a clause allowing you to control the quality of the goods or services provided to the customer under your identifier.

> *Goods manufactured under this agreement shall conform with all governmental regulations and shall maintain a level of quality and merchantability equal to or better than the goods currently being manufactured and sold by Licensor. Licensor shall have the right to enter Licensee's manufacturing and storage facilities on any working day during regular business hours without prior notice to inspect said goods for compliance with this clause.*

As owner of the mark, you're liable for any losses suffered by the consumer as a result of any defect or failure of the product or inadequate service.

In a patent license agreement, the licensor usually won't make any warranty that the invention is worth anything, will work as expected, or that the product or process made under it is effective and safe. There's no legal obligation imposed on the licensor to exert any degree of quality control over the activities of the licensee, making the licensor immune to liability for any of the licensee's failures or misdeeds.

# Assigning Rather than Licensing

Under certain circumstances, and for sundry reasons (such as tax considerations, wanting no further entanglement with the licensee, or because your prospective licensee wants it), you may decide to sell your IP asset and IP rights, under a written document called an *assignment*. Just like a grant deed on a piece of property, the assignment must be notarized (acknowledged before a U.S. consular officer if you reside abroad) to be readily admissible in court. This type of legal paper can be quite short and to the point:

> *For good and valid consideration, hereby acknowledged, I, Jeanne Doe, the owner of U.S. patent no. 9,999,999 for an improvement in motorcycle helmet, hereby assign and transfer my entire interest in said improvement and patent to John Deer, a U.S. citizen residing in Buckeye, Arizona.*

The same wording can be used to transfer a copyright or mark. Just make sure that the description of what's being transferred is complete and readily identifiable (attach a copy or photograph if necessary).

If you're John Deer, you want to record the assignment as soon as possible in the USPTO, or any other appropriate agency. In general, recording cuts off the transferor's right to assign the same asset or right to another person. If you don't record a patent or patent application assignment within three months from its signing, any subsequent assignment takes precedence over yours when it's recorded. Your sole remedy is to sue that weasel Jeanne and try to get some compensation for your losses.

Whether you license or assign doesn't necessarily dictate how you get your money — you can use a lump sum payment or royalty program for either method. However, a royalty program should include an agreement with all the payment and reporting clauses usually found in a license agreement.

# Getting Down to the Government Stuff

You probably thought that after you got your registration, you were through with the government, right? Wrong. Uncle Sam is your partner. Both state and federal agencies regulate some types of license agreements, make sure that all taxes are paid, and act as an antitrust watchdog.

## Recording your document

In general, license agreements don't require filing or registration with government regulatory agencies. However, you can record (don't confuse recording with registering) a patent or trademark license with the USPTO, and a copyright license with the Copyright Office (see Chapter 14), just as you'd record an assignment or other transfer of title. An exclusive licensee wants to record the license to deter infringers and to prevent the licensor from granting a similar license to someone else.

The big exception is a franchise. In most states, you have to *qualify* (have it approved) your franchise scheme before you can offer it to prospective franchisees, proving that you can fulfill the promises you make. In some states, the qualification process is very strict and takes months. After your sell a franchise, it must be recorded with the appropriate government agencies.

Franchising is a very complex operation best handled by an attorney specializing in that field.

## Considering tax advantages

As you know, the government wants a chunk out of any exchange of money. We'd like to alert you to the tax consequences of licensing your IP assets and rights — versus assigning them (see earlier).

For tax purposes, proceeds from a license are usually considered ordinary income. Proceeds from an assignment of assets are treated as capital gains. The IRS may treat some exclusive patent licenses like assignments if the licensor retains little or no control.

When negotiating the transfer of IP assets or rights, consider the lower rate of taxation on capital gains compared to ordinary income. Sometimes, an assignment may be more lucrative than a license when taxes are plugged into the equation. All of these are touchy tax issues; rely on a tax attorney or CPA.

## Avoiding illegal entanglements

To a certain degree, patents, copyrights, and trademarks are monopolies and exceptions to many unfair competition and antitrust regulations. Therefore, the courts and government agencies monitor their use to prevent any coercive practices by IP right owners. The basic rule that will keep you out of trouble can be summarized: Don't leverage your IP rights to obtain advantages not directly related to those rights. The most common faux pas are:

 ✔ **Tie-ins:** An illegal tie-in obligates a licensee to buy something from you that lies beyond the scope of your IP rights. For instance, in the camera example we use in this chapter, you can't obligate the licensee to buy his lenses from you, because your patent doesn't cover the lenses.

 ✔ **Bundlings:** Questionable bundling occurs when you compel someone to take licenses based on several patents or other IP rights or when you bundle different IP assets or rights in a single license or in related ones. This practice is questionable rather than outright illegal because the nature of the wrongful conduct depends upon the circumstances.

 In the camera example, if you have a patent on a lens design and force the licensee to take a license for the lens along with the auto-focusing mechanism that he wants, and there are other sources of lens technology, the license violates antitrust law. However, if the licensee requests a license to make your lens because of its superior design, you're off the antitrust hook. It's also a no-no to obligate your patent licensee to also use your trademark, but if the licensee likes your trademark and asks you to license it along with your patent, there's no harm done.

The main reason to avoid antitrust or anticompetition clauses in your license agreement isn't that Big Brother will charge you with violating the Sherman Act. The government is too busy chasing the corporate big fish to play in your little pond. The problem is that your licensee may have grounds to attack the agreement in any future dispute, sue you, and bring Big Bro into the fray.

# Adopting a Licensing Strategy

Many inventors and other developers of IP assets and rights don't have a clue about how to find a licensee to bring their creations to the market. They often fall victim to unscrupulous invention development companies (see our comments about these guys in Chapter 3). No magic formula will work for everybody, but the best way is to plan your licensing strategy before you pursue IP rights, but if you haven't, all is not lost. If you understand the marketplace, you can develop an effective and lucrative strategy. The first step to a good licensing strategy is understanding market realities. Here are a few observations based on many years serving fledgling entrepreneurs:

 ✔ The more you develop your project, the more you get for it. You generally can't sell an idea or concept. A patented but unproven invention may sometimes be sold or licensed, but not for much. An ongoing business, built around a product, process, or method protected by IP rights can be readily and lucratively sold.

 ✔ Few large companies respond to an unsolicited license offer or proposal.

---

## Patent exhaustion

You must be aware that after your patented product is manufactured and sold by your licensee, you have no right of control over how that product is used by anyone else. Your patent rights are exhausted, and generally you cannot extract additional royalties on subsequent sales or even incorporation into another device.

---

- Most responsible companies don't accept the disclosure of your device or concept in confidence. Check the small print in any so-called non-disclosure agreement offered by a manufacturer. You'll find plenty of escape clauses that render any promise of confidentiality meaningless.

- Manufacturing companies that can directly benefit from your product or process are your most promising licensing candidates. Don't bother with firms that promise to market anything to anybody.

- Don't spend your resources on a product that carries a substantial risk of personal injury without making sure that you or your eventual licensee can obtain product liability insurance at a reasonable cost. This is especially important for medicinal products (especially those to be taken internally), infant toys, baby carriers, some sports equipment, and power tools.

- Computer programs developed in response to a particular manufacturing or processing need are the most welcome.

# Making Beautiful Music Business

The recording, sale, and performance of musical works is a huge, complex industry that relies heavily on copyright law to regulate most of its activities and large-scale licensing of copyrights to distribute its creations.

As a copyright owner, you control and can license reproductions of your song on sheet music or recordings under a *mechanical license,* and its public performance under a *performing license*. You can also authorize a motion-picture studio to use your creation as background music under a *synchronization license.*

You can't possibly enter into licensing agreements with all the record companies, theatres, radio and TV stations, and other organizations that you hope will record, perform, and broadcast your music. Instead, associations of songwriters, music publishers, and recording companies have established complex but very efficient systems to transfer the copyrights and channel a small part of the mechanical and performing royalties back to you.

## Performing licenses and royalties

The bulk of the money you get for your musical creation is from performance licenses and royalties. Songwriter and author organizations collect your royalties every time a musical work is publicly performed or broadcast either live or by recording. The major players are

- ASCAP, One Lincoln Center, New York, NY 10023-7142, phone 212-631-6000, Web site www.ascap.com.
- BMI, 320 West 57th Street, New York, NY 10019-3790, phone 221-586-2000, Web site www.bmi.com.
- SESAC, 55 Music Square, Nashville, TN 37203, phone 615-329-9627, Web site www.sesac.com.

Each of these organizations maintains a list of all the works created by its members. They enter into license agreements with theaters and broadcasting companies to monitor, report, and pay performing royalties, which they then distribute to the authors and music publishers. One half of the royalty goes to the author and the other half to the publishing companies that created the recording or published the sheet music.

Your first step as a songwriter is to join one of these organizations and give it a list of your songs. Due to the instant popularity of your ballad, you can expect a trickle of royalty payments during the first few quarters to turn into a flood of huge checks as every DJ in America spins your CD every hour. You can get a complete application kit and song release forms from your chosen performing royalty association. Some offer online applications.

## Mechanical licenses and royalties

Mechanical licenses allow a company to publish or record your music. There are two types of mechanical licenses:

- A standard, *voluntary license* is one you willingly negotiate and grant on your own to a specific music publishing or record company. Actually, there's very little to negotiate because the royalty rates and modes of payment are pretty standard throughout the industry.
- A *compulsory license* can be claimed by any recording company, without your consent, after you've authorized a company to produce and sell a recording of your work (see Chapter 12).

Most music publishing or recording companies have standard license agreements that don't give you much elbowroom to negotiate terms and conditions. They offer you a pittance for each record or piece of sheet music sold, because they have to pay a royalty to the recording artist, pay for the musicians and recording studio time, and assume other expenses associated with the packaging and sale of the recordings. Songwriters, in general, derive the bulk of their income from performing royalties and, to a lesser extent, from synchronization royalties for the chosen few who are lucky enough to have their music selected by a movie producer.

Your challenge is to maximize the performing royalties you receive. The music publishing company already collects half of your performing royalties — you as the author get the other half. This arrangement is a bit unfair, because the company already receives revenue from the sale of sheet music and recordings. To level the playing field, many songwriters create their own music publishing companies that only deal with real music publishing and record companies. In turn, these other companies agree to give your fictitious company an equal share of the publisher's portion of the royalties. The net result is that you get 75 percent (your 50 percent and your paper company's 25 percent) of the performing royalties.

The creation of a sole proprietorship music publishing company is a mere formality in most states. Ask your performing royalty organization to provide you with a kit to form and register your music publishing company.

The Copyright Act requires the licensee in a compulsory license to provide a monthly report of sales to the copyright owner and also sets the royalty rate. Nobody wants to go through the cumbersome reporting procedure, so some agencies have been created to handle compulsory licenses and act as clearinghouses between the music publishing and recording companies. The royalty rate (slightly lower than the one specified in the statute) and payment schedule are standard. These organizations also handle synchronization licenses and licensing of foreign record companies.

The largest and most popular mechanical licensing organization is The Harry Fox Agency, Inc., created by the National Music Publisher's Association (NMPA), 711 Third Avenue, New York, NY 10017. Their telephone number is 212-370-5330, and their Web site is www.nmpa.org. This site is also a very convenient place to search copyright records.

## Synchronization licenses

A *synchronization license* allows the licensee to use a musical work as background music in a movie, play, video production, or other performance. The name comes from the fact that the music score has to be synchronized with the images and other sounds on the film or other recording medium.

# Copyrights in the electronic age

About every ten years, Congress introduces a major revision of the Copyright Act to keep up with advances in the music business. Congress doesn't necessarily respond to the needs of the songwriters, but to the whims of the big players — the recording and movie companies and the major broadcasters. Over the last 70 years, lobbyists have urged Congress to construct an elaborate legal structure that relies on compulsory license provisions with royalties imposed upon receiving and duplicating instruments, record making, and public transmission.

However, that system is becoming obsolete. The Internet and music-sharing software is threatening the recording industry with near extinction. Peer-to-peer music sharing is a blatant violation of the Copyright Act that hurts the performers and record industry more than the songwriters. You can be sure that a solution will soon be devised; by amending the law to legitimize electronic music sharing and compensate songwriters and record companies in some other way. After that, we'll rewrite this chapter.

If the job is substantial (an entire movie score), if there's an existing relationship between the copyright holder and the producer, or if the holder is a famous composer or songwriter, the copyright holder and the producer may enter into a negotiated license agreement. In other, more anonymous relationships, or when only a few minutes of music are at stake, the producer simply contacts a mechanical license organization and gets a standard license at a standard rate.

# Chapter 21

# Catching Them Rustlers (Infringers)

***

*In This Chapter*

▶ Figuring out what infringement is

▶ Enforcing your IP rights

***

From a legal point of view, your patent, copyright, or distinctive commercial identifier just gives you permission to exclude others from doing something only you can legally do. But this permission has many limits and restrictions. You can't go shoot the meddler or seize counterfeit merchandise. Come to think of it, you'd better not tell anyone that you suspect that person is doing anything wrong until you've jumped through a number of legal hoops. If you can't substantiate your allegations in court, you'll find yourself being pelted with malodorous accusations of unfair practices, in the poorhouse, or both. Our goal is to explain some of the procedures particular to IP litigations and to point you toward the most expeditious and least expensive approaches.

## Determining Infringement

Determining whether an IP right has been infringed requires a careful legal analysis of all circumstances. Going from the least to the most complicated IP rights, we describe their respective infringement tests and how to apply them.

### Violating a copyright

A copyright may be infringed by copying or making adaptations of the protected work, distributing or displaying copies or adaptations, publicly performing a musical or dramatic work, or broadcasting it, and in certain cases defacing, the work (see Chapter 12).

Only the act of copying or adaptation requires special analysis. All other instances of infringement are simply based on cold facts. A recording of your song was played over the radio or it wasn't. Your paper got published or it didn't. Period. But even the test for infringement by copying or adaptation is relatively simple. It only requires a review of the facts and a bit of legal analysis. The infringement test can be summarized in three words: access, expression, and substantial similarity. Ask yourself these three questions:

✔ Did the alleged infringer have access to my work?

✔ Does part of my work constitute a protected expression rather than a pure idea or material already in the public domain?

✔ If the answer to all preceding questions is positive, do the similarities between that part of my work containing protected expression and the infringer's work indicate that partial or whole copying occurred?

If only part of the work was copied, make sure that the copied portion was copyrighted and isn't in the public domain. Example: You design home furnishings and create a pedestal made of a long, fluted Greek column with a Corinthian capital, capped by a square plateau. A competitor comes out with a coffee table supported by a single foot in the shape of a squat and fluted Greek column with the same Corinthian capital as yours. You can prove he visited your showroom, but you can't prove infringement. What he copied was the idea of a Greek column and the Corinthian capital supporting a piece of furniture. The concept of an architectural column in furniture isn't protected by copyright. Corinthian capitals have been around for some 2,400 years. The copyrighted part of your pedestal — its overall harmonious proportions — wasn't copied. (For computer program infringement, review Chapter 12.) Finally, you must make certain that the suspected infringement doesn't fall under one of the exemptions or exceptions listed in Chapter 12.

## *Imitating a commercial identifier*

Determining whether an identifier, trademark, or servicemark is being infringed is a bit more complex than assessing infringement of a copyright. The test is whether there's a likelihood of confusion between your identifier and the alleged infringer's. *Likelihood* doesn't mean possibility but a reasonable expectation that the public will be confused based on court-defined parameters.

Most courts use the test described in Chapter 18, with one additional factor: whether there have been instances of actual confusion. To document instances of actual confusion between the identifiers, keep records of any mistaken calls or inquiries you receive that were meant for the other guy. Also, note any instance where one of your customers ordered or bought goods or services from the infringer, thinking she was buying from you.

Establishing a likelihood of confusion is fairly easy, and the penalties are severe. That's why imitating another's commercial identifier is very risky.

## Running afoul of a patent

Determining patent infringement requires complex and costly legal analysis. We don't expect you to get into that, but we outline the gist of it here.

Don't worry if all the legal mumbo jumbo is hard to understand — like it or not, you'll have to shell out a few thousand dollars for an infringement analysis and even more for a written opinion from a patent attorney anyway.

A patent is infringed if the bad guy's device or process includes all the elements (or a substantial equivalent) listed in any one of the patent claims. In other words, the accused doesn't have to infringe on all claims, just one in its entirety (because each claim defines a distinct area of protected technology).

Dependent claims, ones that refer to one or more previous claims, include all the limitation of the claim they refer to. For example if Claim 3 refers to Claim 2, which in turn refers to Claim 1, then in order to infringe Claim 3, you have to do everything listed in Claims 1, 2, and 3.

The first step in determining patent infringement is determining the scope or coverage of your patent claims. The scope of a claim is strictly limited by its language. Language can be open to interpretation, so both you and the bad guy get to propose your own interpretation of the claims to a judge, who decides the scope of each claim in a *Markman hearing* before the trial begins.

If the claim language is ambiguous, the description, the drawing, and, if necessary, the application file of the patent are used to interpret the claim. Or the judge can receive expert testimony to interpret the meaning of a claim.

Patent owners have a friend in the *Doctrine of Equivalents,* a judge-made rule intended to protect the substance of the patentee's rights. You can establish infringement under this doctrine even if the accused device doesn't literally match the patent's claims, as long as the differences between your patented invention and the infringing one are insubstantial and there's a substantial similarity of function, method, and results.

The Doctrine of Equivalents requires that every component in a certain claim be literally or equivalently present in the accused device or process. An element of little or no importance to the claimed invention can be satisfied by a wide range of equivalent elements not disclosed in the specification. These equivalents aren't limited to elements or process steps that were available when the patent was issued; they can also arise after the patent was issued and before it was infringed. Another important factor to consider is whether persons reasonably skilled in the art would know that the part contained in the patent was interchangeable with one that was omitted. For example, if an element in the claim of an 18-year-old patent recites a telephone handset connected to a wall unit, and the accused device uses a cellphone, the Doctrine would wipe out the difference.

In a recent and very controversial decision, the Court of Appeals for the Federal Circuit (see Chapter 10) has drastically curtailed the application of the Doctrine in connection with claims that have been amended during the prosecution of the patent application in order to get around some prior art. Ask your patent attorney for the latest on that topic, if you really care.

Another tricky aspect in interpreting the scope of a claim is "means plus function" language. Here are some guidelines:

- If a claim expresses a way to perform a specified function, for example, a means for attaching A to B, without describing how to attach the elements or with what, the means are construed to cover the elements described in the specification and its equivalents. For example, if the "means for attaching A to B" is disclosed as a hinge, the means will cover any flexible link such as a strap that could act like a hinge.

- If the "means," or way of performing a function, discloses a physical structure insignificant to the claimed invention, there may be many more equivalent structures than if the characteristics of the structure are critical in performing the claimed function. For example, if an element claimed in the preferred embodiment as a "means for securing together" two pieces of wood is a set of nails, then screws, dowels, dovetails, and other types of joints would constitute equivalent elements if nails aren't critical to the invention's function.

- When interpreting "means plus function" language, an equivalent structure or act cannot embrace technology developed after the patent was issued (as permitted under the Doctrine of Equivalents). For example, the later-developed cellphone may not be considered to be equivalent to a wall-mounted phone claimed as a "means for telecommunicating." Comparison between the proposed equivalent and what's disclosed in the specification must consider the overall structure or process. Accordingly, the accused device may have more or fewer parts than the structure disclosed in the specification, as long as the same function is performed in a substantially similar way.

During the prosecution of a patent, the inventor or his attorney may make concessions, such as restricting the meaning of a term, to avoid rejection because of a prior disclosure. For instance, the phrase "tubular sleeve" may be restricted to tubular elements that are open at both ends, and exclude tubular sleeves that are closed at one or both ends. This kind of concession can be discovered by carefully examining the application file history (often called the "file wrapper"). By the way, such a concession may preclude application of the Doctrine of Equivalents.

A patent claim that addresses a combination of two or more elements or components can be infringed if one of the elements or components is offered, sold, or imported in the United States with the intent to infringe a patent. Note that even if the elements or components are combined outside the United States, there may be infringement.

Don't feel bad if by now you're completely befuddled about those equivalent issues. Many patent attorneys and quite a few judges don't fare any better.

## Misappropriation of a trade secret

One of the most frustrating and infuriating blows that you may experience as a businessperson is the discovery that a former associate or employee has gone over to the competition and is now taking advantage of some commercially sensitive information which you thought was your trade secret. You want to file a lawsuit against the traitor and his new employer to stop them and try to salvage some of your precious information. Indeed, you might be able to obtain a restraining order pending trial enjoining the culprit from spreading or making use of it. Eventually you might obtain a permanent injunction coupled to a judgment for money damages for any loss incurred.

Before you go running for the courthouse, though, you'd better make sure your precious trade secret doesn't fall within one of the exceptions listed in Chapter 4. Protecting and enforcing a trade secret through litigation may not be as costly as suing for patent infringement, but it should be your last line of defense. The best trade secret protection strategy remains a very tight series of in-house safeguards as we recommend in Chapter 4.

# Stopping Infringement Cold

You've done your homework. You are convinced that Tom is copying your copyrighted poster, Dick is using the *Kitty Love* trademark on toastable tarts in derogation of your federally registered *Puppy Love* servicemark for your delicatessen, or Harry is importing, and selling cameras that incorporate your patented auto-focusing mechanism. Now what? Here's what:

- ✔ Take the high road: Go to the nearest federal district court and file an infringement action. Don't forget to bring your checkbook.
- ✔ Look for a special procedure short of full-fledged litigation.

✔ Send a *cease and desist notice* threatening the infringer with a lawsuit if the unlawful activities are not promptly stopped.

✔ Negotiate a friendly settlement that accommodates both parties.

# Taking the high road and going for broke

Suing the infringer is the most effective way to stop an infringement. But it can be very expensive and lengthy, especially if a patent is involved.

### Outline of the proceedings

IP litigation is conducted under the same rules as any other civil matter. The proceedings can be broken down into five phases:

✔ **Temporary relief phase:** You try to obtain a temporary court order restraining the defendant from doing some act that can't be corrected (like cracking Humpty Dumpty), pending further proceedings.

✔ **Discovery phase:** Both parties bombard each other with *interrogatories* (formal or written questions to a witness) requiring an answer under oath, request for admissions and documents, and *depose* (ask to give evidence or testimony under oath) the other guy's prospective witnesses.

✔ **Summary proceeding phase:** One or more of the parties tries to get a judge's decision on a key issue or an *injunction* (court order prohibiting someone from performing a specific act) against an infringing activity. The parties may also submit to voluntary or court-mandated arbitration.

✔ **Trial phase:** The matter goes before a judge or jury.

✔ **Appeal phase:** The party who's dissatisfied with the outcome of a summary proceeding or trial takes the case to a higher court. The outcome of appeal may be a remand of the case to the trial court for a new trial, an affirmation of its decision, or a reversal.

Expending resources and effort upfront to win a temporary relief order or prevail in a summary proceeding may bring the issue to a close before you get to trial. If you win a temporary restraining order or injunction compelling the defendant to stop using your mark pending outcome of the trial, what other option does that defendant have but to use a different mark? He has no reason to pursue the case because, even if he wins a year or two down the line, he doesn't want the trouble and expense of changing his mark again.

### Watching the calendar

You can't sit on your hands forever trying to decide whether to sue an infringer. The *statute of limitations,* the time you have to file a lawsuit in a federal court after an infringement, is six years for patents and three years for copyrights. In trademark cases, the grace period varies as the U.S. court follows the law of the state where the suit is brought. That means you can sue someone for infringing your patent five and one-half years after the patent expires and recover damages for any infringing activity that took place within the last six months of the life of the patent. But be careful; the concept called *laches* prevents you from suing someone when your delay in suing is so long under the circumstances that the accused infringer may have relied on your silence in believing that his device is not infringing.

### Selecting a venue

Litigate in your own backyard for convenience and reduced costs. You may also seek a different venue where the law is more favorable to your case (even federal law varies from circuit to circuit). The defendant, on the other hand, may try to get the action moved to his own district. Things can get very complicated when your complaint includes different types of infringement, multiple defendants living in separate districts, or infringements that occurred in different places. Congress is trying to limit such forum shopping with a law that will assign litigation of a patent in the district of its original owner.

### Praying for paying remedies

Your goal in a lawsuit is a court order that ends the infringing activities. Depending on the type of action and the statute under which you filed your complaint, you may ask for and recover losses due to the infringer's activities; you may also recover the infringer's profit, your attorney fees, and court costs. If the defendant's conduct was egregious, such as intentional patent infringement, you may recover up to three times your losses.

### What's the cost?

Here's a very rough estimate of the average cost to prosecute or defend an infringement action all the way through trial, but short of appeal:

- ✔ Copyright: $250,000 to $325,000
- ✔ Trade secret: $275,000 to $450,000
- ✔ Company identifier or mark: $200,000 to $450,000
- ✔ Design or plant patent: $250,000 to $500,000
- ✔ Utility Patent: $1,000,000 to $4,000,000

You can use these average figures for budgetary purposes, although actual cases can deviate substantially from these estimates. Even large companies try to avoid the cost and the drain of human resources caused by IP litigation. That's why a large majority of IP cases are settled before trial.

### Insuring against litigation

If you just read the list of costs in the previous section, you're probably thinking, "I could never afford to sue someone for infringment. Should I really even bother applying for a patent (or some other IP right)?" Good question. Apart from the other reasons for getting a patent discussed in Chapter 6, the high cost of patent litigation can be minimized through insurance. For a reasonable premium, you can purchase a policy that pays the cost of defending a claim of infringement brought against you or your company and also pays your attorney to pursue infringers of your copyright or patent. What's the catch? If you win your case, the insurance company is entitled to a percentage of any reward granted to you by the court. If you lose, the insurances bears all the litigation expenses, but you may have to pay any award granted to the defendant. The premium for that kind of insurance depends on many factors and is a matter for negotiation with the carrier. Search the Internet for litigation insurance.

## Taking advantage of special remedies

Because of the high cost of a full-fledged litigation, we want to go over some alternate and less costly ways to stop copycats.

### Criminal statutes

The law provides criminal penalties for some IP rights infringements:

- **Federal law:** The federal anti-piracy law provides for punishment of copyright infringement for commercial advantage or private financial gain, as well as the reproduction of recordings or the trafficking in counterfeit recordings, computer programs, and motion pictures. The penalty can be as high as six years in prison and a fine up to $250,000. Heavy fines and prison sentences are also prescribed for theft of trade secrets. The penalty for trafficking in counterfeit goods or services (using a counterfeit mark) can be up to ten years in prison and $2 million in fines for an individual, up to a $5 million fine for a company.

- **State law:** Some states have criminal statutes against the misappropriation of trade secrets and industrial espionage.

Ask your attorney about taking advantage of these criminal statutes by asking for the intervention of the local U.S. attorney, district attorney, or state consumer protection agency instead of filing a civil action. Sometimes, U.S. attorneys or district attorneys can deputize your hired gun to prosecute the infringer on behalf of the people. Imagine your infringer being dragged, handcuffed to the federal pen.

### AntiCybersquatting statute

If you find a domain name on the Web that's confusingly similar to your mark, you may invoke the *AntiCybersquatting Act* to get it cancelled. You must prove that the name was selected and used in bad faith, which means that the infringer knew about your mark and intended to profit from or disparage your mark. You must file this action in a U.S. district court.

If you find a domain name that is similar to your registered mark, you also have recourse to the *domain name dispute-resolution* procedure administered by the Internet Corporation for Assigned Names and Numbers (ICANN). See Document D14 on the CD and log on to www.icann.org/udrp/udrp.htm.

### Getting help from U.S. Customs

If you suspect an unlawful counterfeit importation, you can register your copyright, mark, or company identifier with the U.S. Customs service so that they can seize the targeted goods. You and the goods' owner will be "invited" to appear at a hearing to determine whether the goods should be destroyed or released to their original addressee. This is a much more efficient and less expensive method to bar imported goods than waiting until they appear on the U.S. market and suing the U.S. distributor in a court of law.

### Running to the International Trade Commission

If the infringer is importing the counterfeit merchandize into the United States, you could seek relief from the *International Trade Commission* (ITC) by asking for an order banning importation. The ITC investigates by looking at the validity of your patent, registered copyright, or mark, and then decides whether the importation has an anticompetitive impact on U.S. commerce by infringing your IP rights. Consult www.usitc.gov or your IP specialist. ITC proceedings are quicker and cheaper than a court of law.

## Threatening litigation

Instead of making an immediate beeline for the courthouse, first have your attorney send a stern *cease and desist letter* that demands an immediate stop to all acts of infringement, gives an accounting of all illegal sales, and requests payment to reimburse your losses. What happens next can run from a great disappointment to a big surprise. The infringer can

- ✔ Ignore your letter (the most frequent occurrence). See the section "Taking the high road and going for broke," earlier in this chapter.

- ✔ Contact you to seek an amicable solution, where you forego the payment of damages and the infringer agrees to cease all infringing activities.

- ✔ Drag you to court to defend a declaratory relief action, forcing your attorney to counterclaim (countersue) for infringement. You're back in the litigation circus. In a *declaratory relief action,* the alleged infringer, the plaintiff, asks for a judgment on the grounds that either he's not infringing your IP right or your IP right is invalid. You, the defendant, are no better off than if you'd filed a suit for infringement. Worse, the declaratory relief action could be filed in the infringer's district, forcing you to hire a distant attorney and doubling your litigation costs.

 Be warned that any time you assert your patent in a letter to a suspected infringer, that party can file a declaratory relief action. You can avoid triggering that kind of action by drafting your letter in a nonthreatening manner, offering a license or some other equitable arrangement. Choosing the right language is tricky and best left to an IP professional.

## Negotiating a compromise

In most situations, the sensible approach to resolving an infringement issue is skillful negotiations. That's where attorneys are at their best. The result may be the grant of a very narrow, non-exclusive license to the infringer if the case doesn't involve a commercial identifier. In a trademark infringement, you could offer concurrent use of the identifier in distinct territories or markets. Trust your attorney to balance all the legal and business aspects of the case and guide you to some safe haven, free of tempestuous litigation.

## Enforcing your IP rights abroad

If you think IP litigation is expensive in the U.S., you'll find overseas costs astronomical. In most industrialized countries the Wheel of Justice turns even slower than here. IP-specialized litigators are fewer, and their fees are often higher. In developing nations, IP enforcement institutions are grossly inadequate or nonexistent. Ask your IP guru about the likelihood of successfully and economically litigating your rights in each targeted country. Don't be surprised if she recommends a review by a foreign attorney.

---

### Covering your derrière

Accusing someone of infringing your IP rights on your judgment, without obtaining a written opinion from a knowledgeable attorney, is *prima facie* (presumptive) evidence of reckless behavior, if not willful harassment. If you lose, your cavalier act will be used against you to increase the damages you'll pay. Never accuse anyone without an infringement analysis by a qualified IP attorney. Be sure to get your IP lawyer's opinion in writing. That opinion should refer to, and be based on, a thorough analysis of your patent or trademark application file.

# Part VI
# The Part of Tens

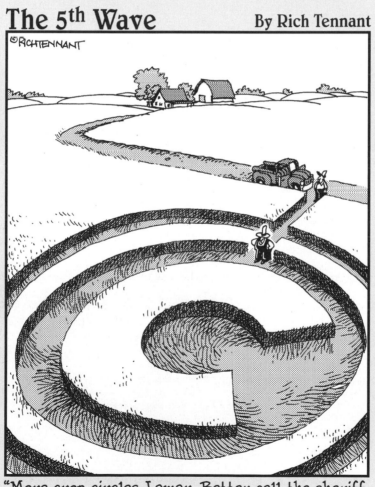

The 5th Wave    By Rich Tennant

"More crop circles, Lamar. Better call the sheriff, them UFO people, and get me a good IP attorney while you're at it."

## In this part . . .

This part contains some great information in easily accessible and digestible lists. Want to know the most common mistakes people make when doing the patent thing? You can check them out here, along with other useful info like frequently asked copyright questions, the ten worst ways to go about naming a company or product, and additional resources that you can use when entering the IP jungle.

# Chapter 22

# Ten Most Common IP Misconceptions

*In This Chapter*

▶ Correcting some frequent misunderstandings about IP rights

▶ Starting on the right foot

*H*ere we cover the most common misunderstandings about the nature of IP rights and how they are obtained. We also show you how to avoid dangerous, and sometimes illegal, acts often committed by inventors, artists, and entrepreneurs who follow the advice of some well-intentioned but ignorant curbside advisor. Over the last 35 years, we've seen too many misinformed individuals get into serious legal trouble when an ounce of knowledge and a bit of caution could have saved the day. Forewarned is forearmed.

## I can apply for a patent by filling out a form and sending it to the USPTO

No way, José. It isn't that simple. A patent application must include a complete disclosure of the invention describing the best mode to practice it. It must also include at least one *claim*, a legal definition of the invention, that will serve as a measuring stick to determine whether an accused device or process falls under the coverage of the patent. See Chapter 8.

## I must file an application to obtain a copyright or a trademark

No governmental agency grants copyrights or trademarks. You have a copyright the instant you reduce an original work of authorship (graphic composition, computer program, piece of music, and so on) to a communicable medium (paper, diskette, DVD, and so on — see Chapter 12).

You automatically get exclusive rights in your geographic area to a distinctive commercial identifier (trade name, brand name, product or package configuration) as soon as you use it in connection with the sale of a product or with rendering a service in the marketplace (Chapter 15). You may, however, apply to the Copyright Office to register a copyright, and to the USPTO or your Secretary of State to register a mark in order to obtain critical procedural advantages when you have to sue an infringer (Chapter 14).

## IP is for creative people, not for a storefront operator like me

Acquiring and protecting IP assets is a must for all types and sizes of businesses. An IP program must be carefully integrated in and tailored to your business plan (Chapters 1–6).

## IP rights are not worth the cost

Your fear of their cost will subside when you realize all the advantages and benefits you can get from exploiting your IP rights. Besides, you may soon find out that you can't do without them (Chapter 1).

## An exclusive IP right is a ticket to expensive litigation

Getting a patent, copyright, or trademark doesn't just give you a license to sue others. These are marketable business assets that can be lucratively exploited (Chapter 20).

## One IP right is all I need

Although a single, well-aimed shot may get the job done, it's better to have a few spare guns of different gauges. Patents, copyrights, trademarks, trade secrets, and contractual rights can be made to work together to give you a full and comprehensive quiver of competition-busting arrows (Chapter 21).

## Minor outside contributions don't matter

IP rights usually vest in their creators, sometimes individually, sometimes jointly. Accepting and incorporating others' suggestions and contributions in your project, no matter how small, can blur the ownership of your assets and throw you into painful and costly disputes.

## A handshake is the best of all agreements

When push comes to shove, your partner, contributor or financier won't remember or contest what that handshake was about. Don't rely on informal arrangements. Get everything on paper and make sure that the rights, expectations, responsibilities, and obligations of each party are clearly spelled out.

## 1 must wait for that ribbon-sealed document before starting business

Nonsense! Don't wait for a patent before commercializing your invention. You may start exploiting your creation as soon as it becomes marketable. Sure, there is some risk of copying and infringement by some early copycat. Under a well-planned, diversified, IP program you'll catch up fast enough. A patent is not a license to manufacture or sell anything. Most IP rights only help you stop the infringing activities of your competitors. They can never absolve you from doing things over which somebody else has a superior exclusionary right.

## With patent pending or in hand 1 can raise money for a share of future returns

The damning word here is *future*. Security laws won't allow anybody to sell a future interest without a license to sell securities. You may sell a fraction of your invention or other kind of creation, or even a share of your IP rights for cash or other form of consideration (a tricky and dangerous step, we must warn you), but not a part of what you might derive from it in the future.

# Chapter 23

# Ten Patent Application Pitfalls

### In This Chapter

▶ Avoiding the most common preparing and filing mistakes

▶ Choosing the right approach

*T*his chapter lists the most common, damaging errors committed by inventors. Because of them, many great inventions never make it to market.

## Choosing a utility patent when other protection fits the bill

A utility patent takes lots of time and money to obtain and even more to enforce against an infringer. Sometimes you can adequately protect many IP assets by less costly IP rights, such as a design patent, plant patent, copyright, trade secret, or trademark. Check out Chapter 6 for information on when and why another type of IP protection could be right for you.

## Filing when you can't afford it

We've seen too many people abandon their patent application midstream for lack of funds. Take a good look at the overall cost (check out Chapter 3 for some handy cost estimates) *before* you begin preparing the application. If you're not sure where the money will come from, and you're not planning to just sell your invention, forget about a utility patent. It's more important to develop a good product and get some early sales. Use your limited resources to develop an effective marketing program, including a blockbuster of a trademark, and look at an alternate and cheaper form of IP protection.

## Going it alone

Unless you received special training, don't think that you can file and pursue a utility patent application without the help of a professional — what you end up with likely won't be worth the paper it's printed on. The worst part is that you won't even know you've messed up on the application until you try to sue someone for infringement.

Reading this book is an excellent first step, but it's not going to make you a competent patent attorney. What it will do is provide you with a basic knowledge base from which you can confidently communicate with the experts, make informed decisions, evaluate the commercial potential of an idea, work with others to protect your businesses IP rights, and do much of the IP legwork, such as gathering a complete background file for your invention and laying out a sensible IP protection strategy. Most important, you'll know to avoid some very damaging faux pas. In some uncomplicated cases, you may be able to conduct preliminary patent and trademark searches and obtain copyright registrations on your own.

## Concealing the past

Too many patents are declared invalid during an infringement trial because the inventor failed to tell the patent examiner everything he or she knew about the background and history of the invention, including prior technology that may be relevant to the issue of patentability. Even if the invention seems entirely new and non-obvious, you have a duty to disclose everything you know. Chapter 8 has information you need to disclose to your IP professional.

## Showing your hand

In the United States, you have only one year to file your patent application after you make the invention public. Most foreign countries give you no leeway at all — you have to file before the invention is public. See Chapter 9 for all the important deadlines to filing a patent application.

Be careful — making an invention public doesn't take much: Bragging about it to your neighbor Clyde may be enough of a public disclosure to blow you out of the game. So get on the ball and file your application as soon as possible — in the meantime, keep your invention under wraps. Treat it as a trade secret, as we explain in Chapter 2, as long as you possibly can and at least until you have a complete patent application on file.

## Naming a non-inventor

Purposely listing someone who didn't contribute to the invention as an inventor is a misrepresentation that can invalidate a patent. The same goes for failing to name a bona fide inventor. Some inventors feel obligated to name their spouses as co-inventors on the mistaken belief that this makes them equal owners of the invention. An employer will want to be listed as an inventor because the employee who came up with the invention was working for him and using his or her facilities, therefore automatically making him or her a contributor. An employee sometimes names the supervisor just to score some brownie points. Some believe that the technician who built the prototype is automatically a co-inventor, although that technician didn't contribute anything beyond standard engineering knowledge. If you faithfully provide your IP professional with all the information listed in Chapter 9, she'll know how to identify the correct inventors.

## Disclosing too little

You must describe your invention with enough detail to allow a person who's skilled in the field to practice (implement) it without undue experimentation. That's called the *enabling disclosure requirement.* You must also describe what you believe is the best way to actually use the invention, not necessarily the way you built your original prototype. Failure to disclose a critical element of the invention, such as where to purchase a hard-to-find component, can be fatal. For example, if you think your new sander works best with a diamond powder coating, but you only described it as using a cheaper glass powder coating, you aren't disclosing the best way to practice the invention.

## Disclosing too much

Some applicants, fearful of failing the *enabling disclosure* requirement (Chapter 8) because they didn't provide enough information, go overboard and describe everything including the kitchen appliances. Anything that a person skilled in the field of the invention can figure out on his or her own is nonessential. We're not talking about the person of ordinary skill defined in Chapter 8, but about a sophisticated expert in the field who understands the technology, is familiar with all the common acronyms, and knows how to anneal a metal, reduce a chemical solution, or modulate a carrier with a waveform without further explanation. Adding superfluous descriptions and drawings to your application ends up costing a lot when you file corresponding applications abroad, because in some countries, you pay according to the number of pages and drawings in your application.

## Bragging

In the summary part of your patent application, don't go bragging about all that your wonderful invention can achieve. Just state its main purpose and let it go at that. In a patent infringement litigation, the defense attorney could invalidate some or all the claims of the patent by demonstrating that the invention didn't really achieve all that the inventor had claimed it could do.

## Waiting too long

Preparing a patent application takes time. Consulting your IP professional close to a filing deadline forces her to rush the drafting of the application at the expense of completeness and accuracy. Attorneys aren't magicians — give her a few weeks to do the job right. It's all to your benefit. More important, don't forget that the inventor who is the first to file his patent application wins over the one who files later.

# Chapter 24

# Ten Practical Copyright FAQs

*W*e couldn't tell you how many times we've heard clients come up with the same misconceptions about copyrights, such as thinking that it's legal to copy less than 30 percent of a copyrighted work, or believing that they can use a recording as background music for an aerobics class because they bought and paid for it. In this chapter are answers to the questions they most often ask.

## I created a dance routine for my school play — is it covered by a copyright?

Yes it is, assuming that you have put it down on some communicable medium (written down on paper, recorded on video cassette or DVD, and so on). Any original, not copied work of authorship such as a piece of writing (including a computer program), a musical composition, a play, a dance or pantomime, a painting, a drawing, a sculpture, a motion picture or other audio-visual creation, a sound recording (even if it is neither new nor written by you), or an architectural creation benefits from copyright protection as soon as it is put down in a communicable form without any other formality. However, registering your copyright is a must in case you need to take action against a copycat. Moreover, you can get greater compensation if you register your work before it's copied (Chapter 14).

## I coined a campaign slogan for the next election — can I copyright it?

No. Names, titles, slogans, and short phrases aren't considered substantial enough to deserve copyright protection. A limerick or other short poem will pass the threshold. In music, a single, original measure may have enough substance. So will a simple line drawing such as a "funny face."

## I have an idea for a TV show — how do I get it copyrighted?

Sorry, but you can't. You can't copyright ideas, concepts, systems, procedures, principles, methods, or discoveries. Copyright protects only the original *expression* of an idea and not the idea itself, so you have to at least write a treatment in order to get a copyright. As you develop the script, copyright attaches as soon as you describe a scene that's a choice among other possibilities (see Chapter 12).

## How much of a copyrighted work can I copy without infringing the copyright?

None. Unless you get permission to use the work from the copyright owner, any copying is infringing. You can't copy a little bit any more than you can be a little bit pregnant. However, with proper permission, you can even modify and adapt the pre-existing copyrighted material.

## I'm designing a Web site — can I use graphics copied from a magazine?

Yes, but there's a catch. You need to get permission from the copyright owner of the material you borrow. Check out Chapter 13 and the section on music in Chapter 20 to find out how and where to get the permission that you need. No permission, no use.

# Can I use a popular song in a video clip of my dog to send to "America's Funniest Animals"?

No. Copying a song from a CD to your videotape would be your first count of copyright infringement. Then every time your tape is played in public or broadcast constitutes another act of infringement. We can hear you saying that everyone does it, and you may be right. But how many tax cheats are in the federal pen as we speak? See Chapter 12 for exceptions and exemptions.

# I'm a teacher — can I copy a page from a book and give the copies to my students?

Yes. This is one of the *fair-use limitations* to a copyright, meaning exactly what it implies. See Chapter 12 for a list of fair-use limitations.

# How long does a copyright last?

It depends. A copyright's life depends on when the copyrighted work was first published or registered. The safe rule is 70 years beyond the life of the author. In the case of an anonymous author, it's the shorter of 95 years from original publication or 120 years from creation.

# Where can I get permission to copy a protected work?

You can find out in this book. To be more precise, read about investigating the status of a copyright in Chapter 13. If you're talking about a musical recording, read about the music business in Chapter 20.

## Can 1 protect software with a copyright and a patent?

Yes. The copyright only protects the ways in which the underlying process is presented by the program instructions, and the patent protects the process itself. While you're at it, you can keep a good part of the program instructions confidential and protect them as a trade secret. (Find out how to preserve the trade secret in a computer program in Chapter 14.) You may also give a distinctive name to your software and get some trademark protection. (Check out Chapter 16 for tips on creating distinctive names.)

# Chapter 25

# The Ten Worst Naming Blunders

Contrary to conventional wisdom, the most popular ways of selecting a company name or a product brand are the worst approaches, and they often spell disaster. On the other hand, the best way to choose the commercial name by which you'll be known is to follow the methodical approach outlined in Chapter 16. You want to coin the most motivating, memorable moniker possible that nobody can copy or imitate — a name that will gain you a loyal customer base and may even provide you with a new and independent source of income. In other words, avoid the wildly popular routes for selecting a commercial identifier that we outline in this chapter.

## Using your family name

Family pride may drive you to name your new enterprise the Bush Company, but you'd limit yourself in many ways. Problems with similar names may lurk in unexpected places. For openers, a surname isn't easy to register as a trademark or servicemark, or to protect against copycats, unless it has some alternate meaning (for example, if you're a scooter manufacturer with the name Dash). Unless your name is unique and memorable, it contains minimal promotional value, and the valuation and transfer of the name upon the sale of the business is often problematic. And in this case, how many customers are not Republicans?

## Mimicking another company's brand

Imitation may be the sincerest form of flattery, but why flatter your competitor? Worse, there's liability for infringing upon another's commercial identifier. Copying is stealing, and penalties can include a seizure of your goods and a court order to change your counterfeit brand name. Copying is the lazy way to avoid the discipline of naming. Be unique. Move to the head of your industry rather than dissolve in the crowd.

## Describing your product or service

This is the most frequent and serious mistake. Do you want to name your company Digital Products (among dozens of Digital This and Digital Thats) or would you rather display uniqueness, brilliance, and creativity with a name like Apple? Should your beer be known as Lite and lose its identity to a gaggle of imitators or sport a shining tiara like Corona? A commercial identifier must be unique and distinctive, and not a mere description of your product that could apply to all other similar products.

A descriptive name is a ticket to the courthouse and to endless, expensive, and time-consuming litigation because it's bound to be imitated eventually by your competitors. The courts have determined that you can't monopolize any part of the language. You can either create a new word out of nothing, such as Kodak, or give a totally new meaning to an existing word, like Crest for toothpaste. See Chapter 15 for more on descriptive versus distinctive names.

## Having brainstorming sessions

Brainstorming monopolizes expensive management time and generates more arguments than deciding on the merits of chocolate versus vanilla ice cream. The result is a predictably colorless compromise that lacks the marketing punch and legal clout you need. Group interaction in naming has its place, but such endeavors need method, structure, and common goals to be effective.

## Holding a naming contest

Holding a public or employee contest to coin a name makes as much sense as practicing medicine by popular vote. It's haphazard at best. And a contest requires a winner, even if the best entry is unsuitable. Have a company picnic instead.

## Ignoring the customer

Insiders are too close to the product and its history to be open minded. A commercial identifier that's effective in the marketplace looks outward; it speaks the customer's language, not the engineer's or designer's. It should motivate your prospect, catch his or her fancy, and be long remembered. Don't focus on your achievement. Consider what will attract the public.

## Creating technobabble

Cold and unpronounceable combinations of Zs and Xs, or meaningless and pseudoscientific monikers like Chloraseptic and Hybrinetics just don't communicate. The minor technical gloss doesn't make up for the lost opportunity to carry a high-impact message to the market several times a day.

## Choosing availability over exclusivity

Just because a name's not already registered doesn't necessarily make it a good candidate for your product or company. If the name isn't strongly enforceable in court, you'll soon be copied and lose goodwill and market share, to the despair of your investors. (Check out Chapter 15 for more info on making your name hold up in court.) Go for the gold, not the tinfoil of an ordinary identifier.

## Relying on the logo

A creative ad and a snazzy logo help the customer remember your commercial identifier. When he or she decides to buy a widget, your name will pop out first. A logo should enhance the impact of a name, but great graphics won't save a weak name. Do your best when coining your identifier and *then* take it to the graphic artist.

## Leaving your mark unprotected

When the time comes to stop a copycat, would you rather limp into court with a wet noodle or swagger in with a bazooka? Registration is your most powerful weapon and should be your top priority. Chapter 18 tells you everything you ever wanted to know about registering your mark. Your registered mark can eventually become incontestable if, after five years, no one has challenged you and you file an affidavit to that effect. Having an incontestable mark gives you an invaluable defense when your success squeezes all those prior name users out of the woodwork.

# Appendix

# How to Use the CD-ROM

## System Requirements

**M**ake sure your computer meets the minimum system requirements shown in the following list. If your computer doesn't match up to most of these requirements, you may have problems using the software and files on the CD. For the latest and greatest information, please refer to the ReadMe file located at the root of the CD-ROM.

- ✔ PC running Windows 98 or later or a Mac running OS X

- ✔ At least 32MB of total RAM installed on your computer; for best performance, we recommend at least 64MB

- ✔ A CD-ROM drive

For more, check out these books published by Wiley Publishing, Inc.: *PCs For Dummies,* by Dan Gookin; *Macs For Dummies,* by David Pogue; *iMacs For Dummies* by David Pogue; *Windows 95 For Dummies, Windows 98 For Dummies, Windows 2000 Professional For Dummies, Microsoft Windows ME Millennium Edition For Dummies,* all by Andy Rathbone.

## Using the CD

To install the items from the CD to your hard drive, follow these steps.

1. **Insert the CD into your computer's CD-ROM drive.** The license agreement appears.

Note to Windows users: The interface won't launch if you have autorun disabled. In that case, click Start>Run. In the dialog box that appears, type **D:\Start.exe**. (Replace D with the proper letter if your CD-ROM drive uses a different letter. If you don't know the letter, see how your CD-ROM drive is listed under My Computer.) Click OK.

Note for Mac Users: The CD icon will appear on your desktop; double-click the icon to open the CD and double-click the Start icon.

2. **Read through the license agreement and then click the Accept button if you want to use the CD. After you click Accept, the License Agreement window won't appear again.**

The CD interface appears. The interface allows you to install the programs and browse the contents with just a click of a button (or two).

# What You'll Find on the CD

We have compiled documents that provide you with comprehensive access to practically all the laws, rules, and regulations pertaining to the acquisition and protection of intellectual property (IP). The material on the CD is not required to understand the book. It's useful but complementary. For easy reference, the CD is organized in six different groups, labeled A through F.

## A. IP resources

**Documents A1–A8:** To be used as references in locating and contacting government administrative agencies and documentary services.

## B. Patent documents

**Documents B1–B19:** Examples of various types of utility, design, and plant patents, giving a glimpse into what final patent look like. These documents illustrate the teachings of various chapters where they are often referred to.

## C. Trademark registrations

**Documents C1–C7:** These registration certificates cover most types of the marks discussed in the book.

# D. Legislation

**Documents D1–D10:** Federal Statutes

**Documents D11–D13:** International IP Treaties and Conventions (documents courtesy of WIPO)

**Documents D14–D15:** Sundry IP-related legislation (document D14 courtesy of I CANN)

These give you the exact laws relating to patents, copyrights, and trademarks as of January 1, 2008. This legislative material is the *black letter law,* before it's interpreted by courts into *case law*, and translated into regulations and rules by Congress and administrative agencies. Most of these interpretations and regulations may be accessed in the first (A) group of documents.

# E. Samples of prosecution files

**Documents E1 and E2:** Prosecution Files

Here are entire "file wrappers" (prosecution files) of a utility patent and a trademark registration, including correspondence between the applicant's attorney and the examiner in the USPTO. The purpose is to acquaint you with the formality, rigorousness, and complexity of the application proceedings.

# F. Application worksheets

**Documents F1–F3:** Application worksheets for a patent, a copyright, and a trademark. Use these to prepare an application, and also as checklists.

# Applications

The following applications are on the CD:

**Adobe Reader from Adobe Systems, Inc. Freeware version:** This is the reader required to view PDF files. For more info, see www.adobe.com/products/acrobat/readstep2.html.

*Shareware* programs are fully functional, trial versions of copyrighted programs. If you like particular programs, register with their authors for a nominal fee and receive licenses, enhanced versions, and technical support. *Freeware* programs are copyrighted games, applications, and utilities that are free for personal use. Unlike shareware, these programs do not require a fee or provide technical support. GNU software is governed by its own license, which is included inside the folder of the GNU product. See the GNU license for more details. *Trial*, *demo*, or *evaluation* versions are usually limited either by time or functionality (such as being unable to save projects). Some trial versions are sensitive to system date changes. If you alter your computer's date, the programs will "time out" and will no longer be functional.

# Troubleshooting

If you have trouble with the CD-ROM, call the Wiley Product Technical Support at 800-762-2974. Outside the U.S., call 1-317-572-3994. You can also contact Wiley Product Technical Support at **http://support.wiley.com**. John Wiley & Sons will provide technical support only for installation and other general quality control items. For technical support on the applications themselves, consult the program's vendor or author. To place additional orders or to request information about other Wiley products, please call 877-762-2974.

# Wiley Publishing, Inc. End-User License Agreement

**READ THIS.** You should carefully read these terms and conditions before opening the software packet(s) included with this book "Patents, Copyrights & Trademarks For Dummies, 2nd Edition". This is a license agreement "Agreement" between you and Wiley Publishing, Inc. "WPI". By opening the accompanying software packet(s), you acknowledge that you have read and accept the following terms and conditions. If you do not agree and do not want to be bound by such terms and conditions, promptly return the Book and the unopened software packet(s) to the place you obtained them for a full refund.

1. **License Grant.** WPI grants to you (either an individual or entity) a nonexclusive license to use one copy of the enclosed software program(s) (collectively, the "Software") solely for your own personal or business purposes on a single computer (whether a standard computer or a workstation component of a multi-user network). The Software is in use on a computer when it is loaded into temporary memory (RAM) or installed into permanent

memory (hard disk, CD-ROM, or other storage device). WPI reserves all rights not expressly granted herein.

2. **Ownership.** WPI is the owner of all right, title, and interest, including copyright, in and to the compilation of the Software recorded on the physical packet included with this Book "Software Media". Copyright to the individual programs recorded on the Software Media is owned by the author or other authorized copyright owner of each program. Ownership of the Software and all proprietary rights relating thereto remain with WPI and its licensers.

3. **Restrictions on Use and Transfer.**

   **(a)** You may only (i) make one copy of the Software for backup or archival purposes, or (ii) transfer the Software to a single hard disk, provided that you keep the original for backup or archival purposes. You may not (i) rent or lease the Software, (ii) copy or reproduce the Software through a LAN or other network system or through any computer subscriber system or bulletin-board system, or (iii) modify, adapt, or create derivative works based on the Software.

   **(b)** You may not reverse engineer, decompile, or disassemble the Software. You may transfer the Software and user documentation on a permanent basis, provided that the transferee agrees to accept the terms and conditions of this Agreement and you retain no copies. If the Software is an update or has been updated, any transfer must include the most recent update and all prior versions.

4. **Restrictions on Use of Individual Programs.** You must follow the individual requirements and restrictions detailed for each individual program in the "About the CD" appendix of this Book or on the Software Media. These limitations are also contained in the individual license agreements recorded on the Software Media. These limitations may include a requirement that after using the program for a specified period of time, the user must pay a registration fee or discontinue use. By opening the Software packet(s), you agree to abide by the licenses and restrictions for these individual programs that are detailed in the "About the CD" appendix and/or on the Software Media. None of the material on this Software Media or listed in this Book may ever be redistributed, in original or modified form, for commercial purposes.

5. **Limited Warranty.**

   **(a)** WPI warrants that the Software and Software Media are free from defects in materials and workmanship under normal use for a period of sixty (60) days from the date of purchase of this Book. If WPI receives notification within the warranty period of defects in materials or workmanship, WPI will replace the defective Software Media.

   **(b)** WPI AND THE AUTHOR(S) OF THE BOOK DISCLAIM ALL OTHER WARRANTIES, EXPRESS OR IMPLIED, INCLUDING WITHOUT LIMITATION IMPLIED WARRANTIES OF MERCHANTABILITY AND FITNESS FOR A PARTICULAR PURPOSE, WITH RESPECT TO THE SOFTWARE, THE PROGRAMS, THE SOURCE CODE CONTAINED THEREIN, AND/OR THE TECHNIQUES DESCRIBED IN THIS BOOK. WPI DOES NOT WARRANT THAT THE FUNCTIONS CONTAINED IN

THE SOFTWARE WILL MEET YOUR REQUIREMENTS OR THAT THE OPERATION OF THE SOFTWARE WILL BE ERROR FREE.

**(c)** This limited warranty gives you specific legal rights, and you may have other rights that vary from jurisdiction to jurisdiction.

**6. Remedies.**

**(a)** WPI's entire liability and your exclusive remedy for defects in materials and workmanship shall be limited to replacement of the Software Media, which may be returned to WPI with a copy of your receipt at the following address: Software Media Fulfillment Department, Attn.: Patents, Copyrights & Trademarks For Dummies, 2nd Edition, Wiley Publishing, Inc., 10475 Crosspoint Blvd., Indianapolis, IN 46256, or call 1-800-762-2974. Please allow four to six weeks for delivery. This Limited Warranty is void if failure of the Software Media has resulted from accident, abuse, or misapplication. Any replacement Software Media will be warranted for the remainder of the original warranty period or thirty (30) days, whichever is longer.

**(b)** In no event shall WPI or the author be liable for any damages whatsoever (including without limitation damages for loss of business profits, business interruption, loss of business information, or any other pecuniary loss) arising from the use of or inability to use the Book or the Software, even if WPI has been advised of the possibility of such damages.

**(c)** Because some jurisdictions do not allow the exclusion or limitation of liability for consequential or incidental damages, the above limitation or exclusion may not apply to you.

**7. U.S. Government Restricted Rights.** Use, duplication, or disclosure of the Software for or on behalf of the United States of America, its agencies and/or instrumentalities "U.S. Government" is subject to restrictions as stated in paragraph (c)(1)(ii) of the Rights in Technical Data and Computer Software clause of DFARS 252.227-7013, or subparagraphs (c) (1) and (2) of the Commercial Computer Software - Restricted Rights clause at FAR 52.227-19, and in similar clauses in the NASA FAR supplement, as applicable.

**8. General.** This Agreement constitutes the entire understanding of the parties and revokes and supersedes all prior agreements, oral or written, between them and may not be modified or amended except in a writing signed by both parties hereto that specifically refers to this Agreement. This Agreement shall take precedence over any other documents that may be in conflict herewith. If any one or more provisions contained in this Agreement are held by any court or tribunal to be invalid, illegal, or otherwise unenforceable, each and every other provision shall remain in full force and effect.

# Index

**• Q •**